CAMBRIDGE TEXTS IN THE
HISTORY OF POLITICAL THOUGHT

───

KUMAZAWA BANZAN
Governing the Realm and Bringing Peace to All below Heaven

KUMAZAWA BANZAN'S (1619-1691) *Responding to the Great Learning* (*Daigaku wakumon*) stands as the first major writing on political economy in early modern Japanese history. John A. Tucker's translation is the first English rendition of this controversial text to be published in eighty years. The introduction offers an accessible and incisive commentary, including detailed analyses of Banzan's text within the context of his life, as well as broader historical and intellectual developments in East Asian Confucian thought. Emphasizing parallels between Banzan's life events, such as his relief efforts in Okayama domain following devastating flooding, and his later writings advocating compassionate government, environmental initiatives, and projects for growing wealth, Tucker sheds light on Banzan's main objective of "governing the realm and bringing peace and prosperity to all below heaven." In *Responding to the Great Learning*, Banzan was doing more than writing a philosophical commentary, he was advising the Tokugawa shogunate to undertake a major reorganization of the polity - or face the consequences.

JOHN A. TUCKER is a professor of history at East Carolina University in Greenville, North Carolina. He specializes in early modern Japanese Confucianism and its varied roles in the intellectual history of Japan. He is the author of *The Forty-Seven Rōnin: The Vendetta in History* (2018), as well as translation studies of Itō Jinsai's *Gomō jigi* (1998) and Ogyū Sorai's *Bendō and Benmei* (2006). He co-edited *Dao Companion to Japanese Confucian Philosophy* (2014) with Chun-chieh Huang, and edited a four-volume series, *Critical Readings on Japanese Confucianism* (2013).

CAMBRIDGE TEXTS IN THE HISTORY OF POLITICAL THOUGHT

Cambridge Texts in the History of Political Thought is firmly established as the major student series of texts in political theory. It aims to make available all the most important texts in the history of political thought, from ancient Greece to the twentieth century, from throughout the world and from every political tradition. All the familiar classic texts are included, but the series seeks at the same time to enlarge the conventional canon through a global scope and by incorporating an extensive range of less well-known works, many of them never before available in a modern English edition, and to present the history of political thought in a comparative, international context. Where possible, the texts are published in complete and unabridged form, and translations are specially commissioned for the series. However, where appropriate, especially for non-western texts, abridged or tightly focused and thematic collections are offered instead. Each volume contains a critical introduction together with chronologies, biographical sketches, a guide to further reading and any necessary glossaries and textual apparatus. Overall, the series aims to provide the reader with an outline of the entire evolution of international political thought.

For a list of titles published in the series, please see end of book

KUMAZAWA BANZAN

Governing the Realm and Bringing Peace to All below Heaven

EDITED AND TRANSLATED BY

JOHN A. TUCKER

East Carolina University

CAMBRIDGE
UNIVERSITY PRESS

CAMBRIDGE
UNIVERSITY PRESS

University Printing House, Cambridge CB2 8BS, United Kingdom

One Liberty Plaza, 20th Floor, New York, NY 10006, USA

477 Williamstown Road, Port Melbourne, VIC 3207, Australia

314–321, 3rd Floor, Plot 3, Splendor Forum, Jasola District Centre, New Delhi – 110025, India

79 Anson Road, #06–04/06, Singapore 079906

Cambridge University Press is part of the University of Cambridge.

It furthers the University's mission by disseminating knowledge in the pursuit of
education, learning, and research at the highest international levels of excellence.

www.cambridge.org
Information on this title: www.cambridge.org/9781108425018
DOI: 10.1017/9781108348911

© John A. Tucker 2021

First published 2021

Printed in the United Kingdom by TJ Books Ltd, Padstow Cornwall

A catalogue record for this publication is available from the British Library.

ISBN 978-1-108-42501-8 Hardback
ISBN 978-1-108-44115-5 Paperback

Contents

Contents

Translator's Note

The cover title of this book, *Governing the Realm and Bringing Peace to All below Heaven*, is an abbreviation of the subtitle of Kumazawa Banzan's *Daigaku wakumon*, here translated as *Responding to the Great Learning*. Banzan's subtitle is highlighted because it more accurately alerts readers to the intensely socio-economic and political content of *Daigaku wakumon*.

The main title, whether romanized as *Daigaku wakumon* or translated as *Responding to the Great Learning*, suggests a dry, abstruse commentary on an obscure Confucian text. Yet nothing could be further from the truth: Banzan's work deals with politics as high drama, offering a vision of peace and plenty for all as the best-case scenario flowing from good government, coupled with, on the other hand, graphic descriptions of chaos, warfare, anarchy, and doom awaiting rulers who ignore the text's wise counsel.

It is tempting to imagine that Banzan presented his text in the guise of a Confucian commentary to hoodwink shogunal authorities ready to outlaw overtly political discussions of controversial issues. But Banzan was not a man given to deceit: he had an early draft, absent any title, sent to the shogunal authorities for their perusal and, incidentally, suffered the consequences for having boldly done so.

The title and subtitle later given Banzan's text are intimately related. The subtitle, *Governing the Realm and Bringing Peace to All below Heaven*, refers to the central goal of rulers as discussed in the *Great Learning* (*Daigaku*), making it a suitable metonym for Banzan's work. In order to best convey the highly political character of the latter, Banzan's subtitle is privileged on the cover, while the present translation of his main title, *Responding to the Great Learning*, is used herein.

像肖山蕃澤熊

Portrait of Kumazawa Banzan from the 1880 edition of the *Sentetsu sōdan,* courtesy of Special Collections, Waseda University Library

Introduction

Speaking Truth to Power: The End of Kumazawa Banzan

Confinement unto death in Koga Castle. Such was the fate of Kumazawa Banzan (1619–1691)[1] following a lifetime of teaching, domain administration, and theorizing on matters related to politics, fiscal policy, civil engineering, disaster relief, religion, literature, ethics, history, education, and national defense. More specifically, Banzan's final years in detention resulted from his summary account of his wide-ranging views – invariably critical of the ruling samurai regime, the Tokugawa shogunate – on how best to administer and govern the realm. Banzan proposed nothing less than a comprehensive, radical reorganization of the Tokugawa polity, one which, if implemented, would have effectively revolutionized the early-modern realm, transforming everything from the hinterlands to the shogun's capital, the socio-economic hierarchy, the spiritual order, the ecological integrity of mountains and rivers, the structure of education, and even the theoretical foundations of the political order. Yet, ironically enough, the revolution would not necessarily have been a progressive one, moving the realm forward toward a recognizable version of

[1] Banzan went by several names during his life. His formal name was Ryōkai. He was also known by his personal name Jirōhachi, and later, Suke'emon. By birth his surname was Nojiri, which was later changed, with his adoption, to Kumazawa. In 1660, he took Shigeyama as his name. The latter, read in Sino-Japanese, is "Banzan." After his passing, "Banzan" became his courtesy name and was most commonly used alongside his surname by adoption, Kumazawa. Hara Nensai, "Kumazawa Banzan," in Minamoto Ryōen and Maeda Tsutomu, eds., *Sentetsu sōdan*, Tōyō bunko, vol. 574 (Tokyo: Heibonsha, 1994), p. 124.

modernity, so much as one returning it to a socio–economic platform of agrarian unity and simplicity wherein the wealth of the nation, that is, the rice harvest, might be more fully shared by all, samurai and farmers alike, while politically reviving a more decentralized, less demanding approach to shogunate–daimyō relations.

Banzan cast his proposals as an expression of the Confucian ideal of "compassionate government" (*jinsei*). An essential corollary was his "grand project for growing wealth," a multifaceted initiative meant to strengthen the realm economically, enabling all within it to enjoy new levels of prosperity and, most importantly, stand prepared to defend the country against foreign invasion. Adding a confrontational edge to his vision of compassionate government, Banzan reminded the Tokugawa regime that rulers who disregarded the welfare of the people ran the risk of losing the legitimating decree of heaven and so faced the prospect of removal and replacement. Even worse, Banzan suggested that the survival of the country was at stake, sketching out in quasi-apocalyptic terms scenarios wherein the world of Tokugawa Japan (1600–1868) might end up in utter anarchy and chaos if his proposals were not acted upon forthwith. Responding to Banzan's proposals, the Tokugawa shogunate declared them outrageous and forthwith sentenced the outspoken Confucian to internment in Koga Castle. Despite his ignominious fate as a scholar silenced in captivity, not a few of Banzan's proposals ultimately anticipated, in general terms, some of the more noteworthy initiatives enacted during the opening decades of the Meiji period (1868–1912) over a century and a half after his passing. Banzan's proposal to return samurai to the countryside to live and work alongside the agrarian estate foreshadowed the early Meiji abolition of the samurai class, and the call for socio–economic unity throughout the land. On another count, Banzan's calls for a reduction in Buddhism and a restoration of Shintō prefigured Meiji religious policies of a similar thrust.

Banzan recorded his thoughts in a provocative work, here translated as *Responding to the Great Learning* (*Daigaku wakumon*). Then, without solicitation, prompting, or coercion, he presented his handwritten text to the Tokugawa authorities. No doubt, Banzan imagined it his professional duty as a sincere Confucian scholar to communicate his ideas, however critical, boldly and forthrightly. The shogunate's reaction was quick and unequivocal: imprisonment for the aged – then 69 – rōnin theorist-critic. Banzan was allowed some freedom, such as strolling around his place of internment, yet still he died, four years later, in 1691, a detained man, effectively cut off from his family, friends, followers, and associates, and surely denied any chance at overhauling the Tokugawa polity which, in his view, was headed toward grave socio-economic peril if not foreign conquest and possible obliteration. As a curious dimension of his punishment, Banzan was buried at a Buddhist temple in Koga,[2] the castle town of his confinement just north of Edo (now Tokyo), the shogun's capital, hundreds of miles from his birthplace, Kyoto, and the Kansai area in southwestern Japan where he spent most of his life. Banzan's separation from Kyoto and its environs in his few remaining years, and then, ultimately, in the finality of death, was for him perhaps the worst part of his punishment.

Some of Banzan's proposals now seem admittedly farfetched. Repeatedly, he warned that Japan faced imminent invasion by "northern barbarians" (*hokuteki*), that is, Manchu tribal forces that were in the process of consolidating their rule over China following the collapse of the Ming (1368–1644) dynasty. Banzan's fear of impending Manchu invasion, though not ungrounded, was surely overblown. In part, his dread was generated by his admiration for shogunal policies dating back to the Kamakura (1185–1336) shogunate, and his knowledge that that earlier samurai regime had been seriously strained by another foreign invasion, that of the Mongols in the late thirteenth century. Banzan advocated a return to some of the more frugal administrative policies of the Kamakura shogunate, and at the same time sought to preclude any possible foreign military challenge of the kind that earlier shook the Kamakura polity.

Yet Banzan's outspoken warnings left him an isolated man: educated Japanese in the late seventeenth century knew of the Manchu conquest of China, but no other scholar of comparable standing sounded the alarm as loudly and repeatedly as did Banzan. On this count alone, those familiar with his thought might have found enough grounds for dismissing his ideas as little more than hysterical exaggerations and alarmist nonsense of an aging, perhaps paranoid scholar. Indeed, other Confucians, including Yamaga Sokō (1622–1685), Hayashi Gahō (1618–1688), and Asami Keisai (1652–1712), saw in the fall of the Ming dynasty evidence of the ethical inferiority of China, a country given to dynastic overthrow, compared to Japan, a sacred imperial realm still led by an unbroken line of

---

[2] The Keienji, a Sōtō Zen temple. While the site has been altered and refurbished several times, Banzan's gravestone dates from the early nineteenth century.

divine emperors. From the perspective of other scholars, the fall of the Ming signaled imperial China's descent into foreign rule and barbarism, not its rise as an imminent danger for Japan.

On the other hand, in the final decades of the Tokugawa and the early years of the Meiji, as barbarians from the north and south, including most notably Czarist Russia and the United States, bore down on Japan, imposing their imperialistic and/or expansionistic agendas on the country, Banzan seemed precocious and farsighted in his awareness, a century and a half before matters came to a head, that foreign domination was a profound threat and that any responsible government should prepare its population to meet such challenges or face the consequences.

Responding to the Great Learning was not published in Banzan's lifetime. Instead, it circulated only in manuscript copies. The work finally appeared, for the first time, in the late-eighteenth century in a woodblock edition, but shortly thereafter was banned by the shogunate. Subsequent editions nevertheless attained some circulation as the power of the Tokugawa to control the press dwindled. As anxieties over impending domination by foreign powers spread in the first half of the nineteenth century, Banzan attained new levels of credibility as a prescient statesman-scholar. Not surprisingly, in the Meiji period, Banzan was far more appreciated as a Confucian scholar and political theorist than he had been in his own life and times.

Yet even before the end of the Tokugawa, some of Banzan's ideas on political economy resurfaced in the world of Tokugawa political thought. At the request of the eighth shogun, Tokugawa Yoshimune (r. 1716–1745), another noteworthy Confucian scholar, Ogyū Sorai (1666–1728), authored a text addressing the social, political, and economic crises of the day. Sorai submitted the text, known to history as *Seidan* (*Political Discussions*), to the shogunate for its consideration. Therein, Sorai suggested that samurai living lives of wasteful indulgence in castle towns, including most notably Edo, be returned to the countryside to dwell and labor alongside the hardworking peasant-farmer population.[3] Sorai's suggestion reiterated Banzan's earlier proposal of essentially the same initiative in socio-economic engineering, though without any mention of Banzan. Oddly enough, the considerable attention given Sorai in contemporary scholarship has left many with the impression that the call for returning

---

[3] For a translation of this work, see Olof G. Lidin, *Ogyū Sorai's Discourse on Government Seidan* (Wiesbaden: Otto Harrassowitz Verlag, 1999).

samurai to the land was his own original proposal instead of a replay of Banzan's.

Any reader of Banzan's *Responding to the Great Learning* well realizes that decades before Sorai offered concrete proposals for addressing the socio-economic and political ills of the Tokugawa regime, Banzan had advanced, in considerable detail, the notion of returning samurai to the countryside as well as a range of other related proposals, effectively pioneering, in early modern times, the genre of practical political theory (*keizaigaku*) that Sorai, Dazai Shundai (1680–1747), and a host of other later early-modern and modern theorists continued. And it should be added that while Sorai did not footnote Banzan in suggesting that samurai be returned to the countryside, he did praise Banzan posthumously as one of the more authentic Confucians of his age.[4] Other Confucian scholars chimed in, admiring and in some cases quoting Banzan's *Responding to the Great Learning*, revealing that despite the fact that a woodblock edition did not appear for nearly a century after the text was drafted, it nevertheless circulated widely and garnered significant favorable attention among some of the scholarly elite of eighteenth-century Japan.

This book presents a new translation-study of Banzan's text.[5] An introductory essay on Banzan's life and thought situates *Responding to*

---

4 For a detailed study of Sorai and Banzan, see Miyazaki Michio, "Kumazawa Banzan to Ogyū Sorai." Parts 1–2. *Kokugakuin zasshi*, vol. 84, nos. 1–2, 1983.

5 For the first English translation, see Galen M. Fisher, "*Dai Gaku Wakumon: A Discussion of Public Questions in the Light of the Great Learning*, by Kumazawa Banzan," *Transactions of the Asiatic Society of Japan*, 2nd Series, vol. 16 (May 1938), p. 263. There is also a more recent translation, into French, by Jean-François Soum entitled, *Questions sur La Grande Étude: Daigaku wakumon*. (Tokyo: Maison Franco-Japonaise, 1995). Soum has also authored a major study of Banzan and Tōju, *Nakae Tōju (1608–1648) et Kumazawa Banzan (1619–1691): Deux penseurs de l'époque d'Edo* (Paris: Collège de France, Institut des Hautes Études Japonaises, 2000). A modern Japanese translation of the *Daigaku wakumon* is in Nishida Taichirō, ed., *Fujiwara Seika Nakae Tōju Kumazawa Banzan Yamazaki Ansai Yamaga Sokō Yamagata Daini shū* (Tokyo: Chikuma shobō, 1970). The present translation is largely based on the text in *Banzan zenshū* (*Banzan's Complete Works*), ed. Masamune Atsuo, vol. 3 (Tokyo: Banzan zenshū kankōkai, 1940), pp. 233–283, as well as on the modern, annotated edition of Banzan's classical Japanese text in Gotō Yōichi and Tomoeda Ryūtarō, eds., *Kumazawa Banzan*, Nihon shisō taikei vol. 30 (Tokyo: Iwanami shoten, 1971). Several early manuscript and woodblock versions of the text are online through the Kokubungaku kenkyū shiryōkan. An undated manuscript copy, including notes throughout in red ink, is online at https://kotenseki.nijl.ac.jp/biblio/200018535/viewer/85?ln=en. An undated woodblock edition is at https://kotenseki.nijl.ac.jp/biblio/100132667/viewer/1?ln=en. A copy of the 1788 woodblock edition is at https://kotenseki.nijl.ac.jp/biblio/100209409/viewer/7?ln=en. The latter includes a new preface, and lists publishers in Edo, Kyoto, and Osaka. A manuscript

the Great Learning in relation to his development as a Confucian theorist and statecraft-thinker, especially as that development crystalized in response to his historical predicament and, most especially, the intellectual and political dynamic of the Tokugawa period. Unlike textbook accounts casting Banzan as one of the period's earliest Wang Yangming (J: Ō Yōmei, 1472–1529) scholars, one profoundly at odds with the wellensconced Zhu Xi (J: Shu Ki, 1130–1200) version of Confucian learning more dominant in his day, this book reappraises Banzan philosophically as a pragmatic relativist, willing to draw ideas and forms of praxis from whatever sources he thought valid and practical, including those of Zhu Xi, Wang Yangming, Nakae Tōju (1608–1648), and others.[6] It is worth noting on this count that Banzan's title was not original: a work compiling Zhu Xi's discussions of the *Great Learning* with his disciples bears the name *Daxue huowen*, which in Japanese is read *Daigaku wakumon.* Presumably, Banzan, who surely knew of that text, understood his own work as, within the context of its unique time, place, and social circumstances, yet another expression of the project earlier advanced by Zhu Xi and his disciples.[7]

In interpreting Banzan as a pragmatic relativist, this book supplements James McMullen's view that Banzan was an idealist.[8] Surely Banzan's lifelong efforts on behalf of compassionate government and socioeconomic prosperity would not have been possible had he not subscribed to high-minded hopes and ideals for the polity, the natural environment, and humanity. Yet Banzan was hardly a philosophically doctrinaire, Panglossian idealist. Instead, he grounded his esteem for ethical ideals such as compassionate government in a pragmatic socio-economic acknowledgment of the contingent, practical realities of time, place,

---

of the 1788 edition, dated to the eleventh month, is at https://kotenseki.nijl.ac.jp/biblio/100199929/viewer/85?ln=en.

[6] Inoue Tetsujirō (1855-1944), in his *Nihon Yōmei gakuha no tetsugaku* (Tokyo: Fuzanbō, 1900), pp. 215–230, pioneered this interpretation of Banzan. While grouping Banzan in with the "Japanese School of Wang Yangming philosophy," Inoue acknowledged that simply classifying Banzan as a Wang Yangming scholar was questionable because, as Banzan himself acknowledged, he drew from Zhu Xi's learning as well. Also, while Banzan began his studies with Nakae Tōju and respected him, he did not typically quote Tōju or recite his views. Most commonly, Banzan put things in his own words. In the end, rather than a doctrinaire schoolman, Banzan was an exceptionally independent thinker.

[7] For a Japanese edition of this text Tomoeda Ryūtarō, ed. *Mōshi wakumon, Daigaku wakumon, Chūyō wakumon,* Kinsei Kanseki sōkan wakoku eiin, shisō 3, hen 5 (Kyoto: Chūbun shuppansha, 1977).

[8] James McMullen, *Idealism, Protest, and the Tale of Genji: The Confucianism of Kumazawa Banzan (1619–91)* (Oxford: Clarendon Press, 1999).

and circumstance, and a realistic understanding, based on his personal experiences, that good can come from any corner. Unlike many Confucian scholars who only sanctioned actions and policies that embodied the highest ethical standards, Banzan was ready to acknowledge the importance of considering, if necessary, expedient measures and temporary fixes as legitimate if not wholly ideal options, depending on the exigencies of human circumstances and the dire needs of the day. As one readily acknowledging the historical variables of time, space, and circumstances as well as the legitimacy of the highest standards and more practical temporary expedients, Banzan is here interpreted as both an idealist and a pragmatic relativist.

Banzan held that everything, including ideas and their practice, should be understood in terms of time, space, and circumstances of rank and order, that is, in terms of the larger geo-historical predicament, problematique, or facticity comprising the overriding, at times determining background informing and affecting every person, event, and moment. In light of his emphasis, especially in *Responding to the Great Learning*, on time, place, and circumstance, the book emphasizes that Banzan, although building on Confucian sources known for their universalistic, trans-temporal and trans-spatial nuances, invariably rendered them in ways expressing the contingent particularity and subjectivity of the early-modern Japanese socio-political environment. Other prominent scholars such as Hayashi Razan (1583–1657), an Edo-based Confucian serving the Tokugawa shogunate, authored politically relevant philosophical treatises as well, though without nearly as much attention to distinctively Japanese subjectivities of time, place, and circumstance. With Banzan, those dimensions in their very particularity were of first-order significance, while otherwise universalistic Confucian notions and their various nuances were, in his writings at least, typically contextualized in relation to them.

The result was that Banzan's writings convey some of the most specifically Japanese expressions of Confucian political thought and action to emerge in seventeenth-century Japan and, for that matter, the Tokugawa period. This is especially evident in *Responding to the Great Learning*, a work that had arguably less to do with the words and passages in the Confucian text, the *Great Learning*, than with Banzan's overall response to that canonical work's utopian goal, "rightly governing the realm [*chikoku*] and bringing peace to all below heaven [*heitenka*]." Banzan's focus on the latter is laid bare in the subtitle to his work – *Another Volume*

on Governing the Realm and Bringing Peace to All below Heaven.[9] Banzan's
subtitle is used here, in abbreviation, as the cover title of this translation-
study of *Responding to the Great Learning* due to its explanatory value,
highlighting the very political nature of Banzan's work. Alternatively,
due to the radical socio-economic and political ramifications of Banzan's
proposals, the main title for this translation-study of Banzan's text might
well have been *A Plan for Restructuring the Realm.* Though this is not a
translation of Banzan's title as such, it aptly captures, along more inter-
pretive lines, what his text was about and what its proposals amounted to
socio-economically and politically.

Banzan's Life, Thought, and Action

Kyoto Confucianism, the Legacy of Fujiwara Seika

Banzan was born in 1619, in the south-central section of Kyoto in Gojō-
chō, the eldest child of a rōnin, Nojiri Kazutoshi (1590–1680), and his
wife, Kame. The same year, Fujiwara Seika (1561–1619), a leading Confucian scholar in the early-Tokugawa, passed away. Seika's legacy as a
relatively independent Confucian based in Kyoto appears to have, in
part, shaped Banzan's philosophical development both in terms of his
independence as a thinker and his admiration for Kyoto's erudition and
civility. As a mature scholar, Seika helped establish the ancient imperial
capital as an alternative center of Confucian learning, one less obliging to
the interests and sensibilities of the newly risen samurai regime than was
Edo, the shogun's capital and increasingly the dominant center of Confucian studies in early modern Japan. Banzan did not, like Seika, remain
in Kyoto the majority of his life. Nevertheless, Banzan did return to the
imperial capital more often than any other center of learning and culture, and envisioned for Kyoto and the sons of its aristocracy, and even
its commoners, an essential role as future educators of the Tokugawa
realm. Simply put, Banzan wanted the teachers of the realm to come
from Kyoto's educated aristocratic elite, spreading the sophistication in

---

[9] Most translations of the *Great Learning* render *chikoku*, or *zhi guo* in Chinese, as
"governing states." Banzan's understanding of *koku* seems best translated as an imperial
"province" rather than state. Banzan's respect for the imperial line and the geo-political
order it defined presumably led him to discuss the polity as composed of provinces rather
than daimyō domains. When he refers to the rulers of the *koku* or provinces, he refers to,
in virtually all instances, the daimyō vassals of the shogunate. Nevertheless, Banzan's text
was not addressed primarily to daimyō as such but instead to the shogunate, prompting
the translation here of its subtitle as "governing the realm."

learning and culture that distinguished the ancient capital throughout the country. Seika never imagined as much, but through his efforts as a Confucian teacher in the imperial capital, he contributed to the growth of Confucianism as well as the educated aristocracy that Banzan planned to enlist and mobilize as teachers for all of Japan.

A transitional figure, Seika, as a young Buddhist monk, first studied Confucianism and Buddhism at one of Kyoto's grandest Zen temples, the Shōkokuji, only to later move toward a more exclusive focus on Confucianism. Seika's evolution accelerated following his encounter with a Korean prisoner of war, Kang Hang (1567–1618), captured during Toyotomi Hideyoshi's invasions of the Korean peninsula in the late 1590s. Kang provided Seika with a wide-ranging introduction to newer expressions of Confucianism that had emerged in China during the Song, Yuan (1279–1368), and Ming dynasties. These had long circulated among Korean scholars, but in Japan made limited headway prior to the early seventeenth century as teachings independent of Buddhism. While mediated by Kang, Seika's Confucianism included, somewhat eclectically, the multifaceted, multi-dynastic developments from China and Korea rather than adhering, along doctrinaire lines, to one school of philosophy or set of ideas formulated in a single dynasty.[10]

Seika promoted the new learning among the educated elite of the imperial capital as well as warrior-leaders and aspiring intellectuals. One of the latter who briefly studied with him, Hayashi Razan, subsequently took a position in Edo as a scholar-secretary in service to Tokugawa Ieyasu (1543–1616), the founding shogun of the Tokugawa regime. From that position, Razan and his progeny, who emerged as hereditary scholar-servants of the shogunate, advanced the fortunes of the new Confucian learning in Edo. Yet unlike Seika, Razan focused on the teachings of Zhu Xi and one of Zhu's last disciples, Chen Beixi (1159–1223) to the relative exclusion of others. In contrast, Seika's thought was wide-ranging and broad-minded, finding value in the teachings of Zhu Xi, his Ming rival, Wang Yangming, and even later followers of Wang such as the late-Ming syncretist, Lin Chao'en (1517–1598). Much the same was true of Banzan's Confucianism, which drew on the ideas of Zhu Xi, Wang Yangming, and other thinkers as their ideas fit the times, locales, and human circumstances of contemporary Japan.

[10] For a translation of Kang Hang's writings, see JaHyun Kim Haboush and Kenneth Robinson, translators, *A Korean War Captive in Japan, 1597–1600: The Writings of Kang Hang* (New York: Columbia University Press, 2013).

Seika's legacy in textual production apparently influenced Banzan at another level. Seika's best-known treatise, *Essentials of the Great Learning* (*Daigaku yōryaku*), was completed in his final year and published posthumously in 1630. In focusing on the *Great Learning*, Seika was at one with many Song, Yuan, and Ming Confucians including Cheng Yi (1033–1107), Zhu Xi, and Wang Yangming, all of whom authored pivotal works on the *Great Learning*. Prior to Cheng Yi, the *Great Learning* was the forty-second of forty-nine chapters in the ancient Confucian classic, *Book of Rituals* (*Liji*). Cheng Yi, however, declared the chapter a separate work unto itself, describing it as "the gateway" to learning. Zhu Xi also privileged the *Great Learning* as a separate text and moreover designated it the first of the so-called Four Books[11] of Confucian study. After Zhu's commentaries on the Four Books became, in the early-fourteenth century, orthodox learning for civil service examinations, the *Great Learning* was studied far and wide by aspiring civil servants and the philosophically astute. Even Zhu's critics, including Wang Yangming, fashioned their interpretations of Confucian learning via their own commentaries on the *Great Learning*, making it arguably the single most important text in post-Song Confucianism.

In *Essentials of the Great Learning*, Seika rightly emphasized the ultimate political importance of the *Great Learning*. There he explained,

> If a student learns this book by heart, he will need no other texts … There is no Confucianism outside this work. Lectures that exclusively focus on the literary arts, so popular these days, are in fact of no use to a ruler. Rulers need only discipline their own mind and heart and try to apply the teachings of the *Great Learning*.[12]

Seika thus agreed with the emerging East Asian consensus recognizing the *Great Learning* as the most primary book in the Confucian curriculum of study. Moreover, he affirmed, as did Banzan, the *Great Learning*'s political importance for rulers.

Following his departure from the Shōkokuji, Seika's studies were sponsored by a samurai lord, Akamatsu Hiromichi (1562–1600), a loyal

---

[11] The Four Books are the *Great Learning*, the *Analects* of Confucius, the *Mencius*, and the *Middle Way*.

[12] Fujiwara Seika, *Daigaku yōryaku*, in Ishida Ichirō and Kanaya Osamu, eds., *Fujiwara Seika/Hayashi Razan*, Nihon shisō taikei, vol. 28 (Tokyo: Iwanami shoten, 1975), p. 44. Translation adapted from Wm. Theodore de Bary, Carol Gluck, and Arthur Tiedemann, eds., *Sources of Japanese Tradition*, vol. 2: *1600–2000* (New York: Columbia University Press, 2005), p. 44.

supporter of the doomed Toyotomi cause at the Battle of Sekigahara in 1600. A month later, the Tokugawa ordered Hiromichi to commit suicide.[13] Having lost his patron as a consequence of the Tokugawa victory, Seika found it difficult to serve the new regime in any capacity. According to Kang's writings, Ieyasu, in an attempt to buy Seika, offered him a new residence in Kyoto along with an annual rice stipend of 2,000 *koku*.[14] Not a man to be bought, Seika refused both.[15] Though only 39, Seika remained in Kyoto, a "retired" scholar, independent of Tokugawa patronage and control, until his passing in 1619. His integrity as an independent teacher was made possible by support from other warriors, often with ties to the defeated Toyotomi cause, including merchants such as Suminokura Ryōi (1554–1614), as well as aristocrats and others in Kyoto interested in his learning. Seika's last decades were ones of modesty, a result of his decision not to peddle himself as a scholar in service to the ruling house whose rise to power entailed the death of his late patron.

Seika's independence need not, however, be explained exclusively in terms of his personal loyalties to fallen opponents of the Tokugawa. Chinese and Korean representatives of the new Confucian learning – new at least for men like Seika – were driven individualists, intent upon offering their insights and thoughts on an ancient tradition of thinking, Confucianism, in an effort to make it more meaningful to present realities. As Seika learned more about Zhu Xi and Wang Yangming, he saw in them examples of intellectual integrity even in the face of exclusion, punishment, and isolation. More immediately, Seika's encounter with Kang Hang, a Korean prisoner of war who remained loyal to his homeland and determined, even at the risk of life and family, to escape from captivity, must have impressed him. Kang's stand possibly inspired Seika to new levels of righteousness in remaining committed to his beliefs rather than stooping to mercenary scholarship. As one apparently loyal in human

[13] For an account of Seika's relationship with Akamatsu Hiromichi, see W. J. Boot, *The Adoption and Adaptation of Neo-Confucianism in Tokugawa Japan: The Role of Fujiwara Seika and Hayashi Razan* (Leiden: Ph.D. Dissertation, 1982), pp. 15-16, 19-20.

[14] One *koku* equals 180 liters or 380 US pints, or five US bushels. Measured in terms of weight, 1 *koku* equals 150 kilograms, or approximately 330 US pounds. The *koku* was a standard unit of measure for rice income during the Tokugawa period. It was generally considered to be the amount of rice that one adult would need in one year.

[15] Evidence of Seika's distance from Ieyasu and the Tokugawa regime appears in the writings of Kang Hang, the Korean prisoner of war whom Seika befriended. According to Kang Hang, Seika helped him and his family escape captivity in 1600 and return to Korea, clearly in violation of the emerging law of the land. Haboush and Robinson, trans., *A Korean War Captive in Japan*, pp. xiii, xix, 95.

relations instead of selfish material gain, Seika embodied Confucian ethics in assisting his friend in learning, Kang Hang, escape from captivity and return to his homeland in Korea.

Also, it must be added that Seika seemingly enjoyed, even in the aristocratic poverty required by his highmindedness as a Confucian scholar, the cultured environment of the imperial capital and its air of ancient civility. With later scholars such as Banzan who gravitated toward the cultured, aristocratic world of Kyoto rather than the upstart, samurai-dominated Edo, Seika's legacy was again apparent.

Relocation and Adoption

In 1626, Banzan's father sent his wife and children to Mito domain to live with her father, Kumazawa Morihisa (d. 1634), a samurai retainer of Tokugawa Yoshifusa (1603–1661), the daimyō lord of that domain. Earlier, Morihisa had served, among others, Shibata Katsuie (1522–1583), a retainer of Oda Nobunaga (1534–1582), and Fukushima Masanori (1561–1624), a retainer of the Toyotomi family. But when Banzan, age 8, arrived in Mito, his maternal grandfather was a retainer of Tokugawa Yorifusa, lord of the domain and son of Ieyasu, founder of the Tokugawa shogunate.

Morihisa adopted Banzan into his family, giving him the Kumazawa family name. As Banzan's surrogate father, Morihisa most likely imparted to Banzan some of the issues that one-time Toyotomi loyalists, as the losers in the Tokugawa rise to power, especially in the wake of the siege of Osaka Castle in 1615, retained. Fukushima Masanori, one of Morihisa's previous lords, had, incidentally, switched his allegiance to the Tokugawa at the Battle of Sekigahara (1600), nimbly negotiating his way into the new age of Tokugawa power. Banzan's early upbringing, in Kyoto and then later in Mito with his grandfather, perhaps predisposed him to a complex loyalty to the Tokugawa as a habitual critic of the regime to which he had somewhat ambiguous cause to feel but so close.[16]

When Morihisa passed away in 1634, Banzan's next move hardly improved his relationship with the still crystalizing Tokugawa order. Family connections in Kyoto enabled Banzan, then age 16, to take up service as a page to Ikeda Mitsumasa (1609–1682), the *tozama* "outer

[16] Akiyama Kōdō, *Bokenroku* (Okayama: Okayama ken, 1901), pp. 1–3. A digital version of the text is available through the Kokuritsu kokkai toshokan dejitaru korekushon at http://dl.ndl.go.jp/info:ndljp/pid/781327. Also, Gotō Yōichi, "Kumazawa Banzan no shōgai to shisō no keisei," in Gotō and Tomoeda, eds., *Kumazawa Banzan*, pp. 467–469.

lord" of a sizable 320,000-*koku* domain, Bizen-Okayama, in southwestern Honshū. Outer lords included those who had opposed the Tokugawa at the Battle of Sekigahara, but successfully came to terms with the new order as vassals, and so were typically kept at a distance from the main centers of power in Kyoto and Edo. Like all vassals, however, *tozama* were expected to render service to the shogunate, affirming, through participation, their subordination within a ceremonial and administrative hierarchy central to the Tokugawa polity.[17] Ikeda Mitsumasa was also, by his strategic political marriage to a granddaughter of Tokugawa Ieyasu, one of the closest "outer lords" to the shogunate. As Mitsumasa's pageboy, Banzan gained additional insights into the uneasy, often complex relationship between Edo and those subsumed within its evolving power structure.

Christianity and the Shimabara Uprising

In Bizen-Okayama, the young Banzan soon gained the trust of his daimyō whom he accompanied to Edo in 1637,[18] while the latter was rendering service to the shogunate. This trip was Banzan's first to Edo, the shogun's capital, already a politico-military boom town centered around the Tokugawa castle. As things turned out, Banzan's time in Edo coincided with a major military challenge, the Shimabara Uprising of 1637–1638, fueled in part by Christian peasants rebelling against the oppressive lord of Shimabara Province, Matsukura Katsuie, on the southwestern island of Kyushu.

Whether Banzan had previously been exposed to anti-Christian sentiments, he was in 1637. That year, his biological father, Kazutoshi, joined the shogunate's forces in putting down the uprising. Also, the shogunate ordered Banzan's lord, Ikeda Mitsumasa, to return to Bizen-Okayama to raise forces to assist in quashing the rebellion. In 1638, Banzan, on his own initiative, left Edo, returned to Okayama, and then, having declared himself of age, requested permission to join Tokugawa forces in the southwest suppressing the Shimabara forces. The rebellion ended

---

[17] Daimyō were required, under the "alternate attendance" (*sankin kōtai*) system, to spend half of the year, or every other year, in Edo, rendering various forms of service to the shogunate. The other half of the year, or every other year, they could return to their home provinces. Still, their wives and children were required to remain in Edo. This requirement was a major drain on daimyō resources. Also, shogunally decreed building projects and other official undertakings were often financed by daimyō funds.

[18] Itō Tasaburō, "Nenpu," *Nakae Tōju Kumazawa Banzan*, Nihon no meicho vol. 11 (Tokyo: Chūō kōron, 1976), p. 51.

before Banzan's request could be acted upon, but his decision, however well intended, to leave Edo without permission was not well received by his daimyō. The resulting strained relations between Mitsumasa and Banzan prompted Banzan's next decision, to relinquish his position with the Ikeda daimyō.[19]

Even at this early stage, Banzan's preference for engaged practical activity as opposed to the life of ceremonial, urban leisure, was evident, as was his distaste for Christianity and his determination to see it eliminated. Later, in chapter 15 of *Responding to the Great Learning*, "Eliminating Christianity," Banzan addressed the topic in some detail, especially as it related to the shogunate's requirement – established after the Shimabara Uprising – that the population register itself at Buddhist temples as a way of ensuring that there were no lingering practitioners of Christianity. While Banzan did not sanction Christianity, he criticized the shogunate's temple registration requirement as a wasteful procedure often administered by a corrupt Buddhist clergy. In his *Accumulating Righteousness, Further Writings* (*Shūgi gaisho*), Banzan described Christianity as a teaching that Japanese had been prepared for by another that he, Banzan, had a distaste for, Buddhism. According to Banzan, "Unless Confucianism prevails and Buddhism is cut off, then Christianity will steal the realm. If that happens, then Shintō and Confucianism will be destroyed, Japan will end up as a country of beasts, and the imperial throne will be lost."[20]

The root of Christianity's appeal, in Banzan's view, was the confusion and poverty of the people. Rather than temple registration, the best way to combat the foreign religion was by a comprehensive program of education for the Japanese people in the fundamentally secular teachings of Confucianism regarding the right ethical way of human relations in this world. Unless this were done, Banzan feared that Christianity would grow because of its resemblance to the other otherworldly teaching that for a millennium had already dominated the realm as a religious force. Ultimately, however, Banzan viewed Christianity as superior to Buddhism and therefore as a real threat to both Buddhism and Confucianism, and of the three, the one that might, if not effectively checked, prevail.[21]

---

[19] Akiyama, *Bokenroku*, p. 4.

[20] Kumazawa Banzan, *Shūgi gaisho*, in Itō Tasaburō, ed., *Nakae Tōju Kumazawa Banzan*, Nihon no meicho, vol. 11 (Tokyo: Chūō kōronsha, 1976), ch. 10, p. 426; *Banzan zenshū*, vol. 2, p. 175.

[21] Kumazawa Banzan, *Shūgi washo*, in Gotō Yōichi and Tomoeda Ryūtarō, eds., *Kumazawa Banzan*, Nihon shisō taikei, vol. 30 (Tokyo: Iwanami shoten, 1971), pp. 222–223. Also, Inoue Tetsujirō, *Nihon Yōmei gakuha no tetsugaku*, pp. 234–237.

Without question, Banzan's concern that Christianity, which he likened to an "internal disease" (*naibyō*), would undermine Japanese political and spiritual culture began to intensify from this pivotal moment. His readiness to break with protocol, leave Edo, and then as a determined volunteer seek to serve in the military suppression of the foreign teaching, gave practical expression to what would become his later theoretical opposition to Christianity.[22]

Other Confucian scholars of the day – including Hayashi Razan in Edo and Matsunaga Sekigo (1592–1657) in Kyoto – criticized Christianity openly, contributing as intellectuals to shogunal efforts to eliminate the foreign religion. In the opening decades of the Tokugawa period, Ieyasu, the founding shogun, had outlawed Christianity and expelled missionaries from the realm. Thereafter, successive efforts by the shogunate and vassal daimyō were made to rid the country of the foreign teaching. The persecution was particularly harsh in Kyoto and on the island of Kyushu where Christian missionaries had earlier established a presence. Banzan's views, while harsh, thus reiterated the strong anti-Christian sentiments characterizing the Tokugawa period. Within anti-Christian discourse, Confucian scholars of all stripes were vocal opponents of the foreign religion, and Banzan, a native of Kyoto and a later retainer, once again, in Bizen-Okayama, halfway between Kyoto and Kyushu, was no exception.

On another count, it is noteworthy that Banzan's 1637 experience in Edo did not transform him into a devoted urbanite, won over by the comforts and amusements of the bustling big city. His readiness to depart the burgeoning shogunal capital and the relative security it offered foreshadowed his later proposals, made in *Responding to the Great Learning*, to reduce the ceremonial and service requirements expected of shogunal vassals and return not only samurai back to the countryside, but most of Edo back into rice fields. Banzan's seemingly incredible suggestion on this count would have effectively reversed, at its epicenter, the urbanization process rapidly transforming the socio–economic and political landscape of Tokugawa Japan.

Study with Nakae Tōju

In 1638, after leaving Bizen-Okayama, Banzan, age 20, moved back to the Kansai, taking up residence in Kirihara village, Ōmi Province (now,

---

[22] Miyazaki Michio, "Kumazawa Banzan no kirishitan ron," *Kokugakuin zasshi*, vol. 85, no. 9. 1984.

Shiga Prefecture), the area where his paternal grandmother's family lived, not far from Kyoto. The years that followed were formative ones for Banzan's education. Reportedly, his father gave him books on military learning. In 1640, Banzan, then 22, first read Zhu Xi's *Commentaries on the Four Books* and apparently was moved by their teachings,[23] resulting in something akin to a conversion experience prompting his commitment to Confucianism. In search of a teacher, he visited Kyoto in 1641, where he learned of Nakae Tōju's work in the nearby village of Ogawa, also in Ōmi Province. Later that year, Banzan visited Tōju twice and then subsequently, in the spring of 1642, heard his lectures on the *Classic of Filial Piety*, the *Great Learning*, and the *Middle Way* (C: *Zhongyong*; J: *Chūyō*). Subsequently, while Banzan's father was traveling to Edo, Banzan, as the eldest son, returned to Kirihara to take care of his family.

Banzan's brief study with Tōju, followed by several years of study on his own while taking care of his family in Kirihara, has prompted some interpreters, largely following Inoue Tetsujirō's (1855–1944) early-twentieth-century writings on Japanese Confucianism,[24] to associate Banzan with the Japanese Wang Yangming school. While there is some truth in this, when Banzan first studied with Tōju in 1641, the latter was only 34 years old, and Banzan a mere 23. Also, Tōju had yet to obtain a copy of the *Complete Works of Wang Yangming*. Their teacher–student relationship only lasted a matter of months and occurred at a time in Tōju's intellectual development when he himself had just begun his move away from Zhu Xi's teachings and toward those of Wang Yangming, but not via Wang's own writings so much as those of Wang Ji (1498–1583), one of the more radical disciples of Wang known for his claim that neither good nor evil resided in the original substance of things.

Equally if not more important for Banzan's development as a thinker was Tōju's advocacy of the unity of Confucianism and Shintō. Similar teachings had appeared even in the Kamakura period, but they became more commonplace in the seventeenth century as thinker after thinker, beginning with Hayashi Razan and Nakae Tōju, endorsed similar ideas.

---

[23] Akiyama, *Bokenroku*, pp. 4–6.

[24] Especially relevant here was Inoue's *The Philosophy of the Japanese School of Wang Yangming* (*Nihon Yōmei gakuha no tetsugaku*), but even Inoue emphasizes how Banzan's thought drew on that of Zhu Xi, and often criticized Wang Yangming's ideas. Though Inoue described Banzan as an eclectic thinker of sorts, who situated earlier thinkers according to their time, place, and circumstances, he did, in the end, tie Banzan to the Wang Yangming school. Later scholarship seemingly lost the nuances of Inoue's analysis, and simply categorized Banzan as a Wang Yangming scholar.

Soon, Yamaga Sokō and Yamazaki Ansai advocated their own versions of Confucian-Shintō unity. Banzan became a central figure promoting this view, a legacy in part of his brief study with Tōju. The same year Banzan attended Tōju's lectures on the *Classic of Filial Piety*, the *Great Learning*, and the *Middle Way*, Tōju had made a pilgrimage to the Grand Ise Shrine, one of the holiest Shintō sites in Japan. Commenting on it, Tōju noted that Ise was devoted to "the primal ancestor of the country and was a place every Japanese should visit." In a poem written on the occasion, Tōju compared the creative work of the high Shintō deity, Amaterasu the Sun Goddess, to that of Fu Xi,[25] a legendary ancient sage figure extolled by Confucians for having invented written Chinese and the trigrams used in the *Book of Changes* (C: *Yijing*; J: *Ekikyō*).

In *Responding to the Great Learning*, Banzan similarly paired the three treasures of Shintō – the jewel, the mirror, and the sword – with the three virtues of Confucianism as explained in the *Middle Way* – compassion (*ren*), wisdom (*zhi*), and courage (*yong*). Banzan added that whatever writing existed in the age of the gods in Japan had been lost, and the three spiritual treasures (*shingi*) were all that was transmitted. Even though the utmost in simplicity, the three treasures were the divine origins of morality and culture, and were endowed with exceptional spiritual significance, lofty, expansive, luminous, deep, mysterious, and profound. Further extolling the three treasures, Banzan added that they conveyed all that was necessary for understanding Confucian methods of mind control and concomitant teachings about government.[26] Banzan's ideas were not identical with Tōju's, but their syncretic approaches, pairing Shintō and Chinese philosophical notions, were similar. In the end, both were arguably as devoted, at the most fundamental level, to preserving and rejuvenating the spiritual beliefs and practices of Japan as they were to Confucianism qua Confucianism. As noted earlier, in Banzan's thinking at least, Confucianism as such was not ideally suited to Japan's environmental circumstances (*suido*).

Tōju also emerged, around the time of Banzan's study with him, as an advocate of Confucian learning as "no different from the [arts of]

---

[25] For an excellent discussion of Tōju's life and thought, see Barry D. Steben, "Nakae Tōju and the Birth of Wang Yang-ming Learning in Japan," *Monumenta Serica*, vol. 46 (1998), pp. 233–263. Also see Gregory J. Smits, "The Sages' Scale in Japan: Nakae Tōju (1608–1648) and Situational Weighing," *Transactions of the Asiatic Society of Japan*, Fourth Series, vol. 6 (1991), pp. 1–25.

[26] Banzan, "Suido kai," *Shūgi gaisho*, ch. 16; *Banzan zenshū*, vol. 2, pp. 279–280.

government by which the world is ruled."[27] This political understanding of Confucianism was echoed in Banzan's later work, especially his *Responding to the Great Learning*. It also meshed well with Banzan's thinking about Shintō religiosity, which viewed government as an expression of ritual (*matsurigoto*). Equally important for Banzan was Tōju's opposition to Buddhism. As of 1631, a decade before Banzan's study with him, Tōju had already criticized Hayashi Razan for submitting to the shogunate's demand that he, Razan, shave his head and wear Buddhist robes as a condition of service. In criticizing Razan, Tōju perhaps sought to appear high-minded even while calling attention to himself and his supposed integrity. At the very least, Banzan's antipathy for Buddhism resonated with Tōju's thought.

Tōju was surely important to Banzan, but in the end Banzan's ideas developed along independent lines. Later, when asked about Tōju's teachings, then referred to as "Jiangxi teachings" alluding to the Chinese province where Wang Yangming had developed many of his ideas, Banzan, in his *Accumulating Righteousness, Japanese Writings*, responded:

> While there is some benefit in them, there is harm as well. It is not clear that those receiving his teachings understand the Confucian classics and their commentaries, nor do they seem to grasp the main ideas of the Confucian way. They declare their own narrow perspectives to be the right ones and, in the process, set forth mistaken views. Nevertheless, they call them the learning of the sage Confucius, leading fools down the wrong path. Prior to Tōju's learning, there was none of this kind of harmful learning. Although it has enlightened many people below heaven about Confucian learning, one finds few among them who are truly fond of virtue. Worse still, more than a few of Tōju's students take great pride in their coarse learning.[28]

When told that he seemed arrogant in espousing his own ideas while only infrequently mentioning those of Tōju, Banzan replied as follows:

> What I have received from my teacher and have not differed with are true moral principles. In response to [changes in] time, place, and social circumstances, insufficiencies in learning and practice begin to develop … Those who come after me will supplement insufficiencies in my learning. And it would be best for them to revise my words and actions if they do not match later times. Yet it is impossible that

---

[27] Ibid., p. 256.   [28] Kumazawa Banzan, *Shūgi washo*, pp. 200–201.

there is even a hair's worth of difference between my teacher, Tōju, and me regarding the true principles of the great moral way. It will be the same with those who rightly follow me.[29]

When asked about the true moral principles of the great way, Banzan replied:

They [true moral principles] state that a person should not do anything that is contrary to righteousness and justice. They also state that a person should not execute another person for minor crimes simply so that they might take control of the realm below heaven. Moral principles have this power because the luminous virtue that we hold as our foundation prompts us to detest what is wrong and to be ashamed of what is evil. The method of the mind consists in maintaining our minds so that we cultivate this luminous virtue and daily make it shine by not doing any wrong to others due to our selfish desires. Such are the true principles in the method of the mind.

Regarding these, not only do my teacher Tōju and I not differ, neither do China and Japan differ. If I neglect these principles, then even if my words do not differ in the least from those of my teacher, then I am not truly a follower of my teacher. Even if one of my followers later declares that my words are mistaken and does not follow them, if they have these true principles in their minds, then they have the same sense of purpose as do I.[30]

Banzan's time with his teacher might have been brief, but it apparently was exceptionally meaningful. The few months with Tōju led Banzan to a vision of the foundations of morality, the basis of his idealism, as well as an understanding that there were contingent factors of time, place, and social circumstances that would result in relative truths that were not always and everywhere expressed in quite the same terms, the basis of his pragmatic relativism. On the latter count, Banzan allowed, he and Tōju were not always necessarily the same, but on the former, he insisted that they did not differ a single iota.

Return to Bizen-Okayama

In 1645, Banzan returned to Okayama domain to take up service in a minor capacity once again to the daimyō lord there, Ikeda Mitsumasa. This time, however, Banzan, 27, was more mature and educated, having

---

[29] Ibid., pp. 254–255.   [30] Ibid.

briefly studied under Tōju, and then having devoted himself to book learning for several years thereafter. Within one year after having arrived in Bizen-Okayama, Banzan distinguished himself as a scholar-samurai and was rewarded with a new role as a chamberlain to Mitsumasa, a position with a stipend of 300 *koku*. By most counts, Banzan had risen quickly, and he continued to do so.

The following year, in the eighth month of 1648, Tōju passed away, age 41. Shortly thereafter, Mitsumasa permitted Banzan to attend Tōju's final services in Ōmi. With Mitsumasa's backing, Banzan went, renewing his ties to the Tōju legacy and making overtures to some of Tōju's disciples regarding service in Okayama domain. Many of them subsequently became Ikeda retainers. Earlier, Mitsumasa reportedly found Tōju's ideas worthy of attention and had invited him to Okayama to serve. Whether Mitsumasa found in Tōju, who had criticized the shogunate's scholar-servant, Razan, a scholar of his own taste is open to question, but the resonance between the powerful outer lord and a marginal, independent-minded Confucian increasingly associated with alleged heterodoxies, as Tōju's learning and Wang Yangming thought came to be viewed by the shogunate and its most obliging vassals, seems more than coincidental.

The Flower Garden Learning Center

In 1641, well before Banzan's arrival, Mitsumasa founded, just outside the walls of Okayama Castle, the Flower Garden Learning Center (*Hanabatake kyōjō*), one of the first domain schools in Tokugawa Japan. Shortly after retaining Banzan, Mitsumasa had him serve as the center's director. Some have suggested that the Flower Garden Learning Center was not so much a school as what turned out to be a private study space for Banzan, his followers, and others interested in his teachings.[31] While that might be so, the center nevertheless marked an important secular development in the history of Tokugawa educational practices, one in which Banzan played an important role as the lead scholar-instructor. Banzan's teachings were wide-ranging, but most distinctive insofar as they included, rather than excluded, Tōju's teachings and ideas associated with Wang Yangming learning.

---

[31] Okayama shi dejitaru myūjiamu, "Kaenkai to Kumazawa Banzan," *Okayama no kyōiku* (Okayama daigaku fuzoku toshokan, 2009), p. 1. Accessed on February 23, 2019, http://www.lib.okayama-u.ac.jp/ikeda/pdf/h21.pdf.

As director of the center, Banzan drafted its "Flower Garden Oath" (*Kaen kaiyaku*), the opening provision of which is indicative of the center's overall nature and purpose as a place of study and learning. The oath suggests that the duty of samurai consists in taking responsibility for the protection and education of the people via exercising intuitive knowledge in the civil and military learning of compassion and bravery.[32] With the oath's reference to exercising "intuitive knowledge [C: *liangzhi*; J: *ryōchi*]," a Wang Yangming ethical teaching, its philosophical identity seemed, at least superficially, cast. As the director of the center, Banzan became, through the oath, more publicly associated in the minds of some with Wang Yangming thought and all the political baggage that went with it. After Banzan's departure from Okayama in 1657, the Flower Garden Center was dissolved. Nevertheless, during his tenure there, it emerged as an educational space where Banzan trained like-minded samurai, many of whom later served in Okayama administration, in his thinking about Confucianism, Shintō, government, culture, and spirituality.

Rifle Command

In 1650, Banzan was also named a domain commander of the Okayama rifle brigade with a stipend of 3,000 *koku*, a tenfold increase over his earlier stipend, making him one of the most favored retainers in the domain. As commander, Banzan emphasized not only the brigade's responsibility to protect and defend the domain, but also the essential unity of the way of the samurai and Confucianism, one wherein responsibility, trust, compassion, and concern for people were taught alongside military formations and the basics of using a rifle. Some of those trained in Banzan's rifle brigade later held administrative positions as village intendants. By 1663, in four Okayama districts, nearly seventy-five village officials were former members of Banzan's rifle brigade.[33]

Banzan also took advantage of his role as commander to relocate some samurai in training to a rural village, Hattōji-mura, strategically located on Okayama's frontier. Though hardly Banzan's intent at the time, this exercise involved, in part at least, what he later advocated for the entire realm, transfer of samurai away from castle towns and back to the countryside to take up life as warrior-farmers. In *Responding to the Great*

[32] Gotō, "Kumazawa Banzan no shōgai to shisō," p. 481.
[33] McMullen, *Idealism*, p. 107.

Learning, Banzan's strong views on this arguably drew from his experiences as an Okayama rifle brigade commander when he personally supervised an analogous relocation.[34]

Banzan's work with the domain rifle brigade paralleled somewhat Wang Yangming's life experiences. In addition to being a philosophical thinker, Wang served intermittently as a military commander who led Ming forces that suppressed several rebellions. On another count, Banzan's work with samurai trained in the use of firearms made him both a more respected and suspected samurai retainer, since the rifle forces that defended the realm could also be marshalled to challenge it. When coupled with his allusions to the, in some corners at least, heterodox Wang Yangming teachings, Banzan appeared, in the eyes of those ready to conclude the worst, a possibly dangerous man with a loyal and militarily trained following. Wang Yangming also had found that his military accomplishments in putting down rebellions soon bred jealousy and slander, resulting in his own eventual exile.

Early Prominence in Edo

In the spring of 1649, Banzan accompanied his daimyō Ikeda Mitsumasa to Edo for the latter's time there in service to the shogunate. While in Edo, Banzan, age 31, emerged as a popular teacher, attracting numerous students including rōnin as well as some daimyō and lower-level retainers of the shogunate. The same year, Banzan completed a short treatise, *Western Inscription for Japan* (*Yamato nishi no mei*),[35] his reformulation of ideas earlier set forth by the Song dynasty thinker Zhang Zai (1020–1077) in his *Western Inscription* (C: *Ximing*; J: *Nishi no mei*). The latter expressed an ethical vision affirming a personal sense of familial oneness with the ten-thousand things of existence grounded in the recognition of heaven as one's father and earth as one's mother, and the plurality of being, including plants, animals, and even inorganic things, as one's brothers and sisters.

Zhang Zai's ideas were incorporated into Zhu Xi's thinking, especially as presented in his philosophical anthology *Reflections on Things at Hand* (C: *Jinsilu*; J: *Kinshiroku*), coedited with Lü Zuqian. Nevertheless, this kind of Confucian mysticism later came to be more associated with

---

[34] Galen M. Fisher, "Kumazawa Banzan, His Life and Ideas," *Transactions of the Asiatic Society of Japan*, 2nd Series, vol. 16 (1938), p. 236. Gotō, "Kumazawa Banzan shōgai to shisō," p. 480. McMullen, *Idealism*, pp. 97–98, 100, 107.

[35] This text is in the *Banzan zenshū*, vol. 5, pp. 117–132.

Wang Yangming's teachings than Zhu Xi's, in large part because Wang included a variation of it prominently in his central writing *Inquiry on the Great Learning (Daxue wen)*. Banzan's readiness to draw on the environmentally sensitive thought of Zhang Zai reflects his relatively nondoctrinaire approach to Confucian learning. Also, Banzan's authorship of this treatise while in Edo reflected, to an extent, his concern for and sense of oneness with the natural order even while residing in the singularly artificial urban density of Edo. In *Responding to the Great Learning*, Banzan took his admiration for nature to new heights, calling for a deconstruction of much of the shogun's capital city for the sake of returning it to agrarian countryside.

In 1651, Banzan again accompanied Mitsumasa to Edo on the latter's duties serving the shogunate. Once again, in Edo, Banzan distinguished himself as a teacher, attracting the attention of many. That year, those seeking instruction included Tokugawa Yorinobu (1602–1671), the tenth son of Ieyasu; the shogunal elder counselor, Matsudaira Nobutsune (1596–1662); the shogunal deputy, Itakura Shigemune (1586–1657), a succession of daimyō including Inaba Masanori (1623–1683), Kuze Hiroyuki (1609–1679), Itakura Shigenori (1617–1673), Nakagawa Hisakiyo (1615–1681), Asano Nagaharu (1614–1675), as well as various lower-level Tokugawa retainers. There was even talk that the then-reigning third shogun, Tokugawa Iemitsu (1604–1651), was considering Banzan for a position within the shogunate. Iemitsu's passing that year, however, ended Banzan's immediate chances for high service.[36] Nevertheless, in a very brief time, he had evidently risen to considerable prominence in relation to his daimyō, his domain of service, and, most fatefully, the shogun's capital, Edo.

Rōnin Uprisings and Razan's Slanderous Critique

Iemitsu's passing in the fourth month of 1651 was followed, later that year, by a failed uprising led by Yui Shōsetsu (1605–1651), an Edo commoner-rōnin who had achieved notice for his efforts in military studies and samurai academies. The latter served not only as training grounds for samurai of all levels, but also, in some instances, as spaces wherein samurai, rōnin, and sundry others shared opinions, hopes, dreams, and

---

[36] Banzan discusses his prominence among the "three lords" (*sanke*), or the heads of families directly related to Tokugawa Ieyasu, around this moment, in *Banzan zenshū*, vol. 2, pp. 113–114. Also see Gotō, "Kumazawa Banzan no shōgai to shisō," p. 482. McMullen, p. 94.

frustrations with the existing order. Despite his commoner background, Shōsetsu was closely associated with rōnin and samurai and so later came to be known, along with Banzan and Yamaga Sokō, as one of "the three great rōnin" of the early Tokugawa period. Working with Marubashi Chūya (d. 1651), a rōnin martial arts instructor, Shōsetsu plotted an insurrection to be launched immediately after Iemitsu's passing and meant to overthrow the Tokugawa shogunate. The conspiracy was uncovered, however, and effectively quashed in its early stages. Chūya and Shōsetsu died in the process, in the ninth month of 1651. The following year, 1652, another anti-Tokugawa plot led by Betsuki Shōzaemon (d. 1652), wherein the shogun's capital was to be set ablaze and the top leadership of the shogunate assassinated, was uncovered. Betsuki and others in the conspiracy were crucified.[37]

Such uprisings intensified shogunal awareness of potentially explosive threats the growing rōnin population posed to Edo and the provinces. The shogunate soon clamped down, monitoring martial arts academies where rōnin sometimes aired their grievances. In 1652, one of the great elders in the shogunate, Sakai Tadakatsu (1587–1662), moved to suppress scholarly gatherings in the domains, fearing that they might be occasions for rallying rōnin discontent.[38] As a prominent teacher serving an outer daimyō, Banzan's even brief references to Wang Yangming teachings such as intuitive knowledge and action, along with his earlier service as commander of a rifle brigade in Okayama, prompted shogunal suspicions. With prevailing anxieties over possible rōnin uprisings, Banzan was apparently viewed, perhaps due to his philosophical independence, as potential trouble, a loose cannon needing a tether.

It did not help Banzan's fortunes that Tōju had in 1631, two decades before, openly criticized Razan for submitting to the shogunal demand that he shave his head and wear Buddhist robes as a condition for service as a scholar. Tōju saw Razan's compliance as a betrayal of the integrity that Confucians – who did not typically shave their heads and wear Buddhist robes – were supposed to embody. By 1651, Tōju was long gone, but his apparent successor, Banzan, was now vulnerable because his profile increasingly resembled that of Yui Shōsetsu and Marubashi Chūya: he was a charismatic teacher leading a samurai school, moreover in an outer province over which the shogunate had limited, remote authority.

[37] Gotō, "Kumazawa Banzan no shōgai to shisō," p. 482.
[38] Kimura Mitsunori, "Nenpu," in Kimura and Ushio Haruo, eds., *Nakae Tōju / Kumazawa Banzan*, Nihon no shisōka, vol. 4 (Tokyo: Meitoku shuppansha, 1978), p. 318.

By this point, the Flower Garden Learning Center had been educating Okayama samurai for several years, producing a cadre of philosophically informed activists ready to extend their intuitive knowledge in administrative practice. Guilt by hazy association seemed sufficient, and just as punishment of Shōsetsu and Chūya had been inflicted, posthumously, on their kin, so, in a convoluted way, might Banzan be punished for his alleged sins as well as those of Tōju in earlier having questioned Razan's integrity.

Soon slanders surfaced in Edo linking Banzan with the rōnin uprisings of 1651–1652, and deceptive teachings that smacked of Christianity. Allegations attributed to Razan suggested that Banzan's teachings were a version of Christianity and had inspired lawless rōnin in their attempted uprisings.

> Kumazawa is a minor official in Bizen-Okayama. With bewitching arts, he misleads those who cannot hear or see for themselves. Those who heed him end up confused and even more ignorant. Yet many have pledged their lives as his followers, gradually becoming part of his cohort. He does not allow them to talk with others who do not share his aspirations. His teachings are essentially a variation of Christianity ... The [rōnin-]bandits [of late] have all heard Kumazawa's bewitching words.[39]

Coming from a scholar serving the shogunate, Razan's remarks virtually indicting Banzan[40] were heeded at the highest levels.

Ikeda Mitsumasa's diary records that he was soon warned by the grand elder, Sakai Tadakatsu (1587–1662), about shogunal displeasure over the rise in Okayama domain of the so-called "Learning of the Mind" (*shingaku*), a reference to Wang Yangming's teachings. Hints were made that the Flower Garden Oath smacked of Christian liturgical formulations. As a result, the oath was soon viewed with suspicion. When it became known that one of Banzan's relatives by marriage had been involved in Betsuki's plot, suspicions intensified. Ikeda Mitsumasa's diary records that he, Mitsumasa, was notified that the shogunate suspected some daimyō, including Mitsumasa himself, who appeared Confucian but were possibly sympathetic to the rōnin and their uprisings.

Two years later, in 1654, while in Kyoto on his way back to Okayama, Mitsumasa was informed by the shogunal deputy in Kyoto, Itakura

---

[39] Gotō, "Kumazawa Banzan shōgai to shisō," p. 482. Also, McMullen, *Idealism*, p. 118.
[40] Ibid.

Shigemune (1586–1657), of Sakai Tadakatsu's order that he, Mitsumasa, be instructed to prohibit "the Learning of the Mind." Despite such warnings, Mitsumasa's trust in Banzan remained unshaken.[41] Perhaps so, but at the same time, except for a brief visit in 1660,[42] Banzan did not return to Edo again until nearly thirty years later when summoned by the shogunate, just before he was sentenced to final confinement in Koga Castle. Though not yet a detained man, Banzan had attracted the attention of the shogunate, and then soon found fame a double-edged sword and himself a watched man.

Disaster Relief and Domain Administration

Soon after, in 1654, Okayama domain fell victim to massive flooding leaving 156 dead from drowning, and a swath of destruction cutting across socio–economic and political lines: losses included 493 samurai houses, 573 homes belonging to foot-soldiers, 443 homes belonging to towns-people, 2,284 peasant homes, and rice fields with a productive capacity of 11,660 *koku*. Bridges, ponds, and irrigation ditches were destroyed in every area of the domain. Starvation took an additional 3,684 lives. Mitsumasa reportedly saw the disaster as heaven's warning to him as the domain lord.[43]

Banzan quickly assumed a leading role in formulating plans for dealing with the disaster. According to Gotō Yōichi, "Banzan became Mitsumasa's right hand man" in coordinating disaster relief efforts. The domain soon opened its storage facilities, making rice available to the starving. Where more was needed, additional grain from neighboring provinces was purchased. Grain stored in Osaka was returned to Okayama for use in continued disaster relief. In many respects, policies later outlined in Banzan's *Responding to the Great Learning* regarding the necessity of maintaining storage facilities in every domain to provide emergency grain in times of disaster echoed the strategies deployed in Okayama in the wake of the 1654 flooding.[44]

James McMullen notes that at one point, "Forty-six percent of the financial aid disbursed to 'districts and towns' by the domain passed through Banzan's hands."[45] When Mitsumasa went to Edo in 1655 to render service to the shogunate, he left Banzan in charge of overseeing

---

[41] Ibid.
[42] Gotō and Tomoeda, eds., "Nenpu," *Kumazawa Banzan*, p. 583.
[43] Gotō, "Kumazawa Banzan shōgai to shisō," p. 484.
[44] Ibid. McMullen, *Idealism*, p. 107.   [45] McMullen, *Idealism*, p. 107.

matters and resolving unanticipated issues and problems. During the recovery effort Banzan led, domain administration was reorganized along more centralized lines. Not surprisingly, many of Banzan's former students staffed new positions in emergency relief. And, much of the relief work done focused on the peasantry, with seemingly scant concern for upper-level samurai. Banzan's involvement in disaster relief and economic reconstruction shaped his thinking about compassionate government and came to inform his proposals outlined in *Responding to the Great Learning.* Conversely, Mitsumasa's administrative efforts toward flood and disaster relief most likely reflected Banzan's practical commitment to those compassionate strategies from early on, as well as his, Banzan's, considerable influence on his daimyō in administering ethically informed government that was more than simply an ideological mask cynically disguising daimyō indifference toward the people.

Resignation

In 1657, Banzan, age 39, relinquished his 3,000-*koku* position in service to Ikeda Mitsumasa. For the next four years, until 1661, he remained in Okayama, living in relative seclusion in a village, Terakuchi-mura. His parents and approximately a dozen followers joined him there. Appreciating the beauty of the location, Banzan called it "luxuriant mountain village" (Shigeyama-mura). The written characters for "Shigeyama" generated, via Sino-Japanese reading, the name Banzan, which he later adopted as his personal name. The words "shigeyama" also alluded to a poem by an eleventh-century Heian aristocrat, Minamoto Shigeyuki, in the ancient compilation of Japanese verse, *Anthology of Old and New Poems* (*Shinkokinshū*, no. 1013), noting the abundant beauty of Mt. Tsukuba. Commemorative stones marking the location of Banzan's dwelling, next to the Shōrakuji, a Shingon temple, are in Bizen City. Gravestones for Banzan's parents are located nearby, behind the temple.

Banzan's time in Shigeyama-mura modeled, on a personal level, his later advocacy of returning samurai to rural areas. Though he did not engage in farming during his retirement, neither did he retreat to a castle town or urban area as he might well have following his relentless work in disaster relief. Banzan's avoidance of strenuous agrarian labor presumably resulted from an injury he sustained in a fall while hunting.[46]

---

[46] Itō Tasaburō, "Tōju Banzan no gakumon to shisō," *Nakae Tōju Kumazawa Banzan*, p. 47.

Complications from the injury left him with a debilitating illness which prevented him from fulfilling his official duties, prompting, according to his account, his decision to resign his post and stipend. Most likely, even before his injury, Banzan was exhausted following two years of relief work.

Other factors contributed to Banzan's resignation. First, shogunal officials had pressured Mitsumasa, following the rōnin uprisings of 1651–1652, to end Banzan's role in domain education. While Mitsumasa remained a faithful supporter, from the perspective of Edo powerbrokers, Banzan was a liability for the Okayama daimyō. Resentment from within Okayama over Banzan's quick rise to power did not help. Worsening matters, Banzan's readiness to move away from established patterns in government that privileged samurai over the peasantry elicited opposition from the warrior elite in the domain. Opposition led to innuendo and even accusations about egregious waste and mismanagement. At one point, rumors circulated that certain domain samurai wanted Banzan dead. Surely Banzan understood that for the sake of his health and well-being a lower profile would be advantageous.

Before resigning, Mitsumasa allowed Banzan to adopt his, Mitsumasa's, third son, Ikeda Masatomo (1649–1714), as his heir. There were good reasons for Mitsumasa to do this since it meant that, upon Banzan's resignation, his 3,000-*koku* fief would return to the Ikeda. In *Responding to the Great Learning*, Banzan criticizes hereditary stipends and suggests that they last no longer than one generation. Considered in that light, his resignation issued out of a sense of his responsibility not to misuse domain resources for his own personal gain, especially when he no longer felt capable physically of tending to his responsibilities. At the same time, by adopting one of his daimyō's sons, Banzan became even closer to his daimyō than ever before.

Coinciding with Banzan's resignation in 1657 was the passing of Hayashi Razan, longtime Confucian scholar in service to the first four Tokugawa shoguns. Razan had advanced, gradually, the fortunes of Zhu Xi-style Confucianism in Edo for nearly six decades. Though never a strict orthodoxy, Razan's bookish interpretations of Zhu Xi thought prevailed in Edo far more than did the activistic Wang Yangming teachings. Yet most importantly, Razan had set in motion a hereditary line of Hayashi scholars that, one generation after the next, built upon his gains, incrementally growing the presence and power of Zhu Xi learning. While Razan's clout was limited, he was, as his mean-spirited remarks about Banzan showed, no friend of Banzan's nor the least bit sympathetic to the kind of quick learning for which claims to intuitive knowledge allowed. And just as the outer lords were, in the mid-seventeenth century, still vassals the shogunate kept either at a distance or under administrative surveillance, so did Razan seek to make sure Banzan knew he was a watched man, not welcome in Edo, nor in Okayama domain for that matter. Even after Razan had passed, his successors close to the shogunal halls of power continued his efforts in compromising the abilities of samurai and rōnin intellectuals who seemingly posed a threat, philosophical or professional, to them.

Pressure from on high continued, but it was not always from the Hayashi. Shogunal elder, Hoshina Masayuki (1611–1673), half-brother of the third shogun Iemitsu, and close advisor to the fourth shogun Ietsuna, was, even more than the Hayashi, a stern advocate of Zhu Xi-style Confucianism. Masayuki and the Hayashi were not at one on philosophical issues, especially after Masayuki became a patron of Yamazaki Ansai (1619–1682) and his more exclusivistic approach to Zhu Xi learning. Both agreed, however, that Wang Yangming teachings were anathema, and that their prominence in domains such as Okayama needed to be undone. Banzan, age 39, was a casualty of this struggle for philosophical power.[47] For the time being, at least, he retreated to the countryside for rest and recuperation.

Kyoto and Imperial Culture

In 1659, two years after his resignation from service in Okayama domain, Banzan stayed briefly in Kyoto, meeting a number of court nobles including the scholar-aristocrat Nakanoin Michishige (1631–1710).[48] In the spring of 1660, Banzan traveled to Edo at the invitation of Nakagawa Hisakiyo (1615–1681), the daimyō of Oka domain in Bungo Province, apparently with the blessing of Mitsumasa. That winter, Banzan served in Oka as an advisor on matters of domain administration.[49] The following year, 1661, he returned to Kyoto and took up residence near the Kamigoryō Shrine, just north of the imperial palace. The same year, Itō Jinsai opened a private school in Kyoto, pioneering a new dimension of

---

[47] Wajima Yoshio, "Kanbun igaku no kin, sono Hayashi mon kōryū to no kankei," *Nihon Sōgakushi no kenkyū* (Tokyo: Yoshikawa kōbunkan, 1988).

[48] For a study of Nakanoin and Banzan, see James McMullen, "Courtier and Confucian in Seventeenth-Century Japan," *Japan Review*, no. 21 (2009), pp. 11–23.

[49] Gotō, "Kumazawa Banzan shōgai to shisō," pp. 499–500.

Kyoto Confucianism at odds with the Hayashi in Edo, the leanings of Hoshina Masayuki as shaped by Yamazaki Ansai, also in the shogun's capital, and finally those of Nakae Tōju earlier espoused just outside of Kyoto, in Ōmi. Although not a hundred schools, Confucian philosophical thought was blossoming with every decade of peace, prosperity, and cultural growth.

Banzan remained in Kyoto for the next six years, until 1667, reading and discussing Japanese history and literature with court nobles and scholars, as well as studying Japanese music, including two string instruments, the *biwa* and the *koto*, revealing along the way a talent for music. Banzan also taught many of Kyoto's elite, including a dozen prominent nobles, as well as lesser aristocrats, samurai, physicians, and townspeople. During this period, he began work on his commentary on the *Tale of Genji*. At odds with many earlier commentators, Banzan interpreted the court romance novel, written by a courtesan, Murasaki Shikibu (c. 973–c. 1031), in radically Confucian political terms. In Banzan's view, the novel was not simply a great work of literature, but a "resource for his own times," one that had "universal relevance" in its depiction of the age of royal rule before the country came to be dominated by a military class. In the shining prince Genji, Banzan envisioned an exemplar of "humanity and creative altruism."[50] While Banzan's time in Kyoto led him to a deeper appreciation for imperial culture, Shintō, Japanese poetry and music, and other aspects of aristocratic refinement, it was only following his years in the ancient imperial capital that he completed his study of the *Genji* and most of his other works on ancient culture, including a novel, *Tale of Miwa* (*Miwa monogatari*).

In *Tale of Miwa*, Banzan showcases his thinking about time, place, and circumstances, and in the process, his leanings toward relativism. The novel features three speakers who voice different perspectives on Japanese spirituality, the origins of the people, its imperial line, and its divinities. One speaker, a senior priest at a Shintō shrine, affirms literal belief in accounts of the age of the gods (*kami*) found in the histories of ancient Japan, insisting that the emperor is the descendant of the heavenly gods, and that the spirit of the country must be divine. Because *kami* are sagely and virtuous, Amaterasu and then the earliest emperors were full of virtue as well. Consequently, there was no need to borrow anything from China. In the view of the priest, "Shintō is the foundation,

[50] McMullen, "Courtier and Confucian," p. 15.

the Confucian way comprises the branches and leaves, and Buddhism is the fruit" of Japanese spirituality.

In opposition, two samurai express a contrary view. They note that Kyushu is close to Korea and China, and that there have been exchanges between the two lands. As a result, the way of Kings Wen and Wu, two ancient sage kings in China, entered Japan along with many other dimensions of Chinese culture and civilization. Through the study of Confucianism, Japanese came to understand the moral way. Rationalizing and historicizing Shintō, the samurai thus portray Japanese spirituality as in large part derived, in its principles and sensibilities, from neighboring China.

An aristocrat, however, delivers what seems to be Banzan's view, negotiating an affirmation of indigenous Japanese spirituality and yet recognizing the unmistakable resonance with Chinese religio-philosophical thinking by means of appealing to a universal essence and particular manifestations. Without attributing to it a particular country of origin, the aristocrat states that "the way of great emptiness," also known as "the spiritual way of one foundation in heaven and earth," is the source of the way of the sages in China and the way of gods and emperors symbolized in the three treasures of the imperial throne. In the case of Japan, while the three treasures came to be paired with the three Confucian virtues – compassion, wisdom, and courage – they existed before Japanese had learned those words. In effect, through the aristocrat's view, Banzan preserves both the particularity of Japan and China, while accounting for both by reference to a transcendent universal, "the way of great emptiness."[51] The aristocrat's views are not, however, presented dogmatically. Instead, the dialectical progression of the tale suggests that the various perspectives are generated, and to a certain extent valid, for those representing different times, places, and circumstances.

Yet Banzan's innovative, even iconoclastic interpretations of imperial history, literature, and culture also brought trouble: in 1667, Makino Chikashige (1607–1677), the shogunal deputy in charge of Kyoto, had Banzan, then 49, expelled from the imperial capital, supposedly because

---

[51] This analysis is based on Gotō, "Kumazawa Banzan no shōgai to shisō," pp. 504–506. The *Miwa monogatari* is in *Banzan zenshū*, vol. 5, pp. 207–290. For other discussions, see Bitō Masahide, *Nihon hōken shisōshi kenkyū* (Tokyo: Aoki Shoten, 1966), p. 222. Also, McMullen, *Idealism*, pp. 411–412, and Kate Wildman Nakai, "The Naturalization of Confucianism in Tokugawa Japan: The Problem of Sinocentrism," *Harvard Journal of Asiatic Studies*, vol. 40, no. 1 (1980), pp. 190–194.

of his standing as a rōnin. Banzan first relocated to the Yoshino Mountains south of the imperial capital, again taking refuge through a retreat to the countryside. Shortly after, he moved to the area of Kaseyama Castle in Yamashiro Province, living there in seclusion. Although the real reasons for his expulsion from Kyoto remain unclear, speculation is that Banzan was driven away by the same forces that had earlier exiled Yamaga Sokō from Edo. In both cases, Hoshina Masayuki, advisor to the shogun and patron of Yamazaki Ansai, a Zhu Xi purist scholar who detested Sokō's learning and any version of Wang Yangming thinking, is suspected of having sanctioned if not engineered their exile for the sake of driving out heterodoxies and facilitating dominance of the variety of Zhu Xi learning advanced by Yamazaki Ansai.[52] At the time, Ansai was spending half his time in Kyoto, and half in Edo. It is therefore conceivable that Ansai was behind Banzan's troubles as well, and that by working through his patron, Masayuki, he was ridding both the shogun's capital and the imperial capital of prominently troublesome philosophical opposition which happened to be, in both cases, of rōnin status and therefore highly vulnerable. Most likely, Banzan's outspokenness had also landed him on the wrong side of some of the aristocracy with whom he studied the *Genji*. Rumors circulated that Banzan was an enemy of Buddhism, and even that his inclination toward Wang Yangming teachings, however superficial, was simply a mask for his sympathy toward Christian teachings. Groundless though these accusations seem to have been, they and others had been voiced before, making them, via repetition, even more credible for some. Whatever the real reason for his expulsion, Banzan clearly had upset not a few powerful people and so came to suffer the consequences.[53]

Semi-Exile in Akashi

By 1669, Banzan had negotiated his relocation in banishment to Akashi, a castle town west of Kyoto, near the area to which the shining prince Genji, in the novel, had been exiled. Instrumental in securing Banzan's preferred place of exile was Itakura Shigenori, the shogunal deputy in Kyoto who had, in 1651, studied briefly with Banzan when the latter was in Edo otherwise assisting his daimyō, Ikeda Mitsumasa. Yet

---

[52] For an in-depth study of Sokō and Banzan, see Miyazaki Michio, "Kumazawa Banzan to Yamaga Sokō," *Kokugakuin zasshi*, vol. 82, no. 8, 1981.

[53] Gotō, "Kumazawa Banzan no shōgai to shisō," p. 511.

even with Shigenori's support, Banzan was not able to secure exoneration enabling him to return to the imperial capital. The best Shigenori could do was arrange a pleasant place of exile for Banzan. This suggests that there must have been other forces higher, possibly the shogunal regent, Hoshina Masayuki, and his scholar-vassal, Yamazaki Ansai, still intent on marginalizing Banzan. Nevertheless, it was during this period that Banzan completed work on his study of the *Tale of Genji* (*Genji gaiden*).

In Akashi, Banzan lived in exile, but not heavy-handed detention, under the watchful supervision of a daimyō, Matsudaira Nobuyuki (1631–1686), a Tokugawa relative. Although banished from Kyoto, Banzan was allowed to move about with permission. Just two months after moving to Akashi, he was permitted to travel to Okayama to officiate at the ceremonies honoring Confucius held on the opening of a new domain school there. The following year, Okayama founded the Shizutani Academy, the first domain-supported school for the education of commoners. Although typically credited to Ikeda Mitsumasa, Banzan's earlier role in the educational development of Okayama and his later advocacy of education in *Responding to the Great Learning*, suggest that credit for such educational advances in Okayama domain was, at least indirectly, his.[54]

In 1672, Banzan published one of his major works, *Accumulating Righteousness, Japanese Writings* (*Shūgi washo*). A second, considerably expanded edition appeared before his passing. From the start, however, *Accumulating Righteousness, Japanese Writings* affirmed both the eternal and universal nature of the way – understood as consisting of the three bonds (ruler–subject; father–son; husband–wife) and the five constants (compassion, righteousness, propriety, wisdom, and honesty) as well as the relativity inherent in expressions of them in relation to time, place, and circumstances of rank and status. Banzan left no doubt that the way existed before anything and would continue to exist long after reality as it then existed was gone. In that respect, the way was constant, universal, and eternal, transcending time, place, and circumstance. On the other hand, human creations such as the fundamentals of civilization, laws, rites, and music were meant to approximate the way, and necessarily corresponded to the time, place, and circumstances in which they originated. As such, they were subject to change, modification, elimination, and innovation as particular, subjective expressions of the universal way.

---

[54] Akiyama, *Bokenroku*, pp. 6–9.

According to Banzan, these factors – time, place, and circumstance – were key determinants in assessing the validity of received traditions, wisdom, rules and regulations, and approaches to realizing success in the world.[55]

Banzan insisted that even the laws and regulations of the sages of antiquity, when no longer appropriate to the time, place, and circumstances of contemporary problems, should not be deemed expressions of the way. Conversely, efforts to impose ancient laws on present-day humanity simply because they were attributed to the sages, regardless of their resonance with contemporary time, place, and circumstances, were contrary to the way. In this regard, Banzan's *Accumulating Righteousness, Japanese Writings* sets forth a dialectic of universalistic idealism and conditional relativism that while affirming the abiding, eternal reality of the fundamentals of morality, left ample room for contingent modifications as required by and appropriate to the exigencies of time, place, and circumstance.[56]

In emphasizing the importance of these contingent factors, Banzan continued a line of thought Tōju developed in his *Discussions with an Old Man (Okina mondō)*, which in turn was shaped by the ideas of a late-Ming follower of Wang Yangming, Wang Ji.[57] And, Banzan's *Accumulating Righteousness, Further Writings*,[58] a text he began during the early 1670s but edited and expanded until his final days, further developed these same views. In addition to continuing themes from *Accumulating Righteousness, Japanese Writings*, Banzan emphasized subject matter such as the importance of mountains, rivers, and forests for the realm, declaring them the foundations of the country, thus according them a level of ultimate political importance more typically reserved for the people. Implicit in Banzan's view, however, was the belief that humanity could not exist in any suitable manner without active respect for and cultivation

---

[55] A modern edition of the *Shūgi washo* is in Gotō and Tomoeda, eds., *Kumazawa Banzan*, pp. 7–404. Another modern edition is in Itō, *Nakae Tōju Kumazawa Banzan*, vol. 11, pp. 175–309.

[56] Gotō and Tomoeda, *Kumazawa Banzan*, pp. 7–404. Also, Itō, *Nakae Tōju Kumazawa Banzan*, pp. 175–309.

[57] Yamashita Ryūji, "Nakae Tōju's Religious Thought and Its Relation to 'Jitsugaku,'" in Wm. Theodore de Bary and Irene Bloom, eds., *Principle and Practicality: Essays in Neo-Confucianism and Practical Learning* (New York: Columbia University Press, 1979), pp. 307–336.

[58] The translation of *Shūgi gaisho* here follows that of Richard Bowring, *In Search of the Way: Thought and Religion in Early-Modern Japan, 1582–1860* (Oxford: Oxford University Press, 2017), p. 82.

of the best interests of the surrounding environment, including in Japan's case mountains, rivers, and forests. Degradation of the latter, in Banzan's view, marked the beginning of the end of any political community. Similar ecologically oriented themes appeared prominently in Banzan's *Responding to the Great Learning* wherein the integrity of the natural world is emphasized, and ways in which to maintain the vitality of forests, mountains, rivers, and arable land are outlined.

Exile-Detention in Yamato Province (1679–1687)

In 1679, the shogunate relocated Banzan's supervising daimyō, Matsudaira Nobuyuki, former lord of Akashi Castle, to another location in the Kansai, Kōriyama Castle (now Yamato Kōriyama). Banzan, still in Nobuyuki's custody, was permitted to reside in rural Yata village just outside Kōriyama Castle, in Yamato Province (now, Nara Prefecture). During the years that followed, Banzan, then in his sixties, was allowed to take excursions every so often, making his time in supervision not terribly restrictive. In 1683, Banzan received an invitation from Hotta Masatoshi (1634–1684), the shogunal great elder, with overtures of possible service to the shogunate. Then 65, Banzan went to Edo but firmly refused the offer. Rather than accept and enjoy the more urbane life a shogunal stipend might afford, Banzan, apparently unwilling to serve the shogun – Tokugawa Tsunayoshi (1646–1709), for whom he had little respect – returned to Yamato, close to his birthplace, Kyoto, and the cultural region he most admired. As things turned out, Banzan's refusal was a wise choice: the following year, in 1684, Masatoshi was assassinated in Edo Castle in one of the most shocking political murders of the Tokugawa period.

Masatoshi's overture was made possible by the passing, in 1682, of Yamazaki Ansai, perhaps the most charismatic and politically scheming, even somewhat Machiavellian Confucian teacher of his day. Ansai's insistence, as a Confucian scholar, on fidelity to Zhu Xi's teaching attracted many, but not Banzan. The hardships Banzan faced in the decade and a half prior were in part due to Ansai's considerable power over philosophical discourse in Edo and Kyoto. However, following the death of Ansai's patron, Hoshina Masayuki, in 1672, Ansai's power declined as evidenced in the shogunate's pardon of Yamaga Sokō, whom Masayuki had earlier exiled from Edo. Nevertheless, while alive Ansai and his patron Masayuki had made life difficult for those whose teachings differed from his own.

In 1684, a year after refusing Masatoshi's offers, Banzan visited Kyoto twice, once in the third lunar month, and then again in the tenth. The following two years, 1685 and 1686, Banzan, in his late sixties, made similar trips to Kyoto in the spring and autumn. In 1687, he enjoyed two brief trips to Kyoto, one in the second lunar month and another in the fifth. His frequent travels might have been prompted by a growing awareness on his part that his time was growing short. Earlier, in 1682 the same year Ansai died, Banzan's former daimyō, Ikeda Mitsumasa, who had also helped supervise Banzan's exile for over a decade, also passed away. Two years prior, Banzan had lost his father, age 91.

In addition to travel, Banzan continued to work on several manuscripts, bringing them to varied states of completion. In 1686, he finished, for the most part, work on three texts: *Brief Explanation of the Great Learning* (*Daigaku shōkai*), *Brief Explanation of the Analects of Confucius* (*Rongo gekan shōkai*), and *Commentary on the Great Treatise of the Book of Changes* (*Keiji denkai*). Banzan also made plans for publishing a revised and expanded version of his *Accumulating Righteousness, Japanese Writings*.

Well along in years and relatively isolated from the realities of the times, Banzan remained fearful of an imminent foreign invasion by northern barbarians, that is, the Manchus. Earlier, he had expressed concerns about the same while serving Ikeda Mitsumasa. Worried that such an invasion would soon become a disastrous reality, Banzan voiced his concerns to his son-in-law, Inaba Hikobei (1659–1734), claiming to do so not for fame or personal gain but instead "for the sake of his country, Japan." Banzan's son-in-law was then a retainer of the daimyō, Kitami Shigemasa, a chamberlain and close confidant of the fifth shogun, Tsunayoshi. Banzan apparently asked his son-in-law to share his anxieties with Shigemasa. Most likely Banzan hoped that Shigemasa would in turn inform the shogun.

In his letter dated the first of the eighth month, 1686, Banzan, writing from his residence in Yata to his son-in-law, Hikobei, in Edo, explained:

> I do not know what will become of our transitory existence during this year. However, for the sake of Japan (*Nihon no tame ni*) saying nothing about matters would be criminal …
>
> Quite possibly, the Tartar tribes (*Dattan*) living north of China will come down next year or the year after. If they come next year and if the authorities have not prepared by the eighth, ninth or at latest the tenth month of this year, by the eleventh or twelfth month

the situation will be beyond [the abilities of even the great generals of China who long ago sought to defend that land] ... The Tartar tribes will come suddenly and without warning. There is not the slightest evidence of the necessary preparations ... However, unless we begin preparations during the fall of this year, we will not be ready for the battle to come next spring or summer.[59]

Banzan added that if the shogun's chamberlain was interested in his thoughts, he would write them out, probably fifty to sixty pages' worth. Banzan added that he had considered discussing these matters with Matsudaira Nobuyuki, but sickness had kept him from doing so.

Responding to the Great Learning addresses the supposed invasion of Japan by northern barbarians repeatedly. There is no question that the list of contents Banzan mentioned to Hikobei was essentially that of the work later known as *Responding to the Great Learning*. According to Inoue Michiyasu, Banzan proceeded to draft the text after having sent the letter to Hikobei, finishing it around the ninth month of the following year, in the autumn of 1687.[60] Presumably he did so in the hope that the shogun's chamberlain, upon hearing of it, would share it with the shogun, Tsunayoshi, who might in turn wish to read the text, or perhaps even meet with Banzan and discuss the supposedly imminent dangers facing Japan. Quite possibly, Banzan imagined that he might be elevated to high office, one responsible for coordinating emergency measures needed to provide for national defense and internal prosperity.

Nearing his own end, Banzan felt compelled to speak. Not sharing his thoughts, he suggested, was criminal. That very statement, however, suggests that Banzan also realized that in sharing his proposals, he might well be charged with high crimes vis-à-vis the shogunate. Rather than recoil, once again Banzan spoke out, but no response, at least not from the shogun's chamberlain, came.

---

[59] Inoue Michiyasu, an early twentieth century scholar of Banzan's life and thought, is credited with piecing together the documentation establishing these connections. Kumazawa Banzan, "Letter to Inaba Hikobe," *Banzan sensei shokan jūi.* Excerpt quoted from Gotō, "Kumazawa Banzan no shōgai to shisō," p. 530. Ian James McMullen, "Kumazawa Banzan and 'Jitsugaku': Toward Pragmatic Action," in Wm. Theodore de Bary and Irene Bloom, eds., *Principle and Practicality: Essays in Neo-Confucianism and Practical Learning* (New York: Columbia University Press, 1979), p. 337. Also, McMullen, *Idealism,* p. 415. For Inoue's writings, see Inoue Michiyasu, *Banzan kō* (Okayama: Okayama-ken, 1902); Inoue, *Banzan sensei ryakuden* (Kogamachi, Ibaraki-ken: Kogakyō yūkai, 1910); and Inoue, *Banzan sensei shokanshū* (Tokyo: Shūseidō, 1913).

[60] Gotō, "Kumazawa Banzan no shōgai to shisō," p. 531.

Yet the matter somehow did come to the attention of one of Banzan's followers, Tanaka Magojurō, a low-level Tokugawa retainer then serving as a shogunal censor. Magojurō asked Banzan for his thoughts about government affairs, which prompted Banzan to send him a copy of his manuscript. After deliberating over what to do, Magojurō, realizing the sensitive nature of Banzan's text and his responsibility to report it, contacted the elder counsellors and turned a copy of the text over to them. Foreshadowing what was yet to come, Magojurō was stripped of his position as shogunal censor for having hesitated before reporting receipt of Banzan's text to the elder counsellors. Realizing the sensitive, even problematic nature of the text, later known as *Responding to the Great Learning*, some of Banzan's students had referred to it as "a secret writing" (*hisho*).[61] Their assessment of its nature and how it most likely should have been handled was not, apparently, mistaken.

Final Confinement in Koga Castle (1687–1691)

In the eighth month of 1687, Matsudaira Tadayuki (1674–1695), successor to his father as the daimyō supervising Banzan's custody, was relocated to Koga Province, north of Edo. He soon instructed Banzan to proceed to Koga as well. Tadayuki was acting on directives from the shogun's chamberlain, Makino Narisada (1634–1712).[62] Consequently, Banzan, in the ninth month, departed Yata but first stopped near Kyoto, in Fujinomori, to part company with friends and followers in and around the imperial capital. Most likely, he realized that he might not be seeing them again.

The following month, Banzan arrived in Koga, no doubt exhausted by the lengthy trip from the Kansai. He might well have imagined that finally he had been heard and the opportunity to address the shogunate on a range of matters was at hand. However, shortly after arriving he learned that the occasion was otherwise. Banzan was permitted to write one of his friends in Kyoto, Kitakōji Toshimitsu, noting that he had arrived in Koga. Banzan must have said more because Kitakōji

---

[61] One of Banzan's high disciples among the Kyoto aristocracy, Kitakōji Toshimitsu, in his diary, *Toshimitsu nikki*, referred to Banzan's "twenty-one-chapter secret text." The standard version of the *Daigaku wakumon* includes twenty-two chapters. Nevertheless, the diary entry is thought to have been to Banzan's *Daigaku wakumon*. Tomoeda Ryūtarō, "Shūroku shomoku kaidai," in Gotō and Tomoeda, eds., *Kumazawa Banzan*, pp. 590, 592. Itō, "Tōju Banzan no gakumon to shisō," p. 45.

[62] McMullen, *Idealism*, pp. 441–442. Gotō, "Kumazawa Banzan no shōgai to shisō," p. 532.

responded, acknowledging Banzan's misgivings and advising him to "trust in the decree of heaven," an indication that fate might be at hand. Later in the tenth month, Banzan was informed that he was prohibited from traveling to Edo, and that he was to remain in Koga indefinitely. Initially, at least, the shogunate was not expressing its condemnation of Banzan in any harsher terms.[63]

Subsequently, in the twelfth month of 1687, Banzan was informed of a shogunal decree placing him in confinement in the southeastern extreme of Koga Castle. According to the shogunate's verdict, Banzan was to be allowed no travel outside Koga, and nothing more than license to stroll around his place of confinement. He was not allowed to conduct correspondence with anyone, nor was he to have visitors from outside the domain. Even within Koga, he was only allowed to associate with those with whom he had good reason to associate. And of course, there would be no visits to Kyoto, nor to any other part of Japan. He was allowed the company of his wife, Ichi, but she passed away, age 55, in the following year, 1688, the first year of the Genroku period. This personal loss compounded Banzan's punishment. Together, they had had ten children, four sons and six daughters.

The shogunate's verdict stated that it found the writing Banzan had sent to Tanaka Magojurō offensive. In the shogunate's judgment, the untitled text was of "no interest whatsoever." Worst of all, from the perspective of the authorities, it was "not appropriate"[64] for Banzan to have written and submitted such political writings to the shogunate. He was, after all, a rōnin who had been living in the custody and supervision of a daimyō for two decades, not an official advisor to the shogunate or any of its trusted vassals.

The message was, in part, that if the shogunate had wanted advice, it would have sought it. Furthermore, it would not tolerate the writings of a scholar proposing what amounted to a wholesale reorganization of government, society, the economy, as well as the educational and spiritual realms. Also, Banzan's somewhat apocalyptic vision of a coming invasion by northern barbarians must have seemed, to the shogunal authorities,

---

[63] Gotō, "Kumazawa Banzan no shōgai to shisō," p. 528. Also, McMullen, *Idealism*, pp. 441–442.

[64] This account is from a memorandum by a Koga samurai, Tsutsui, that the early twentieth century Banzan scholar, Inoue Michiyasu, introduced. Quoted from Gotō, "Kumazawa Banzan no shōgai to shisō," p. 529. Also, see McMullen, *Idealism*, p. 443, for another translation.

the product of a disturbed if not deluded mind. True, the Manchus had taken control of China in the wake of the fall of the Ming dynasty, but their conquest there had occurred four decades earlier, and still there was no credible intelligence suggesting an imminent move against Japan. Banzan's alarmist calls on this count impaired, it seems, his credibility on virtually all others.

Banzan's confinement was real, yet also relatively mild. Then again, for a 69-year-old scholar in failing health, being cut off from contact with the remainder of the world was emotionally debilitating if not torturous. In *Accumulating Righteousness, Japanese Writings*, Banzan left a brief statement conveying his more noble sentiments while imprisoned at Koga Castle.

> I have been slandered repeatedly by various parties. As a result, I am no longer free to visit with friends who have come from afar, or even discuss morality and virtue with those nearby. Others might see me reduced to confinement and think that I am suffering in distress. However, in my mind and heart, I am most aware of the blessings I have received from heaven.
>
> It is indeed true that seeing a clear moon in exile is something to be desired. The quiet moonlight seen by those who have escaped from the world is something that people still bound up in it can only hope for. It is precisely because I am in exile now that I can see the moon that glows beyond the everyday floating world.
>
> Even if a person is wealthy, of high rank, and worldly, if he knows in his mind and heart that he has indeed committed crimes and misdeeds, then he will suffer. But the person who has been [falsely] accused of crimes and so feels no shame will never lose sight of the vast and lofty original substance of their minds and hearts.[65]

Such testaments suggesting that a wrongly victimized party free from guilt could continue to enjoy peace of mind were not unusual. They allude back to the opening passage of the *Analects* where Confucius asks, "Is it not the princely man who, when ignored, is not disturbed?" By "ignored," Confucius referred to the fact that contemporary rulers had not heeded his ideas about government and ethics. Yet Banzan's fate went well beyond Confucius': not only were his ideas ignored, he was being punished for them. By paraphrasing Confucius and seeing his own predicament in relation to that of the ancient sage, Banzan found solace

---

[65] Banzan, *Shūgi washo*, p. 376.

in noble sentiments affirming the ultimate importance of a clear conscience regardless of exile and confinement.

Following Banzan's death in 1691, the daimyō of Koga Province, Matsudaira Tadayuki, had his remains interred at the Keienji, a Sōtō Zen temple, next to the grave of his wife, Ichi. However, both were buried, as Banzan wished, according to Confucian rites. Banzan had impacted many in his turbulent, often controversial life, but in the end died in detention, excommunicated from his friends, his remaining family, and followers in the Kansai, as well as from his mission of working for the sake of his country.

The Genre: Political Economy (*keizaigaku*)

Before his final detention, Banzan's draft text circulated among his disciples and followers, going by various names. In his *Commentary and Questions on the Classic of Filial Piety* (*Kōkyō gaiden wakumon*), completed by 1690, Banzan mentioned having written *Responding to the Great Learning and Bringing Peace to the Realm below Heaven* (*Daigaku heitenka no wakumon*) for those intent on governing. By that point, the work had evidently been given a version of the title by which it would be known, for the most part, to history.[66] Initially, however, it was not commonly referred to as *Responding to the Great Learning*. Surviving manuscript copies and diary accounts reveal that it was, early on, something of a confidential if not secret writing known variously as *Discussions of Political Economy* (*Keizai ben*), *Gleanings from Political Economy* (*Keizai jūi*), *New Discussions of Government and Political Economy* (*Shinsei keizai ben*), and *Essentials of Politics and Viable Administrative Measures* (*Keizai katsuhō yōroku*). In each case, the alternative titles announced, via the word *keizai*, Banzan's central concern with politics, political economy, statecraft, and political philosophy.

In modern Japanese, *keizai* refers to economics and matters related to the economy. However, the components, *kei* and *zai/sai* first emerged in meaningful proximity in a fourth-century Chinese Daoist text, the *Baopuzi*, by the Eastern Jin dynasty scholar, Ge Hong (283–343), in speaking of "ordering the world and helping the common people" (C: *jing shi ji su*; J: *keise saizoku*). Later, in the Sui dynasty (581–619), the Confucian scholar Wang Tong (584–618), in *Discussions of Master*

---

66 Kumazawa Banzan, *Kōkyō gaiden wakumon, Banzan zenshū*, vol. 3, p. 76.

Wenzhong (*Wenzhongzi*), brought the components together, noting that in rites and music there is "a way of ordering and helping" (*jingji zhi dao*; *keizai no michi*) that, more fully stated, consists in "ordering the world and helping people" (*jing shi ji min*; *keise saimin*). In the Song dynasty (960–1279), the Confucian scholar Wang Anshi (1021–1086) and a growing number of other scholar-statesmen likewise spoke of *jingji*, or *keizai* in Japanese, as an abbreviated reference to "ordering the world and helping people," that is, vis-à-vis matters related to politics, government, and socio-economic administration.[67]

Centuries later, with the ongoing introduction of Song Confucian literature, Tokugawa writings on statecraft and political economy multiplied. Prominent examples from the early eighteenth century include Ogyū Sorai's *Political Discussions* (*Seidan*) and his *Plan for an Age of Great Peace* (*Taiheisaku*), reportedly written at the request of the eighth Tokugawa shogun, Yoshimune (1684–1751). Sorai advocated some radical proposals like the ones Banzan had earlier advanced, including returning samurai to the countryside. However, unlike Banzan, who proposed his ideas without invitation, Sorai only wrote at the request of the shogun, Yoshimune. One of Sorai's followers, Dazai Shundai (1680–1747), also authored a noteworthy work in the *keizai* genre, *Writings on Political Economy* (*Keizai roku*, 1729).[68] In Shundai's case, however, he did so without shogunal invite, assuming the more headstrong strategy of Banzan.

Decades before Sorai and Shundai, Banzan had pioneered the genre in the late seventeenth century with *Responding to the Great Learning*. The early aliases for the latter make its East Asian genre clear, but the contents even more so. In the work, Banzan introduces accounts of political legitimacy as well as administrative policies at the shogunal and domain levels that could, in his view, alleviate the socio-economic hardships facing the population, and secure the defense of the realm. Banzan also outlines other policy proposals that would stimulate production of wealth and prosperity as well as educate the population at large. Insofar as Banzan's *Responding to the Great Learning* pertains to the interplay of political

---

[67] Morohashi Tetsuji, "Keizai," *Dai Kan Wa jiten*, p. 9211.

[68] For a translation of Sorai's *Seidan*, see Lidin, *Ogyū Sorai's Discourse on Government (Seidan)*. Lidin lists Banzan as the first of the five great authors of works in the *keizaigaku* genre in Tokugawa Japan. For a study of Shundai's text, see Tetsuo Najita, "Political Economism in the Thought of Dazai Shundai (1680–1747)," *Journal of Asian Studies*, vol. 31, no. 4 (1972), pp. 821–839.

thought, political administration, and the socio-economic well-being of the governed, it stands as the major pioneering work in the development of the *keizaigaku* genre in early-modern Japan.

Sorai, an important contributor to the genre, knew of his predecessor, Banzan, and expressed respect and admiration for him as a man of learning and talent. Shundai also acknowledged reading Banzan's *Responding to the Great Learning* as a youth. In his *Writings on Political Economy*, Shundai quoted Banzan's discussions of the growing problem of samurai debt and its magnitude in his own day, reportedly greater than all the gold and silver in Japan combined.[69] Other eighteenth- and nineteenth-century Tokugawa thinkers also recognized Banzan as one of the great political writers of the age. In Meiji Japan, as modern scholars began tracing the beginnings of the study of political economy, Kumazawa Banzan's name almost invariably was at the top of the list.[70]

In *Responding to the Great Learning*, Banzan warned rulers against the consequences of misrule and reminded ministers of their responsibility to remonstrate with their rulers when the latter erred. The ideal Banzan upheld was compassionate government, sometimes referred to as "benevolent government" or "humane government." Although he did not define it as such in *Responding to the Great Learning*, Banzan apparently meant by compassionate government a concern for the economic

[69] Other Tokugawa intellectuals who went on record praising Banzan included the eighteenth-century physician-scholar Nagatomi Dokushōan (1732–1766) who declared Banzan one of the four great samurai of his age. Another follower of Sorai, Hattori Nankaku (1683–1759), stated, "I read Kumazawa Ryōkai's discussions of political economy (*keizaisetsu*) ... [and his analyses] were nothing like the empty talk of other scholars." Also, a student of Shundai, Yuasa Jōzan (1708–1781), and late-Tokugawa pro-imperial activist-scholars such as Fujita Yūkoku (1806–1855) and Yokoi Shōnan (1809–1869), expressed respect for Banzan. As Inoue Tetsujirō notes, despite his issues with the shogunate, Banzan was well regarded by many Tokugawa thinkers. Inoue, *Nihon Yōmei gakuha no tetsugaku*, pp. 201–203.

[70] Soeda Juichi, "Conditions of Study of Political Economy in Japan," *Kokka gakkai zasshi*, vol. 6, no. 79 (1893). Soeda viewed Banzan as a physiocrat. Also, Kawakami Hajime (1879–1946), "Essay on the Theory of Political Economy in the Tokugawa Period," *Kokka gakkai zasshi*, vol. 17, no. 191 (1903), listed Banzan as the first in a succession of thinkers including the likes of Ogyū Sorai, Satō Nobuhiro (1769–1860), and others. In the early twentieth century, the Nihon bunko series included a volume on Banzan, featuring a modern printing of his *Daigaku wakumon*. The first volume of *Kinsei shakai keizai gakusetsu taikei* (*Compendium of Early Modern Learned Discussions of Society and Economics*) is the *Collected Works of Kumazawa Banzan* (*Kumazawa Banzan shū*, 1935), edited by Nomura Kanetarō, and it presents Banzan's *Daigaku wakumon* as its opening text. See Honjo Eijirō, "Development of the Study on the History of Japanese Economic Thought," *Kyoto University Economic Review*, vol. 29, no. 2 (1959), pp. 1–2.

and overall well-being of the people and the realm. It is tempting to add that, for Banzan, compassionate government culminated, in a philosophical and practical way, with the ruler identifying with all aspects of existence and forming one body with them. After all, Wang Yangming, in his *Inquiry on the Great Learning*, suggested such an understanding of compassion and Banzan surely knew of it. But Banzan does not endorse this quasi-mystical, ethico–metaphysical understanding of compassion in *Responding to the Great Learning*. Instead, he associates compassionate government with, in part, initiatives meant to expand wealth and economic prosperity, as well as advice on how best to prevent human suffering from floods, famine, droughts, and other disasters including possible invasions by northern barbarians.

Banzan's concern for the realm extended to maintaining the vitality of its mountain forests, rivers, and streams, which he called the very foundations of the state. Banzan repeatedly criticized the wastefulness of the alternate attendance system requiring vassals of the shogun to maintain residences in Edo and reside there half of every year or every other year. In advocating what amounted to socio–economic engineering, Banzan set forth revolutionary policies that would have entailed a wholesale restructuring of the realm. Rather than resort to mere philosophical abstractions, Banzan's grasp of compassionate government was defined concretely and specifically, in terms of the times, places, and pressing political circumstances of his day.

Banzan also called on the shogunate to do away with Christianity, the internal foreign threat, by restoring Buddhism and Shintō as spiritual teachings capable of filling the needs of the population with integrity and honor. Banzan proposed that secular schools be established for the essentially Confucian education of the samurai elite and the rest of the population, at times sounding as if he envisioned all being enrolled and educated together for the sake of realizing an enlightened realm, peaceful and well governed. Throughout his text, Banzan additionally emphasized, again along ancient Confucian lines, elevating men of talent and abilities in governing rather than privileging a hereditary elite with positions of power they were often unfit to fill. In effect, Banzan criticized the hereditary order generally, suggesting instead that real ability be the determining factor in one's fate. Simply put, in advocating compassionate government, Banzan was calling for nothing less than a reorganization of the realm, one so radical in scale that his apparent hope that the shogunate would heed his words and act on his proposals seems, despite his presumed sincerity, profoundly naive.

Instead, the shogunate had Banzan interned in Koga Castle. Its verdict ended up being more than a passing fancy. A century later, in 1788, an Osaka publishing house, perhaps thinking that Banzan's writings were no longer problematic, published, for the first time in the Tokugawa period, *Responding to the Great Learning.* However, the following year – which happened to be the first of the Kansei period during which a high shogunal official, Matsudaira Sadanobu, led a purge of heterodox forms of learning – the shogunate banned sale and circulation of Banzan's text.[71] Banzan's book thus ended up being one of the most consistently silenced if not censored publications of the early-modern period.

Only as the old regime moved toward crisis and then collapse were two later Tokugawa editions of *Responding to the Great Learning* published, in 1848 and then in 1863, but even those were kept quiet for fear of another round of censorship. The last Tokugawa edition went by an alias, *New Discussions of Government and Political Economy* (*Shinsei keizai ben*), but included on the opening page of its first volume, the title, *A Discussion of Political Economy, also known as Responding to the Great Learning: Another Volume on Governing the Realm and Bringing Peace to All below Heaven.*[72] Then as before, the opening chapters of Banzan's text must have appeared to many as downright revolutionary. His calls throughout the work for a systematic overhaul of the polity were surely even more so.

Although many of the details of Banzan's proposals were rather dated by that point, on other counts his line of thought seemed more pertinent than ever and surely more than Banzan himself might have imagined. Indeed, some of Banzan's proposals remained relevant until well after the Meiji Restoration when some were approximated if not enacted, in one way or another, by the innovative imperial regime. Banzan's call for returning samurai to the countryside was a first step in their demotion

---

71 Itō, "Tōju Banzan no gakumon to shisō," *Nakae Tōju Kumazawa Banzan*, p. 43. Several months elapsed between the first publication of the text and the shogunate's decision to ban it. As a result, many copies of this edition came to circulate. The *Nihon shisō taikei* version of *Daigaku wakumon* is based on this edition. Waseda University holds a copy dated 1788. The title listed on the table of contents is *Responding to the Great Learning: Another Volume on Governing the Realm and Bringing Peace to All below Heaven* (*Daigaku wakumon: chikoku heitenka bekkan*).
72 "Kaidai," *Banzan zenshū*, vol. 3, pp. 12–13.

as a privileged, hereditary estate, carried forward in the Meiji with their eventual abolition as a class followed by an imperial call for all peoples of the nation to unite as one, regardless of matters of birth. Banzan's critiques of Buddhism also foreshadowed, along unfortunate lines, the Meiji attack on Buddhism in the name of elevating Shintō as a state religion. Also, Banzan's calls for the establishment of schools throughout the realm as a means of uplifting all areas with an infusion of education and cultural enlightenment from an elite group of teachers trained in the imperial capital was a harbinger of the Meiji move to found a national school system led by teachers trained at imperial universities, broadcasting a new form of government, one sanctioning both enlightenment and political control through education.

Parallels in Confucian Existentialism: Banzan and Wang Yangming

Textbook accounts of Banzan typically identify him as an advocate of Wang Yangming teachings in early-modern Japan. The preceding biographical sketch acknowledges some basis for this: Banzan studied, albeit briefly, with Nakae Tōju, the so-called founding figure in the Japanese Wang Yangming movement. Closer examination of Tōju's thought and that of Banzan makes it clear that while Tōju and Banzan did, to an extent, admire Wang, neither was as exclusively devoted to Wang's thinking as facile labels might suggest. Nevertheless, a look at Wang's life and thought is worthwhile because, doctrinaire allegiance aside, Banzan's life did echo Wang's as much as, possibly more than, did his philosophical ideas.

More than the merely coincidental, Banzan and Wang shared ground in what might be called the Confucian existential quest, or the search for and discovery of the meaning of existence in knowing their obligations as Confucians and acting upon them with commitment and vigor, defining for their lives greater meaning and authenticity thereby. Existentialism, of course, refers to a branch of philosophical inquiry and practice concerned with the meaning of existence, if there is any, and, if there is, how to realize it with authenticity. Banzan's answer, and before him, Wang's, was that human existence has meaning through active engagement of the inborn ethical goodness of human nature with the myriad things of the world. Rather than withdraw from reality, Banzan and Wang threw themselves into existence via direct ethical action as

Confucian scholar-administrators, ever ready to act on behalf of what they thought right, and to remonstrate for the same. As a result, both men endured repeated punishment in exile. While substantial portions of their lives were spent isolated from the socio-political arena, their periodic isolation was due not to a flight from engaged authenticity so much as a consequence of the extent to which they invested their existence in practical, righteous engagement with the flawed reality they confronted. Banzan and Wang both affirmed through action that outspoken integrity and remonstration with the unethical were integral to their authentic being as Confucian scholars, and as a result, each man paid a real and substantial price.

Wang was born in 1472 in Zhejiang Province in east central China to a family of scholar-officials. Wang's father served the Ming dynasty as an official in the Ministry of Rites before being exiled after offending a powerful eunuch. An exceptional student, Wang nevertheless earned the highest degree in the Ming civil service examination system in 1499, proving his relative mastery of Zhu Xi's thought which, during the Yuan dynasty, had been designated as the official subject matter for testing. As a Ming official, Wang served in various capacities until being banished in 1506, for, as with his father, offending a eunuch. In exile in remote southwestern China, Wang developed, contrary to Zhu Xi and others, his own understandings of Confucianism.

Wang emphasized the primary role of the mind and heart in action. For Wang, "the investigation of things" meant not, as with Zhu Xi, investigating external things one by one, but rather investigating things by grasping their principles as they constituted the human mind itself. In effect, for Wang, investigating things meant investigating the mind. Similarly, for Wang, "the extension of knowledge" was achieved not as Zhu Xi claimed by incremental advances in knowledge of external things or by extended book learning and textual study, but instead by using the intuitive ethical knowledge each person has at birth. Wang stressed that active engagement with the world need not wait on years of book study. Instead, he insisted that with action, our intuitive ethical knowledge emerges fully evident, and through that intuitive knowledge, action is rightly directed. Existential authenticity, then, was realized via human nature in action.

Exercise of intuitive ethical knowledge, according to Wang, culminates in a person's realization of oneness with the myriad things of the world, a realization that enables the enlightened agent to engage the world with care and compassion. Ultimately, this engaged realization culminates, for Wang, in the achievement of sagehood. Zhu Xi spoke of sagehood but conceived its attainment as something real but at the same time rare, virtually beyond the reach of the common lot. With Wang, however, everyman has the potential for sagehood in the here and now. Emphasizing this, Wang reportedly quipped that the streets were full of sages.

Wang's exile ended in 1510. It was followed by a period of success in administrative, military, and philosophical ventures. Between 1514 and 1516, Wang served as an official in Nanjing and attained some renown as a thinker at odds with Zhu Xi. One of their more important differences concerned the *Great Learning*. Rather than follow Zhu Xi, who added a substantial section to the ancient text written by one of his Song dynasty predecessors, Cheng Yi, explaining "the investigation of things," Wang insisted on respecting the "ancient version" which, of course, never included Cheng Yi's remarks or Zhu Xi's commentary. Wang's thinking about the *Great Learning* later culminated, toward the end of his life, in one of his most representative philosophical expressions, *Inquiry on the Great Learning* (C: *Daxue wen*; J: *Daigaku mon*). While the title of Wang's text is similar to that of Banzan's *Daigaku wakumon*, the two works differ profoundly in content. Despite Wang's claim to be following the ancient text, he interprets the *Great Learning* in terms of his earlier-mentioned notion of realizing oneness with all things. Banzan's *Responding to the Great Learning* is mostly concerned with practical political proposals for reorganizing the polity of Tokugawa Japan, although there are several significant allusions to the *Great Learning* in his work as well. However, the politically confrontational portions of the *Great Learning* that Banzan emphasized were not the ones that Wang had focused on first and foremost.

Between 1515 and 1516, Wang emerged as a man of action, suppressing several rebellions in Jiangxi and Fujian Provinces. In doing so, he presided over the recruitment of troops, a reorganization of the local military, and implementation of a family registration system. In 1519, Wang gained new fame as a military commander by successfully subduing a rebellion led by an imperial prince, Prince Ning. At the end of the year, Wang was rewarded with appointment as the new governor of Jiangxi Province. Yet Wang's victory brought jealous reactions from the inner circle of the imperial court. Rumors surfaced that Wang succeeded because he had been conspiring with Prince Ning in the first place to overthrow the Ming dynasty and then turned on Prince Ning in support of the Ming. Wang defended himself, but still ended up a persona non grata at the Ming court.[73]

Between 1521 and 1527, Wang lived in seclusion while hostile attacks and ridicule continued. Worst of all, his teachings were prohibited. Despite his disfavor at court, when rebellions broke out in Jiangxi in 1528, Wang was called on to quash them. Thereafter, he continued his philosophical work, authoring, between 1527 and 1528, his *Inquiry on the Great Learning*. Wang died the following year, 1529, while returning from a military expedition suppressing rebels in Jiangxi. Wang's enemies at the court did not cease their attacks even after his death. Instead, they charged that prior to his passing, Wang had left his post without permission. As a result, Wang's hereditary privileges were revoked and his ideas condemned as "strange doctrines." Nearly forty years later, however, Wang's titles were posthumously restored. By imperial decree, sacrifices were also to be offered to Wang at Confucian temples.[74]

Wang's life-course was not unlike Banzan's. Both were men of action who, in part due to their bold engagement with the world, found themselves in trouble repeatedly with the ruling elite. Rumors, jealous slander, and philosophical resentment seem to have followed them. Their biographical details vary significantly, but both lived under the surveillance of the authorities who seemingly at every turn were ready to clamp down on their power and influence. Also, in terms of their key texts, both men authored studies of the *Great Learning*, yet in neither case were those studies strict commentaries on the text itself so much as expositions of philosophical visions grounded in their unique forms of practical experience and distinctive understandings of intuitive ethical knowledge.

Wang and Banzan focused on the *Great Learning* arguably because Zhu Xi had made so much of the text. Rightly or wrongly, Zhu had taken the text, once a mere chapter in the *Book of Rituals*, and declared it a book in its own right, one that Confucius himself had transmitted. Zhu even declared the *Great Learning* the first and most primary book in the Confucian curriculum. Given Zhu's elevation of the *Great Learning*, Wang and Banzan were arguably compelled to address it, even if only in name, as a means of advancing their understandings of Confucianism.

---

[73] Wing-tsit Chan, trans., *Instructions for Practical Living* (New York: Columbia University Press, 1963), p. xxvii.

[74] Ibid., pp. xxviii–xxix.

The elevation of the *Great Learning*, from book chapter to premier Confucian text, thus continued with both Wang and Banzan. The *Great Learning* lent itself well to Banzan's ends because, unlike Wang, he sought to advance a primarily political message and the *Great Learning* offered a ready protocol for realization of his grand political proposals. In its opening chapter, the *Great Learning* explains that its philosophical program climaxes in nothing less than "governing the realm and bringing peace to all below heaven." The latter phrase became the subtitle to Banzan's text, specifically indicating the dimension of the *Great Learning* to which he was most directly responding.

Banzan and the *Great Learning*

The first English translation of Banzan's text, authored by Galen M. Fisher and published in 1938, rendered the title as "Certain Questions respecting *Great Learning*."[75] Fisher was right in rendering *wakumon* literally as "certain questions," but in Banzan's work the questions opening each chapter are typically little more than formulaic prompts for his essay-answers. Because Banzan's text lacks an ongoing dynamic interplay of interlocutors and author-teacher, the result is neither dialogue nor dialectic so much as often pro forma questions followed by relatively polished, conclusive essays on the political responsibilities of rulers and their ministers, the socio-economic organization of the realm, taxation and currency, environmental concerns, administrative policies related to clergy and religious institutions, disaster prevention, foreign threats, and education as a way of uplifting and assisting in governing the populace.

Fisher recognized the discrepancy between title and actual content in a follow-up observation where he stated,

> In reality, however, it is an exposition on the views of a radical economist respecting the acute problems which confronted the Tokugawa shogunate during the latter part of the seventeenth century ... It embodied the practical experience of a student of the Chinese classics who, because of his rugged non-conformity, had spent more than half his manhood in exile. Its criticism of the ruling powers was as daring as it was original and pithy. It is easy to understand why the work offended the Tokugawa authorities, and was long suppressed. In a score of passages Banzan rebukes the shogunate and the daimyō

[75] Fisher, "*Dai Gaku Wakumon*," p. 263.

for their stupidity and self-indulgence. It was the defiant counsel of one who loved the truth and country more than personal liberty.[76]

Fisher thus acknowledged that Banzan's text was not really a commentary on or discussion of the *Great Learning* as such, but instead a series of confrontational policy proposals that were as offensive to the existing powers as they were honest, penetrating analyses of the problems confronting them.

There is much truth in Fisher's analyses. Yet he adds a subtitle – *A Discussion of Public Questions in the Light of the Great Learning* – that, while perhaps a good summary, bears little similarity to Banzan's own subtitle which so well clarifies his work's real textual ties to the *Great Learning*. Banzan's text most meaningfully pertains to the *Great Learning* insofar as it addresses the grand political project mentioned in that work's opening lines. There, a Confucian vision is presented regarding how a ruler might provide for "governing the realm and bringing peace and prosperity to all below heaven." Taking this vision as its subtitle, Banzan's work immodestly, perhaps, suggests that its central concern is nothing less than the socio-economic and political well-being of the entire realm below heaven.

The *Great Learning* claims that this grand vision can be achieved by a ruler through self-cultivation wherein the ruler's mind, thoughts, and will are made correct, his knowledge extended, and the myriad things of the world are exhaustively investigated. Via this protocol, a ruler can, supposedly, bring peace and good government to the entire world. The *Great Learning* thus relates:

> The ancients who wished to illuminate luminous virtue throughout all below heaven first ordered their states. Wishing to order their states, they first regulated their families. Wishing to regulate their families, they first cultivated their persons. Wishing to cultivate their persons, they first rectified their minds and hearts. Wishing to rectify their minds and hearts, they first sought to make their thoughts sincere. Wishing to make their thoughts sincere, they first extended their knowledge.
>
> The extension of knowledge consists in the investigation of things. Once things are investigated, knowledge is extended. Once knowledge is extended, thoughts are made sincere. Once thoughts are made sincere, minds and hearts are rectified. Once minds and hearts

---

[76] Fisher's foreword in *"Dai Gaku Wakumon,"* p. 263.

are rectified, people can engage in self-cultivation. Once people can engage in self-cultivation, families will be regulated. Once families are regulated, states will be governed. Once states are governed, the realm below heaven will realize peace and prosperity. From the son of heaven down to the masses of people, all must consider self-cultivation the root of everything else. When the root is chaotic, what springs from it cannot be well ordered.[77]

The grand political project of the *Great Learning* thus moves from investigating things, to knowledge, the mind and heart, the self, the family, governing the state, and finally climaxes in the achievement of peace and prosperity for the entire realm below heaven.

In *Responding to the Great Learning*, Banzan says virtually nothing about the *Great Learning*'s teachings on self-cultivation, investigating things, extending knowledge, and so forth. However, he does not broach that content arguably for a good reason. *Responding to the Great Learning* emerged as the last of three works that Banzan, in his final decade, authored on the *Great Learning*. Banzan's previous two works were *Japanese Explanation of the Great Learning* (*Daigaku wakai*), completed in 1685, and *Brief Explanation of the Great Learning* (*Daigaku shōkai*) completed in 1686, and published in 1689.[78] In the latter, Banzan explains the *Great Learning*, clause by clause, in some cases word by word, focusing mostly on the text itself with rare references to contemporary circumstances.

With *Responding to the Great Learning*, which amounted to yet "another volume" on the *Great Learning*, Banzan sought to outline his thoughts about how the domains of Tokugawa Japan should be governed and how the entire realm below heaven might be brought to a state of peace and prosperity. In that sense, Banzan's work is "responding" to the *Great Learning*. However, Banzan's responses are not presented in terms

---

[77] *Daigaku*, Uno Tetsuto, ed. (Tokyo: Kōdansha, 1999), pp. 34–38. Translation based on Wing–tsit Chan, trans., *A Source Book in Chinese Philosophy* (Princeton, NJ: Princeton University Press, 1963), pp. 86–87, with significant modifications.

[78] Banzan's *Daigaku wakai* and *Daigaku shōkai* appear in volume 3 of the *Banzan zenshū*, immediately before the *Daigaku wakumon* and after Banzan's *Kōkyō shōkai* (*Brief Account of the Classic of Filial Piety*) and *Kōkyō gaiden wakumon* (*Explanations of the Classic of Filial Piety*). Banzan's *Brief Explanation of the Middle Way* (*Chūyō shōkai*) is the last text presented in that volume. In a note at the end of his handwritten manuscript of the *Daigaku shōkai*, Banzan refers, incidentally, to his *wakumon* on the *Great Learning*, establishing that the text was his. This note is included in the *Daigaku shōkai* edition found in the *Banzan zenshū*, vol. 3, p. 217. See "Kaidai," *Banzan zenshū*, vol. 3, pp. 8–9. However, there is no surviving manuscript from Banzan's hand of the *Daigaku wakumon*.

of notions such as "illuminating luminous virtue," "self-cultivation," "making the ideas sincere," "correcting the mind," "investigating things," or "extending knowledge," but rather by reference to the fundamental Confucian political approach first advanced in the *Mencius*, that of "compassionate government." Banzan's central message is that compassionate government is a political imperative for the sake of saving the realm from internal socio-economic collapse and external conquest.

In one of his lengthier works, *Accumulating Righteousness, Japanese Writings*, Banzan clarified his overall understanding of the *Great Learning*. In response to the question of why the Confucian *Analects* focuses on compassion while the *Great Learning* emphasizes knowledge, Banzan analyzed the differences between the two works not in terms of right and wrong, but rather in terms of their time, place, and circumstances, noting that Confucius offered his instruction on compassion directly to those who would listen, making it his central message. By the time the *Great Learning* was composed, Confucius had passed away and it was unknown when another sage would appear. The *Great Learning* therefore emphasized knowledge and wisdom instead of compassion. Knowledge, in Banzan's view, is the spiritual luminosity of virtue while compassion is its foundation. Though he does not say as much, Banzan presumably understood knowledge to be the intuitive knowledge, or the inborn moral conscience and ethical sensibility of humanity that Wang Yangming and Nakae Tōju extolled as a faculty of the mind ready at birth for use in dealing with people and things of the world at large. The *Great Learning*, in supposedly emphasizing this form of knowledge, served to illuminate and clarify human ethics, providing through intuitive ethical knowledge the real foundation for self-reflection and self-scrutiny.

Modifying Zhu Xi's views, Banzan added that with the sage Confucius gone, people who engaged in learning took the *Great Learning* as "the gateway" for their entry into virtue, while the *Analects'* teachings on compassion served as "the inner chambers" of virtue.[79] If Banzan's analyses of the *Analects* and the *Great Learning* are applied to *Responding to the Great Learning*, then the latter text can be seen as his attempt to synthesize the teachings of the *Analects* and those of the *Great Learning* by way of the *Mencius* and its advocacy of compassionate government, thus bringing them to bear on the social, political, and economic problems challenging the Tokugawa realm.

---

[79] Kumazawa Banzan, *Shūgi washo*, p. 134.

Zhu Xi on the Great Learning

Banzan's studies of the *Great Learning* followed the contents of the "old text," i.e., the text that appears as a chapter in the *Book of Rituals*. For a millennium, that was how the *Great Learning* was known, as one chapter in the *Book of Rituals*. The same was true with another chapter later known as a text unto itself as the *Middle Way* (*Zhongyong*). In his reinterpretations of Confucianism, Zhu Xi elevated the two chapters as books in their own right, and added prefaces, emendations, and detailed commentaries to each. Expanding on the thinking of an earlier Song dynasty Confucian scholar, Cheng Yi, Zhu Xi called the *Great Learning* the gateway to learning and the first of the Four Books. The *Middle Way*, in his new curriculum, was the last of the Four Books and its most metaphysical.

In a questionable move, Zhu included as a "supplement" to the main text – not as part of his commentary – a passage by Cheng Yi explaining the "investigation of things." Zhu justified this textual alteration of the *Great Learning* by claiming that a portion of the original text had been lost and needed replacement. In Zhu's mind, Cheng Yi's passage filled the gap nicely. Zhu also reinterpreted a crucial word in the opening of the *Great Learning* by suggesting that the phrase, "love the people" (*qin min*) be read as "renew the people" (*xin min*). That, he claimed, was the correct understanding of it.[80] Zhu's alterations of the *Great Learning* were subsequently criticized by many who charged that he was taking unwarranted liberties with if not rewriting portions of the classics. No doubt they were right.

Zhu Xi's understanding of the *Great Learning* was countered by Wang Yangming who did not accept his alterations. Though hardly the majority, a fair number of later Confucian thinkers, in China, Korea, and Japan, also challenged Zhu's revisions. Banzan joined them, presenting his commentaries as explanations of the old text rather than Zhu's emended text. Arguably, in following the old text, Banzan revealed his standing as a follower of Wang's views, at least regarding the *Great Learning*.

However, Banzan did not criticize Zhu for his emendations, he simply did not follow them. When pressed by his disciples about Zhu, Banzan was characteristically gracious, noting that Zhu had done what he did in response to the time, place, and circumstances in which he

---

[80] For a study of Zhu Xi's thinking on the *Great Learning*, see Daniel K. Gardner, *Chu Hsi and the Ta-hsueh: Neo-Confucian Reflection on the Confucian Canon* (Cambridge, MA: Harvard University Asia Center, 1986).

lived, attempting thereby to revive the truth of Confucianism against the mistaken foes of the day. While the latter went unidentified, Banzan most likely meant Buddhism. Like Zhu, Banzan had little use for contemporary Buddhism, and frequently took the opportunity to criticize its latter-day failings. That aside, Banzan's willingness to contextualize historically Zhu Xi's emendations of the *Great Learning* reveals his, Banzan's, own pragmatic relativism: without judging right or wrong, Banzan viewed Zhu as a man who did what he thought was necessary, in response to his historical predicament.

Banzan's decision to address the old text of the *Great Learning* need not be viewed as an indication that he was following Wang Yangming. After all, one of the supposed founding figures in Zhu Xi Confucian studies in the early seventeenth century, Fujiwara Seika, authored his own interpretation of the *Great Learning, Essentials of the Great Learning*, following the old text instead of the one that Zhu had groomed as his signature expression of Confucian learning.[81] When Hayashi Razan later wrote a summary of Zhu's views, *Writings on the Three Virtues* (*Santokushō*), he too followed the older version of the *Great Learning*. Nevertheless, both Seika and Razan have been cast as followers of Zhu Xi. Due to the controversial nature of Zhu's emendations of the *Great Learning*, it seems that utter fidelity to Zhu on that text was not taken necessarily as an absolute indication of one's philosophical lineage.

Despite textbook characterizations of Tokugawa thought in terms of doctrinaire schools, individual thinkers were less given to following rigid orthodoxies as spiritual slaves than to finding their own answers by drawing from various, seemingly disparate sources including Zhu Xi, and Wang Yangming, and others. Yet in focusing on the *Great Learning* as a work apart from the *Book of Rituals*, even Wang owed much to Zhu Xi and his earlier textual reorganization of the Confucian curriculum. Whether acknowledged or not, the post-Song plethora of East Asian writings on the *Great Learning* reflected Zhu's view, following his philosophical predecessor Cheng Yi, that the *Great Learning* was the first text students of Confucianism should master. Banzan likewise treated the *Great Learning* as a premier work, eminently worthy of serious comment and consideration.

---

[81] De Bary, Gluck, and Tiedemann, eds., *Sources of Japanese Tradition*, p. 44. Richard Bowring, "Fujiwara Seika and the *Great Learning*," *Monumenta Nipponica*, vol. 61, no. 4 (Winter 2006), pp. 437–457. A modern edition of Seika's text is in Ishida and Kanaya, eds., *Fujiwara Seika/Hayashi Razan*, pp. 41–78.

Banzan's Brief Explanation of the Great Learning

Much as Zhu did in his commentaries on the *Great Learning*, Banzan wrote into his *Brief Explanation of the Great Learning* a substantial amount that arguably had little or no basis in the original text. A few examples will suffice. In explaining the *Great Learning*'s remark "the one who wishes to govern a state must first regulate their family," Banzan notes that the "family" referred to here is that of "the emperor." He adds that much the same applies to the various lords of the realm, but disparages the common people as ones who, even if they attain wealth and rank, will continue to behave poorly. Only if the ruling elite, and primarily the imperial family, establish good customs, might the remainder of the realm reap the benefits and be well governed. This is because, Banzan claims, the emperor and the lords of the realm are the teachers of the samurai and the common people.[82]

In his *Brief Explanation of the Great Learning*, Banzan's admiration for the Japanese imperial line and its potential role in the polity is evident. Compared to the disrespect later Japanese Confucians such as Ogyū Sorai showed the imperial throne, Banzan's outspoken esteem for it is noteworthy. Banzan's thinking on this count was surely a byproduct of his upbringing in and around Kyoto, as well as his continued contacts with the ancient imperial capital throughout his adult life. Added to that was his acquired admiration for the aristocratic cultural expressions of Kyoto, including Murasaki Shikibu's *Tale of Genji*, as well as court music and poetry.

Regarding the *Great Learning*'s remark, "things have their roots and branches," Banzan explains that "things" refer to everything in the world below heaven, and that the root or origin of heaven and earth is "the spiritual way of great emptiness" (*taikyo no Shintō*).[83] Here, Banzan's regard for Shintō, again a likely byproduct of his time in Kyoto and at the shrines there catering to imperial spiritual culture, enters his accounts of the *Great Learning*. In a summary explanation of "governing the realm and bringing peace to all below heaven," Banzan suggests that it consists in "following ranks and circumstances in loving people and thereby embracing the reality of their oneness [literally, 'one-body']."[84] In affirming a vision of becoming one with all things, Banzan shows sympathy with one of Wang Yangming's central teachings. Yet no mention is

---

[82] Kumazawa Banzan, *Daigaku shōkai, Banzan zenshū*, vol. 3, p. 187.
[83] Ibid., p. 185.   [84] Ibid., p. 186.

made of Wang as Banzan's source. Banzan might have just as well cited the all-embracing vision of one of Zhu Xi's predecessors, Zhang Zai, author of the "Western Inscription" (*Ximing*), because after all, Banzan wrote a commentary on the same work entitled *A Japanese Commentary on the Western Inscription*. Zhang Zai opened his "Western Inscription" by declaring that heaven was his father, earth his mother, all people his brothers and sisters, and the stuff that fills all between heaven and earth, his body. In effect, Zhang Zai's was a more poetic expression of the vision of oneness that Wang Yangming later affirmed. Significantly enough, Zhu Xi included Zhang's way of thinking within his own formulation of Confucianism, making the vision of oneness part of his perspective long before Wang did much the same in the Ming.

Banzan's all-embracing vision was in fact relatively selective. *Responding to the Great Learning* makes it clear that he was not interested in forming one body with the so-called northern barbarians whose imminent invasion he warned against. Banzan's sense of oneness with things was most real vis-à-vis the natural beauties of Japan's mountains and rivers, its imperial culture and its Shintō religiosity, yet considerably less so with foreign threats, Buddhist clergy, and Christianity. At the same time, Banzan did, on occasion, note that when viewed from the grandest metaphysical and ethical perspective, insofar as heaven and earth are the father and mother and give birth to humanity, the people of China (*Chūgoku*), Japan (*Nihon*), the Ainu (*Ebisu*), and the northern barbarians are all brothers. Yet such all-embracing social statements are not characteristic of Banzan's *Responding to the Great Learning*, while his discussions of the threat posed by northern barbarians are far more so.

Later, in commenting on a line from the *Book of Poetry* quoted in the *Great Learning*, "the realm of one thousand miles is where the people rest," Banzan gives a brief account of the ancient Japanese imperial realm, one wherein harmony and centrality naturally prevailed and military and civil virtues, rites and music infused the customs of the people. During this idyllic age, samurai wanted to serve their ruler, farmers wanted to till his fields, and artisans and merchants wanted to work in his towns. Therein the minds and hearts of the people rested. Such, Banzan suggested, was the state of things in Japanese antiquity.[85] In this passage, Banzan sounds like the legendary Daoist philosopher Laozi, describing

[85] Ibid., p. 196.

simple village life in a time when people were so at one with the way that they never wanted to leave their homes. Not surprisingly, Banzan's critics claimed that some of his ideas were from ancient Daoist texts. And rightly so: Banzan's accounts of the *Great Learning* drew on diverse sources, including some that had no necessary relation to the *Great Learning* other than Banzan's contextualization of them therein.

Banzan's Japanese Explanation of the Great Learning

As a short work reinterpreting the *Great Learning*'s ethico-epistemological protocol for right government, Banzan's *Japanese Explanation of the Great Learning* anticipates *Responding to the Great Learning*. In its opening pages, Banzan explains that regulating families, governing the state, and bringing peace to all below heaven involve following the circumstances of things and "loving people and embracing the reality of our oneness [literally, 'one-body'] with them."[86] By focusing on the old text of the *Great Learning* and "loving the people" rather than Zhu's reading of it as "renewing the people," Banzan's compassionate leanings – which inform the translation of *jinsei* (sometimes rendered as "benevolent government" or "humane government") here as "compassionate government" – emerge as a core emotive theme in his thinking about the *Great Learning*. Banzan's intent was not, presumably, to distinguish himself as a doctrinaire associate of this or that form of Confucianism, but instead simply as a scholar of the way, interpreting Confucian philosophy and practice according to the needs of his time, place, and circumstances.

Though Buddhism is not mentioned in the *Great Learning*, Banzan takes the opportunity to criticize it in his *Japanese Explanation*. First, however, he praises Confucius as a sage who taught the way of kings and was concerned for those below him. On the other hand, Buddhist teachings discarded emperors and called on the faithful to abandon their families. In the end, those teachings would mean the ruin of a state. Banzan adds that Buddhism entered China and brought harm to it. After it entered Japan, the Japanese way of the gods (literally, Shintō) was damaged and the country nearly brought to ruin. Banzan charges that Buddhism had brought no benefits to the realm below heaven, not even one, even though countless injuries resulted from it.[87] Banzan expands the

---

[86] Kumazawa Banzan, *Daigaku wakai, Banzan zenshū*, vol. 3, pp. 219–220.
[87] Ibid., p. 222.

lxvi

political critique of Buddhism initiated in his *Japanese Explanation of the Great Learning* in *Responding to the Great Learning.*

Commenting on "the investigation of things," Banzan mentions neither Cheng Yi nor Zhu Xi, but clearly differs with their externally oriented epistemological approach by instead explaining it along more internally focused lines as "overcoming one's own selfish tendencies." Moreover, Banzan views the "extension of knowledge" not as a matter of understanding the principles of external things in the world, but rather in behavorial terms as "returning to ritual propriety." In offering these accounts, Banzan, as he acknowledged, was reinterpreting key notions in the *Great Learning* by reference to Confucius' teachings to his most promising disciple, Yanzi, on "compassion" (*jin*). In that context, Banzan also praised modesty as a virtue of heaven, enabling it to give life, and of earth, enabling it to nourish life. In the way of the gods (Shintō), fullness is cursed but modesty and yielding is blessed, and likewise in the way of humanity, pride is despised and modesty, adored.[88] On these counts, Banzan had moved some distance beyond the interpretations of Zhu Xi and Wang Yangming.

In Banzan's *Complete Works*, compiled well after his passing by later followers intent on preserving his writings, *Responding to the Great Learning* appears after Banzan's other two works, *Brief Explanation of the Great Learning* and *Japanese Explanation of the Great Learning*. The three texts, uneven in style and content, do not seem to have been meant as a trilogy, but nevertheless ended up as a set of sorts reflecting Banzan's ongoing concern with that important Confucian text. Chronological accounts of Banzan's life suggest that his *Japanese Explanation of the Great Learning* was written first, in 1685, followed by, in 1686, his *Brief Explanation of the Great Learning*, and then finally his *Responding to the Great Learning*. No doubt, his *Japanese Explanation* is the least refined, more a draft than a polished work. On the other hand, his *Brief Explanation* is a more thoughtful commentary, interpreting and explaining the text, line by line. With *Responding to the Great Learning*, however, Banzan is not so much systematically addressing the doctrines and passages of the *Great Learning* as launching his own exposition of the text's overall political mission, governing the realm and bringing peace and prosperity to all below heaven, with a keen awareness of his historical time and its predicament, his geopolitical place and its challenges, and his circumstances

---

[88] Ibid., p. 227.

of status and birth, and the crossroads they presented him. In *Responding to the Great Learning*, Banzan does allude to portions of the *Great Learning*, but without calling attention to the extent to which his comments might be viewed as expositions of the text, preferring instead to present his allusions to the *Great Learning* as expressions of his own thinking as grounded in that text.

Many of the topics addressed in *Responding to the Great Learning* are also addressed, in varying degrees, in Banzan's *Accumulating Righteousness, Japanese Writings* and his *Accumulating Righteousness, Further Writings*. Quite possibly, Banzan compiled *Responding to the Great Learning* by bringing together essays he had authored over the years, the remainder of which later went into the two larger anthologies. However it was completed, Banzan gave his final work a name reflecting its thematic relationship to governing, thus tying it to the *Great Learning* and linking it inevitably to his two earlier writings on the same text, as well as to a host of writings by Japanese, Chinese, and Korean scholars on that brief but seminal work defining a protocol for governing the realm and bringing peace to all below heaven.

Banzan's Accumulating Righteousness *and the* Great Learning

In *Accumulating Righteousness, Japanese Writings*, Banzan discusses the *Great Learning* often. One essay opens with a simple question, "What are the essentials of governing the realm and bringing peace and prosperity to all below heaven?" Banzan's response is to the point: "For the sake of the realm and all below heaven, the essential thing is employing men of talent and ability in government."[89] Banzan sees this as crucial because men of talent will understand what is necessary and beneficial for the people of the realm in order that peace and prosperity might be realized for all. One of the most repeated teachings of *Responding to the Great Learning* concerns the importance of finding men with talent, that is, men with a propensity for governing well who can contribute to the realization of compassionate government.

In a follow-up essay, Banzan discusses the three most important things for a ruler who wishes to govern a state. This time drawing on the *Analects* (12/7), Banzan notes that food, an army, and the trust of the governed are the three necessities for governing. In the *Analects*, however, Confucius said that an army would be the the least essential, followed

---

[89] Kumazawa Banzan, *Shūgi washo*, p. 228.

by food. His reasoning was that without the trust of the people, a government would not be able to stand. In Banzan's response, the absolute necessity is food, because without food a military cannot be sustained and, more importantly, a people cannot be expected to refrain from all manner of behavior subverting the realm. Next in importance is the military because without it, Banzan reasons, chaos will ensue. Finally, with food provided and military order realized, the trust of the people will follow.[90]

Banzan's inversion of Confucius' ranking is striking. Banzan's assessment of the relative importance of these three most likely reflected his work in Okayama following the devastating flooding that reduced many to poverty and starvation. From his work in disaster relief, Banzan knew first-hand the importance of having sufficient food for civil behavior. It was also something he likely had gathered from the *Mencius* (3A/3) and its exposition of "compassionate government" (C: *renzheng*; J: *jinsei*). There, Mencius explained "the way of the people" is such that they will have a "reliable mind and heart" if they have a "reliable livelihood." Yet if people have no reliable livelihood, or at least food to eat, there is nothing that they will not do. Therefore, if one expects people to be moral, they must be able to provide for themselves. Mencius proceeded to explain how land could be distributed along egalitarian lines as a first step toward realization of compassionate government. In *Responding to the Great Learning*, Banzan's main concern is not with implementing the well-field system[91] so much as with economic policies that would maximize the material well-being and sustenance of everyone in the realm. In this regard, his understanding of compassionate government draws, with modifications, on the *Mencius* and, most especially, the Mencian imperative of ensuring a sufficient livelihood for all.

Compassionate government for Banzan, then, was more than platitudes about self-cultivation and ethical instruction: it involved practical matters like building retention ponds to prevent destructive flooding; adjusting taxation to provide relief for the peasantry; reconfiguring the currency so as to maximize the value of rice and prevent waste of edible crops; cultivating healthy forests, mountains, and rivers; regulating Buddhist clergy to ensure their integrity; restoring Shintō religiosity; returning samurai to the countryside; limiting urban growth; eliminating Christianity; reducing the alternate attendance requirements for daimyō rendering

---

[90] Ibid., pp. 246–247.   [91] See translation, Chapter 12, n. 1.

service to the shogunate; preparing for possible invasion by northern barbarians; and establishing an educational program uplifting the cultural literacy and civility of the population. As these topics are broached successively in *Responding to the Great Learning*, Banzan's text appears less like a commentary specifically on the *Great Learning* itself, and more fully like a response to the political challenge of the *Great Learning*: how to find a way to govern the realm and bring peace and prosperity to all below heaven.

Early Tokugawa Studies of the Great Learning

Banzan's three studies were part of a larger literature on the *Great Learning* that emerged in the early Tokugawa period. The plurality of interpretations offered reflected in turn the extent to which the rise of Confucian learning in the early seventeenth century resulted in a relative boom in individual philosophical statements authored by various thinkers personally engaging the new discourse and its primary texts. The plurality also indicated the multifaceted nature of the learning, and how claims to orthodoxy were contested by the diverse perspectives that emerged from various socio–economic corners of the realm.[92]

While Banzan's text sought to address political matters as they pertained to the entire country, often referring to it as "Japan" (*Nihon*), his analyses issued most particularly from his experiences in southwestern Japan, in Okayama domain, as a samurai–retainer of a daimyō somewhat distant from Edo, and then later, in and around Kyoto, as a controversial rōnin–scholar watched by the shogunate. Banzan's Confucian voice, then, was one from the hinterlands, relatively speaking, formerly in service to an outer daimyō. By extension, Banzan, then, was arguably what might be called a *tozama* scholar, one who ultimately had to recognize the relative power of Edo–based shogunal Confucians such as the Hayashi, and then later, Edo transplants, including Yamazaki Ansai, but who himself subscribed to views that differed significantly from theirs. Following his resignation from service to the Ikeda, Banzan's standing then as a rōnin scholar left him more vulnerable than ever. Nevertheless, he was determined, as an authentic Confucian responding to his existential predicament, to offer his advice on how governing should proceed if the country were to attain peace, prosperity, and security for all. In doing so,

---

[92] For a detailed study of the *Great Learning* in Japanese early-modern intellectual history, see Minamoto Ryōen. *Edo no Jugaku Daigaku juyō no rekishi* (Tokyo: Shibunkaku, 1988).

he seems to have disregarded the very factors that he otherwise emphasized – time, place, and circumstance – and landed himself in considerable trouble even as he affirmed, at another level, his very authenticity
as a scholar concerned about the political welfare of the realm and the
socio-economic well-being of the people therein.

Fujiwara Seika and the Great Learning

As noted earlier, one of the first Tokugawa studies of the *Great Learning*
was *Essentials of the Great Learning* authored by a Kyoto scholar, Fujiwara Seika, in the early seventeenth century. Though typically cast as
Zhu Xi Confucians, neither Seika nor his student Hayashi Razan were
blind followers of Zhu and indeed both included many insights and
interpretations that had no precedent in Zhu's writings. Seika, for example, drew on a Ming dynasty commentary by Lin Zhao'en (1517–1598),
Correct Meanings of the Great Learning (Daxue Zhengyi zuan), a work
noted for its syncretic approach to Confucian learning, often pairing the
latter with Buddhist and Daoist notions. An autonomous thinker, Seika
did not follow Zhu Xi's view that "loving the people" should be understood as "renewing the people." In veering from Zhu on this count, Seika
endorsed the Wang Yangming view that the old text, that is, "loving the
people," should be accepted, without Zhu Xi's emendations. Razan,
it might be added, did the same in his *Writings on the Three Virtues*.[93]
Although not purebred adherents of Zhu Xi learning, for the most part
Seika and Razan would be grouped closer to Zhu, especially when their
writings are compared with those of Banzan which, while hardly statements of utter fidelity to Wang Yangming, did recognize teachings –
such as the extension of intuitive knowledge – that were often considered, however simplistically, as ones quintessentially Wang Yangming.

Hayashi Razan on the Great Learning

Razan also addressed the *Great Learning* in his brief work, *Writings on the
Three Virtues (Santokushō)*. Although Razan claimed Seika as his teacher
and sought thereby to enhance his scholarly standing in the early Tokugawa via that association, the explanations of Razan and Seika varied
considerably in style, content, and most especially, socio-political context. Nevertheless, Razan, like Seika, devoted substantial attention to the

---

[93] Hayashi Razan, *Santokushō*, in Ishida and Kanaya, eds. *Fujiwara Seika/Hayashi Razan*,
p. 172.

Great Learning and, moreover, left several additional studies of it including his *Explanation of the Great Learning* (*Daigaku kai*), *Summary of the Great Learning* (*Daigaku ryaku shō*), and *Vernacular Explanation of the Great Learning* (*Daigaku waji kai*).[94]

Most interesting, however, was Razan's essay, "Variant Editions of the *Great Learning*" (*Daigaku ihon kō*). There he noted that the *Great Learning* had been a part of the *Book of Rituals* ever since the Han dynasty. However, it was centuries later in the Song that a variant edition appeared including corrections and alterations that Zhu had made in the text. From that point on, there was an "old text," based on the *Book of Rituals*, and another, Zhu's text, that stood apart from the *Book of Rituals*. Notably, Zhu's text came to be studied widely by those aspiring to service in the imperial bureaucracy. Later, with the Ming dynasty, scholars such as Wang Yangming, contrary to Zhu Xi and the Song scholars, returned to the old text, denying it needed revisions, alterations, or supplements, even while proceeding to interpret it in terms of their own thinking about "extending intuitive knowledge." From that point forward, Confucian scholars discussed the *Great Learning* over and again, in more and more detail, with some defending Zhu's views and others lining up behind Wang.[95]

Razan does not strongly defend Zhu's views. And, when Razan's other writings on the *Great Learning* – which follow the old text, but not Wang's interpretations – are considered, it seems that over time he developed questions about Zhu's alterations, even while remaining, for the most part, more an admirer of Zhu's positions than any others. Here again, it seems, that school lines as previously drawn in Tokugawa intellectual history have been overly simplistic and even misleading about the extent to which doctrinal fidelity ever prevailed. That aside, Razan does not mention factors of time, place, and circumstance, but clearly his study of variant editions develops a historically contextualized analysis of the texts, one that anticipates the kind of thinking more characteristic of Banzan.

Nakae Tōju on the Great Learning

Banzan's focus on the *Great Learning* perhaps grew from his brief study with Nakae Tōju, a pioneer in advocating Wang Yangming thought in

---

[94] See *Razan sensei bunshū*, vol. 2 (Kyoto: Heian kōkogakkai, 1918), pp. 203–204, 208, for postscripts to these writings.

[95] *Razan sensei bunshū*, vol. 2, pp. 306–307.

Tokugawa Japan. Tōju is best known, however, for his emphasis on filial piety as a sense of reverence and respect not only for one's parents and grandparents, but for heaven and earth as the father and mother of all humanity, and then, ultimately towards the primeval "great emptiness" (C: *taixu*; J: *taikyo*), the source and foundation of heaven and earth. Tōju's account of filial piety went even further, positing the existence of an "august supreme monarch" (C: *huang shang di*; J: *sumeragi jōtei*) ruling over great emptiness and all creation, and to whom ultimate filial reverence was owed.[96] Tōju developed these ideas in his major work *Discussions with an Old Man* wherein he recognized the *Great Learning*, along with the *Classic on Filial Piety* and the *Middle Way*, as books that any student of Confucianism should read.[97]

Like Banzan, Tōju wrote three texts explaining his views: *Thoughts on the Great Learning (Daigaku kō)*, *Commentary on the Great Learning (Daigaku mōchu)*, and *Explanation of the Great Learning (Daigaku kai)*.[98] In these, Tōju discusses "luminous virtue" as what resides in the center of the mind and heart, but also as what penetrates the great emptiness of the cosmos and embraces heaven, earth, and the ten thousand things of reality. Following the old text rather than Zhu Xi's emended version, Tōju interpreted the phrase "loving the people" literally as affirming an intimacy with and love for people at large. The "extension of knowledge," he explained, was the process whereby our innate intuitive knowledge engages the world in our practical relations with things.

As in *Discussions with an Old Man*, Tōju's *Explanation of the Great Learning* affirms his egalitarian views, especially regarding humanity and the project of learning. At odds with the hereditary, hierarchical divisions defining Tokugawa society, Tōju declared that "regardless of distinctions in rank, respect, and esteem, there was not an iota of difference between people, from the emperor, various lords, and samurai down to the common lot of humanity."[99] Although described as a Wang Yangming scholar, Tōju's ideas on the great emptiness and the august supreme monarch can be traced more to the late-Ming dynasty thinker,

[96] Yamashita, "Nakae Tōju's Religious Thought," pp. 307–336.
[97] Nakae Tōju, *Okina mondō*, in Itō, ed., *Nakae Tōju Kumazawa Banzan*, pp. 167–168.
[98] For a more complete listing of the works written during the Tokugawa period on the *Great Learning*, see Zhang Wenchao, ed., *Jiang hu shi dai jing xue zhe zhuan lüe ji qi zhu zuo* (Taipei: Wan juan lou, 2014) where myriad such writings are listed. Those discussed here amount to a sampling of the more relevant ones.
[99] Nakae Tōju, *Daigaku kai*, quoted from Kimura Mitsunori and Ushio Haruo, *Nakae Tōju Kumazawa Banzan*, Nihon no shisōka, vol. 4 (Tokyo: Meitoku shuppansha, 1978), p. 123.

Wang Ji, a disciple who further developed Wang Yangming's teachings, rather than to Wang Yangming himself.

While some of Tōju's thinking is apparent in Banzan's *Brief Explanation of the Great Learning*, it is not cited prominently in *Responding to the Great Learning*. And, as has been noted earlier, though Banzan studied briefly with Tōju and early on counted him as his "teacher," in the end Banzan stressed that his thinking had developed along independent lines, in response to his time, place, and circumstances, and that that was as Tōju would have expected it to be. One crucial difference between the two was that Tōju passed in 1648, just four years after the collapse of the Ming dynasty and the beginning of the Manchu conquest of China. At the time, successful Manchu rule of China was hardly a foregone conclusion. Four decades later, toward the end of Banzan's life, Manchu power was well established, resulting in the relative credibility of a possible Manchu invasion of Japan, something that Tōju had never imagined but that Banzan was obsessed with unto death. This difference alone in their time, place, and circumstances resulted in a considerable variance in their philosophical concerns and practical engagement with the polity.

Along other lines, Banzan criticized students of Tōju who did little more than recite their teacher's sayings and criticize others for not doing so. Rejecting that doctrinaire approach, Banzan declared that he had not sought to found a school and moreover "had not even a single disciple."[100] By this, Banzan conveyed his modesty as well as his belief that learning was, in the end, not a matter of repeating verbatim what had been said in the past, but adapting the truth of ancient wisdom and knowledge to ever-evolving contemporary circumstances.

Itō Jinsai on the Great Learning

The most provocative writing on the *Great Learning*, one that questioned not just one emendation or the other, but rather the wholesale integrity of the text itself, appeared in 1685, one year before Banzan completed his *Brief Explanation of the Great Learning* and *Responding to the Great Learning*. Itō Jinsai's *Established Text of the Great Learning (Daigaku teihon)* challenged virtually all previous literature on the *Great Learning* by arguing that, whether considered as a chapter in the *Book of Rituals* or as the first of the Four Books as defined by Zhu Xi, the *Great Learning*

---

[100] Banzan, *Shūgi washo*, ch. 2, pp. 38–39.

was not a text Confucius had transmitted and was not, in effect, a legitimate expression of Confucian discourse.

In formulating his argument, Jinsai designated the two most ancient texts of Confucianism, the *Analects* of Confucius and the *Mencius*, as his standards for judgments regarding orthodoxy. Jinsai claimed that the *Analects* was the most perfect writing in the entire world below heaven, and even the greatest work ever in the entire universe. The *Mencius*, in his view, occupied a subordinate position as a commentary on the *Analects*. Jinsai then noted that nowhere in either the *Analects* or the *Mencius* did the sequential formula presented in the opening paragraphs of the *Great Learning* appear. In those paragraphs, the *Great Learning* explains that those wishing to make evident luminous virtue and thereby govern the realm and bring peace and prosperity to all below heaven, that is, those intent on ruling, must first cultivate themselves by making their minds correct and their thoughts sincere, and should achieve that by extending knowledge and investigating things.[101] Such a formulaic protocol, Jinsai insisted, was foreign to the *Analects* and the *Mencius*. Its absence from the latter two texts meant, in Jinsai's view, that the *Great Learning* was not part of the Confucian lineage of learning.

Most importantly perhaps, Jinsai related that while the words "luminous virtue" appear in the ancient classics, neither Confucius nor Mencius ever spoke of them. The ancient classics wherein those words appear suggest that they are attributes of the sage-rulers, not ones that any person might hope to embody or exhibit. Conversely, Confucius and Mencius taught compassion (C: *ren*; J: *jin*) as a moral practice that all people should seek to embody, but in the *Great Learning*, it is exclusively associated with rulers. In Jinsai's view, the author of the *Great Learning* was simply using words as he wished without necessary regard for the teachings of Confucius and Mencius.

On another count, Jinsai notes that the *Great Learning* introduces the notion of "a great way [C: *da dao*; J: *daidō*] for growing wealth and prosperity." Confucius, however, never mentioned this. In the *Analects* (16/1), Confucius did acknowledge that if resources were divided

---

[101] John A. Tucker, "Skepticism and the Neo-Confucian Canon: Itō Jinsai's Philosophical Critique of the *Great Learning*," *Dao A Journal of Comparative Philosophy*, vol. 12, no. 1 (March 2013), pp. 11–39. Itō Jinsai, "The *Great Learning* is not a Confucian Text," *Gomō jigi*, translated in John A. Tucker, *Itō Jinsai's Gomō jigi and the Philosophical Definition of Early Modern Japan* (Leiden: Brill, 1998), pp. 233–244. A digital copy of the 1685 woodblock edition of Jinsai's text is online on the Kokubungaku kenkyū shiryōkan site at https://kotenseki.nijl.ac.jp/biblio/100160961/viewer/30?ln=en.

equally, there would be no poverty, and if society were ordered harmoniously, there would be no scarcity. That, Jinsai insists, was Confucius' teaching, but he said nothing about a "great way." Here, Jinsai's remarks are especially relevant to Banzan's text because *Responding to the Great Learning* refers to "the great way" a number of times suggesting a grand socio-economic program whereby the realm would be enriched, and all would share in prosperity. While an important notion in Banzan's text, Jinsai asserts that it has no place in Confucian discourse.

Finally, Jinsai critiques the *Great Learning* claim that there is profit (C: *li*; J: *ri*) in righteousness. Jinsai condemns this view as fundamentally at odds with the words and ideas of Confucius and Mencius. Both declared that their only concerns were with moral teachings and ethical behavior, and explicitly denied any interest in profit. In endorsing the profit mentality even by tying it to moral practice, the *Great Learning*, in Jinsai's view, was some distance from the teachings of Confucius and Mencius. Although Jinsai confessed that he did not know who wrote the text, he insisted that it was not, as Cheng Yi and Zhu Xi asserted, "a remaining work of Confucius." Instead, Jinsai speculated that the *Great Learning* was the product of a degenerate age when heterodoxies prevailed and came to be mixed with the ideas of Confucius and Mencius. By Zhu Xi's day, distinctions between heterodoxies and the original Confucian teachings had become so blurred that Zhu Xi mistook the *Great Learning* for a Confucian writing and elevated it as the first of the Four Books and the gateway to Confucian learning.[102]

Whether Banzan knew of Jinsai's work before his own writings on the *Great Learning* were completed, is unclear. However, given that Jinsai spent his entire life in Kyoto as a teacher-scholar and attained some renown as a Confucian, it is difficult to imagine that Banzan did not at least know of it. On the other hand, while Banzan was born in Kyoto and returned often, enjoying the erudite, civil culture that existed there, he was also a man of action, often elsewhere for extended periods, either in service to a lord or in the custody of a lord, living in seclusion as a banished man. Still, when in Kyoto, Banzan apparently made his mark, and must have come to the attention of Jinsai. Later, Ogyū Sorai, according to the late-Tokugawa work *Sentetsu sōdan* (*Discussions of the Early Confucian Philosophers*), linked the two men in one of the most memorable and amusing remarks of that age, noting "that if Kumazawa's knowledge and

---

[102] Itō Jinsai, "The Great Learning is not a Confucian Text," pp. 233–244.

Itō Jinsai's emphasis on practice could be combined with his [Sorai's] own learning, then the eastern sea (Japan) would have its first sage." In another remark, less prideful, Sorai stated, "among the Confucian giants of the last hundred years, Kumazawa was a man of talent, and Itō Jinsai was a man of learning. The others are not worth mentioning."[103]

That Sorai would reportedly link the two Kyoto scholars, but that they, as contemporaries, did not seem aware of each other, is unusual but perhaps explainable. Jinsai possibly heard of Banzan's troubles with the Kyoto authorities and so distanced himself from the controversial scholar because he understood just how provocative his very own ideas might appear from the perspective of the same authorities. Not wanting to invite presumption of guilt due to association, and surely not relishing the thought of exile into the hinterlands, Jinsai might have maintained reserve and a relatively low profile as a scholar-teacher, aware that Banzan's tendency was toward being outspoken, even pugnacious. Then again, by the time of Jinsai's writing on the *Great Learning*, Banzan was an aging scholar living in exile outside Kyoto and, despite his occasional visits and contacts with learned men in Kyoto, was most likely out of touch with the latest developments in Confucian studies there. On the other hand, Banzan remained a man of action until the end, one who might not have paid Jinsai's logical assessments of the *Great Learning* any mind even if he knew of them. Whether the *Great Learning* was a text that Confucius had left or not made no difference. It set forth valuable ideals, leaving Banzan with the task of proposing a strategy for their realization consistent with the time, place, and circumstances of his day.

If Banzan did know of Jinsai's critique of the *Great Learning* and simply ignored it, he was not alone. Despite the discrepancies and philosophical inconsistencies that Jinsai noted between the *Great Learning* and more ancient, authentic Confucian works, few later scholars – other than his own disciples – accepted Jinsai's judgments as the final word. The philosophical charisma that Zhu Xi and later Wang Yangming recognized in the *Great Learning* continued strong, Jinsai's views notwithstanding.

Banzan as an independent thinker

Banzan fully realized the differences between Confucius' teachings in the *Analects* and those of the *Great Learning*, but rather than elevate the *Analects* and abandon the *Great Learning*, he saw them as different

[103] Hara Nensai, "Kumazawa Banzan," pp. 132–133.

expressions relating to different times, spaces, and circumstances, legitimate in their own way given the relative historical crucibles from which they sprang. Banzan was apparently not as concerned about the purity of school lineages and discourse as he was about good ideas, from whatever provenance, and most especially, their real practicality. In Banzan's view, the *Great Learning*, in setting forth the goal of governing the realm and bringing peace to all below heaven, advanced a valuable agenda that would necessarily be responded to differently by different thinkers in different times.

Banzan was an independent-minded thinker who respected his predecessors but coupled that respect with an unwillingness to be confined by their thinking as if he and they lived in the same time, space, and circumstances. Appreciating his historical predicament and that of those who came before him, Banzan selected from earlier ideas those he deemed most credible and practical. In *Accumulating Righteousness, Japanese Writings*, Banzan rejected any facile categorization of his learning. He stated:

> I do not draw my views from Zhu Xi or Wang Yangming. I draw from the ancient sages. What has been transmitted in the lineage of the way is the same with Zhu and Wang. Their words reflect their historical predicaments. The truths of their teachings complement one another as do matching tallies.
>
> Zhu and Wang are not really different. For the sake of rectifying evil evident in his day and to rid the world of confusion and doubt, Master Zhu emphasized fully understanding rational principles. As a result, he did not discuss introspection and self-vigilance. Responding to the evils of his historical circumstances, Master Wang stressed introspection and self-vigilance, but did not emphasize fathoming principles.
>
> In practicing introspection and self-vigilance as a means of self-cultivation focusing on the inner mind, I draw on Wang Yangming's explanations of intuitive moral knowledge. In warding off confusion and doubt, I rely on Master Zhu's emphasis on comprehending rational principles. The doubts and misgivings of students differed during the time of Zhu and Wang, but with adjustments for time and circumstance, are their teachings not the same?[104]

Banzan's views of Zhu and Wang, then, were shaped by his understanding of their historical predicaments and his estimation of their

[104] Banzan, *Shūgi washo*, p. 141.

response to the same. Rather than declare one right and the other wrong, Banzan recognized in each thinker's ideas real philosophical value. Banzan was harsher on Nakae Tōju. He allowed that Tōju's learning combined strengths from the teachings of Zhu and Wang, but also made it clear that he had no use for Tōju's accommodation of Buddhism. The unity of the three teachings, so evident in Tōju's thought, had no appeal to Banzan. Even more critically, Banzan stated that Tōju's followers often showed no real knowledge of the classics of Confucianism, nor the major teachings of the way. In the end, Banzan stated that despite claims about Tōju's teachings having prompted everyone below heaven to practice the way, people who were fond of virtue were indeed rare.[105] From Banzan's perspective, Tōju's teachings had, then, done little to bring about real change.

Banzan added that he rarely repeated Tōju's words as such, even though he had learned much from Tōju. The teaching about the importance of time, place, and circumstance was one that Tōju emphasized, but in following that very teaching, it was only natural, in Banzan's view, that his own expressions would differ from Tōju's as surely as their time, place, and circumstances differed. In much the same way, Banzan acknowledged that his followers should not simply repeat his words but instead they should respond to their own predicaments with their own observations. In interpreting anew his teacher Tōju's words in response to his own historical circumstances, Banzan claimed he was most fully repaying his debt to Tōju.[106]

Banzan added that while some people referred to his learning as the "learning of the mind" (*shingaku*), he thought that label inappropriate. Instead, he insisted that "the way is the way, and learning is learning. Unfortunately, when names are applied, one-sidedness often results." Banzan saw Zhu and Wang as addressing different historical circumstances with each, in their own way, providing answers for their times. Banzan added that there had been a developmental progression in Confucian learning wherein each stage contributed to the growth of the next. Han dynasty commentaries made possible the rise of the Song dynasty "study of principle" (*rigaku*), and Song developments in turn made possible the rise, in the Ming, of the methods of the mind (*shinpō*), which in turn contributed to his own progress along the path of virtue. Banzan noted that while discussions had become more complex, it was doubtful

[105] Ibid., p. 200.   [106] Ibid., p. 254.

whether later scholars matched the ancients in virtue. Nevertheless, Banzan made it clear that in his view Zhu Xi and his predecessors in Song learning were all "one body with the sages."[107]

Further historicizing Confucian philosophical developments, Banzan added that after the first emperor of the Qin dynasty attempted to burn all the Confucian classics, it was necessary for Han scholars to focus their work on textual studies and commentaries, recreating as best they could the philosophical literature that the Qin had attempted to eradicate. Thereafter, with the appearance of Buddhist heterodoxies, it became necessary for Song Confucians to emphasize the study of principle as a means of dispelling misunderstandings that the Buddhists had spread. Once confusion had been dispelled, Ming Confucians then focused on introspective methods of mind control and cultivation.[108] Via historical contextualization, Banzan thus cast Confucianism as a growing, evolving set of teachings, continually adapting to the temporal and environmental predicaments faced and thereby giving rise to new and progressive expressions. Reviewing the changes in Confucian teachings, Banzan recognized value in each developmental stage without narrowly confining himself, along exclusive, dogmatic lines, to any single one.

Elsewhere in *Accumulating Righteousness, Further Writings*, Banzan compared Zhu Xi and Wang Yangming, in a relatively fair and judicious manner, without taking sides. When asked whether Zhu Xi and Wang Yangming were "worthies," Banzan replied:

> Master Zhu can, presumably, be called a great scholar and a worthy. Through his commentaries on the classics, he made enormous contributions, and so he stands as the most renowned of all commentators, ancient and modern. Regardless of whether his commentaries were faithful to the minds and hearts of the ancients, his writings were meant, from the start, for beginners who needed ethical explanations that were meaningful and intelligible to them. On that count, later students of Confucianism are indebted to him for his efforts ...
>
> Master Wang was, presumably, a scholar who possessed both culture and military learning. He earned fame as a great general. He was also a worthy. He further developed Mencius' teachings about intuitive knowledge and intuitive abilities and emphasized, in the process, introspection and self-vigilance. Wang's legacy for later students practicing introspection was not shallow.[109]

[107] Ibid., pp. 14–15.   [108] Ibid., pp. 15–16.
[109] Banzan, *Shūgi gaisho*, ch. 6, *Banzan zenshū*, vol. 2, pp. 106–107.

In addition to recognizing significant contributions in the thought of both men, Banzan also recognized their weaknesses.

Master Zhu went to excess with broad learning and study. As a scholar, he focused on learning principle but remained reserved regarding methods of the mind. Books are comparable to rabbit tracks in the snow while rabbits are like the mind. Commentaries on Confucian classics are like commentaries on our minds. When one gets the rabbit, its tracks are no longer useful. When one gets one's mind, the classics are no longer necessary. The path to penetrating the mind can be full of expansive stops, but once one has gotten the overall idea, one should be able to grasp the mind ... Zhu's learning was excessively devoted to commenting on passages, and so became obsessed with the principles of words and phrases, often losing touch with the mind ... As a result, it did make major contributions to the study of the classics. However, the methods of the mind are some remove from the classics. Thus, Zhu Xi's learning came to be viewed as a crime against the sagely Confucian teachings.

Master Wang went overboard with compassion and self-vigilance and so ended up appearing very much like those who emphasize heterodox learning and Buddhist enlightenment. Those who saw Master Wang's excesses as wasteful and wrongheaded judged him to be a criminal as well ... Both men were worthies insofar as they recognized the principles of heaven as their minds, left off selfish human desires, and deemed it wrong to seize control of the realm if it involved mortal injury to even a single innocent person. In that sense, Zhu and Wang can be called worthies.[110]

Banzan readily acknowledged that the disciples of Zhu and Wang had real faults, and were by far inferior compared to the teachers they claimed to follow. Again, in *Accumulating Righteousness, Further Writings*, Banzan stated:

Those partial to Zhu's learning praise him. Those partial to Wang's learning praise him. Neither Master Zhu nor Master Wang were common men who were simply fond of fame and reputation. They were both princely, refined men who thought primarily of virtue. They both thought in terms of doing away with evil practices of their day and illuminating the way of the sages.

However, when we look at those who belong to Zhu's school and Wang's school, they are neither fond of virtue nor interested

---

[110] Ibid.

in accomplishing anything. They simply want to argue over who is right and who is wrong. Thus, the learning of the sages has not been realized.

Although the fundamental thinking of Zhu and Wang was to make the way of the sages manifest in the world, it has actually become more obscure. This was not the intent of Zhu and Wang. Would they not be saddened by these shows of partiality and exclusive praise? ...

The contributions of these two men to the sagely learning have not been minor. However, when we only follow one of them, harm results ... Those who seek the original minds of these two masters will reap benefits and incur no harm.[111]

Despite his overall respect for Zhu in relation to the historical development of Confucian thinking, Banzan questioned the extent to which Zhu's learning was appropriate to Japan. Banzan added that while advocates of Zhu's thought claimed to practice the methods of sages and worthies, their minds and hearts were often the very same as those of ordinary common people.[112] It should be emphasized, however, that Banzan's view of Zhu's learning as ill-suited to the cultural environment of Japan should not be construed as an indication that he opposed it. After all, Banzan referred to Buddhists as barbarian heretics but added that their teachings were appropriate to Japan. More than either Confucianism or Buddhism, Banzan saw Christianity, a teaching he wanted eliminated, as even more appropriate to Japanese circumstances. Yet there can be no doubt that Banzan opposed Christianity and Buddhism, and saw in Confucian teachings a way that would uplift Japan out of its complacency and to a new and more ethical time, place, and circumstance.

Insofar as Banzan's works added to the overall prestige of the *Great Learning* as a gateway to virtue, and simultaneously clarified the political dimension integral to the *Great Learning*, he was arguably following both Zhu and Wang and any number of other commentators who had, through their explanations, altered and enhanced thereby the very text they claimed to be faithfully explaining. In *Responding to the Great Learning*, however, Banzan was concerned minimally with epistemological questions related to the investigation of things or with the ethical mysticism of forming one body with all things, and instead was far more concerned with providing a comprehensive account of how good

---

[111] Ibid., pp. 139–140.   [112] Ibid., p. 177.

government might be effectively and actively achieved in his day, fully taking into consideration contingent factors such as the historical age in which he lived, the place, that is, Japan, to be governed, and the socio-political, economic, and religio–philosophical circumstances prevalent within that time and place.

Responding to the Great Learning: A Synopsis

Banzan's ideas in *Responding to the Great Learning* grew largely from politically oriented sections of the *Great Learning* as well as other Confucian philosophical writings such as the *Mencius*. Despite their importance for Confucian political thinking, the passages in the *Great Learning* most pertinent to *Responding to the Great Learning* were not ones previously emphasized by Zhu Xi, Wang Yangming, or most other later commentators. Banzan does not explicitly cite the relevant passages as such, and in some cases barely alludes to them, leaving their relationship with his work unclear to all except the Confucian cognoscenti. Much the same is true of Banzan's text and the *Mencius*, although this might seem less peculiar because Banzan's title does not call attention to the text's special relationship with the *Mencius*. Modern readers lacking familiarity with the *Great Learning* and *Mencius* will likely wonder just how they are related, if at all, to Banzan's *Responding to the Great Learning*. To clarify these ties as well as the content of Banzan's text, relevant background material in the *Great Learning* and *Mencius* is here underscored in tandem with a summary of Banzan's core ideas.

Banzan's foreword announces that *Responding to the Great Learning* proposes "viable measures" (*katsuhō*) that might save the country from its contemporary predicament. While "save" might seem too dramatic a word here, it must be emphasized that Banzan saw Japan as on the verge of economic implosion, with debt totaling more than all the gold and silver in the country, and on top of that facing the prospect of imminent invasion by northern barbarians. Simply put, Tokugawa Japan was, in Banzan's view, hovering over profound crisis if not impending doom and, without exaggeration, in need of rescue and salvation.

Making matters worse, Banzan viewed government measures (*hō*) then in place – those established by the Tokugawa shogunate – as contributing to if not causing the problems facing the country. In response to the times, the place, and the socio-economic and political circumstances, Banzan proposed a series of new measures that would, in his view, rescue

Japan from disaster and lead it to a new age of prosperity and security. Because these measures were specific to Japan's circumstances, one could not have found them earlier, in a different time and place, in either Japan or China, nor in ancient times or relatively modern. In a word, they were unprecedented and yet uniquely appropriate to Banzan's own day and the country's predicament. While some of the guiding principles of the *Great Learning* such as governing the realm and bringing peace and prosperity to all below heaven were surely relevant at an inspirational level, Banzan's practicable measures were not to be found as such in the *Great Learning* or any other ancient Confucian text.

Realizing the politically challenging nature of the proposed measures, Banzan stated that their realization would depend upon having the right person in government, one who could understand Japan's dire predicament and enact the measures forthwith. Until then, they would of necessity remain hidden and secret. Apparently in presenting a draft of the text to the shogunate, Banzan imagined either that the time had come and the right person was in place, or that his time was running out and that he would need to voice his proposals for the sake of the country, regardless of the consequences. The latter, it seems, was most likely the case. Had he kept the text to himself, a secret, at least until after his demise, he presumably would have passed his final years with far more liberty of movement and association than confinement and isolation in Koga brought him. However, by following that safe, self-centered course, he would have done nothing to help save the realm from the socio-economic and political disaster looming ahead.

Chapter 1, "The Heaven-Decreed Duty of the People's Ruler," is the most controversial of the entire work due to its account of "the people's ruler" and its radical remarks regarding the conditional nature of his legitimacy. While most Confucian literature refers to a ruler simply as a ruler (*kun*), Banzan refers to the ruler as "the people's ruler" (*jinkun*), that is, not as a ruler who rules in his own right, nor one designated by the imperial throne, but instead as a ruler whose standing is intrinsically related to and even derived from the people he governs. In speaking of the ruler in this way, Banzan echoes the *Great Learning*, section 7, wherein the words "the people's ruler" are used in reference to King Wen of the Zhou dynasty, otherwise described as an ideal ruler who governed his people with honesty and fidelity. There, the *Great Learning* adds "the people's ruler abides in compassion." Banzan's distinctive designation for the ruler also resonates with the *Mencius*, which suggests that while heaven decrees that certain individuals serve as rulers, the people serve as the eyes and ears of heaven, expressing the will and decree of heaven, which in effect makes them, the people, arbiters of the fate of their rulers.

The *Mencius* (1A/6) also uses the term, "the people's ruler" in its opening chapter. There, Mencius responds to a question posed by King Hui of Liang, identified by Mencius as one who did not appear to be "the people's ruler." Nevertheless, King Hui asks Mencius, who can give a ruler his throne? Forthrightly, Mencius answers, "Everyone in the realm below heaven gives it to him ... if there were a person who did not take pleasure in killing people, all people below heaven would gather around him ... The people would return to him irrepressibly, just as water rushes downwards." Mencius' pointed use of the term "the people's ruler" – in effect suggesting that King Hui was not such a ruler, and so not truly legitimate – thus reveals that, far from a mere euphemism for a sovereign, the term "the people's ruler" is one that affirms the decisive role of the people in relation to the ruler and his standing as such, as well as the responsibilities of the people's ruler to those over whom he rules.

Chapter 1 is equally controversial in stating, as a matter of cosmopolitical fact, that if the ruler forsakes his heavenly-decreed responsibilities to rule as the father and mother of the people and in accordance with compassionate government, then he will be removed and replaced by someone more suited to the task. Here, Banzan again draws on the *Mencius* which makes it clear that the people play a central role in deciding who "the people's ruler" will be. In Banzan's view, rulers are legitimate only if they preserve the decree of heaven which in turn is contingent on their real concern for the welfare of the people. When that concern is neglected, heaven sends warnings. If the wayward ruler continues to disregard his responsibility toward the people, then ultimately heaven, acting through natural events and human agency, will replace the individual who, at that point, will have effectively forfeited his right to rule.

Banzan's analysis of political legitimacy was profoundly at odds with the shogunate's. In its view, the line of shoguns or samurai rulers beginning with Tokugawa Ieyasu, founder of the Tokugawa line, had been appointed by the Japanese emperor to serve as practical governors of the realm. Their position depended neither on heaven nor the people. The shogun was, simply put, the emperor's shogun, not the people's shogun. Rather than endorse the Tokugawa understanding of shogunal legitimacy, Banzan drew on ancient Confucian literature to affirm a more humanistic, people-centered, and surely conditional account of legitimacy that emphasized the ruler's responsibility to govern paternalistically, as the father and mother of the people, and humanely, in accordance with the principles of compassionate government. Equally emphasized in Banzan's account were the consequences met by rulers who abandoned their responsibilities to the people and ignored the warnings of heaven as communicated through its earthly surrogate, the people.

Without question, Banzan's remarks about "the people's ruler" were made in reference to the shogunate in Edo and, by extension, daimyō in the domains, not the emperor in Kyoto. Banzan's extensive writings on what he calls Shintō make it clear that he saw the imperial line as sacrosanct and not subject to heaven's decrees. It is questionable whether Banzan believed the emperor to be of divine descent, but he surely held that the imperial line had a spiritual standing. It was most certainly not, therefore, the line of contingent, secular rulers discussed in Banzan's writings on "the people's ruler." Although confrontational, Banzan's opening discussion is cast in abstract, even universalistic Confucian terminology, referring to "the people's ruler" and "the people" without, at least at that point, identifying them as specifically Japanese. However, there can be no doubt about who Banzan was discussing. Surely, his challenging, even radical remarks about "the people's ruler" were one reason for his final exile. Whether the shogunal authorities read past the first chapter is questionable because there alone was more than enough outrageous political discourse to justify banishment of the aged but still offensive and troublesome scholar.

In addition to the *Mencius*, the *Great Learning* provides Banzan with a substantial textual basis for his aggressive, populist political theory. The relevant material in the *Great Learning* appears in section 13, where the *Great Learning* addresses the grand political culmination of the text, governing the realm and bringing peace and prosperity to all below heaven. While Banzan does not explicitly cite that portion of the *Great Learning*, it is there that his thinking on the conditional nature of a ruler's legitimacy has a strong textual foundation. Section 13 relates the following:

> It is said, "... The great decree [of heaven] is not easy to maintain." This shows that, by gaining the people, a state is gained, and, by losing the people, a state is lost. Therefore, the ruler is careful about his own virtue. If he has virtue, he will have the people. If he has the people, he will have the realm. If he has the realm, he will have

wealth. If he has wealth, he will have resources for necessary expenditures.

Virtue is the root of everything, wealth is what flows from it. If the ruler makes the root secondary, and the wealth that flows from the root his primary concern, he will end up struggling with his own people [over wealth], leading them to thievery. For this reason, when a ruler [selfishly] amasses wealth for himself, he is effectively forcing his people to flee elsewhere [in search of sustenance].

On the other hand, when a ruler distributes wealth among the people, he establishes a way to bring his people closer together. Accordingly, when the ruler's words are crooked, people will speak to him in the same way. And when the ruler acquires wealth by crooked means, he will end up losing it due to people's crookedness.

In the *Book of History*, the "Announcement to Kang" observes, "The decree [of heaven] is not permanent." That remark conveys the fact that with goodness, a ruler obtains the decree of heaven, and with depravity, he loses it.

Although Banzan does not cite Section 13 of the *Great Learning*, it presents solid grounds for his opening description of the ruler as the people's ruler, and the ruler's legitimacy as contingent upon his willingness to rule with care and compassion for the people just as fathers and mothers show their children. Though paternalistic and condescending, Banzan's thinking about the ruler's responsibility emphasizes, without declaring the people sovereign, that rulers who neglect the people are doomed.

Banzan's central theme in *Responding to the Great Learning* is the importance of administering the realm according to the principles of compassionate government. The latter notion, distinctively Confucian, traces back most distinctively to the *Mencius*. Confucius in the *Analects* never mentions the two-word compound, even though he often discussed compassion and government separately. Nor does the *Great Learning* mention the compound "compassionate government." In making this notion his central message, Banzan links *Responding to the Great Learning* as closely to the *Mencius* as to the *Great Learning* itself.

In the *Mencius*, compassionate government is often a code word for right rule, virtuous rule, and the kind of government that secures for a ruler the support of the people, and for the people, their well-being. More specifically, Mencius (3A/3) associates compassionate government with socio-economic reform of a radical sort. After noting that people cannot be expected to have a constant mind and heart devoted to moral behavior if they do not have a constant livelihood, Mencius suggests that a system of equitable land distribution be an integral part of compassionate government. Significant here is that Mencius understood compassionate government not simply as a set of moral platitudes, but as an ethical way of governing that provides for the economic well-being of the population and a secure material foundation for a moral polity. Banzan does not advocate, as did Mencius, an overall redistribution of land, but he does propose reforms meant to create a realm wherein the people are more adequately provided for, materially and economically, in terms of daily sustenance and livelihood, as well as educationally, culturally, and in regard to national defense. For Banzan, as for Mencius, compassionate government meant government that cares about the material as well as the ethical well-being of the people. Banzan's corollary message is that rulers who neglect compassionate government and the best interests of their people will face the consequences, as decreed by heaven and as executed by the people.

Chapter 2, "The Heaven-Decreed Duty of the People's Ministers," like Chapter 1, advances a people-centered agenda. It does so by referring to the ministers of the realm not as the ruler's ministers but as "the people's ministers," as if they in some sense represented the interests of the people rather than those of the ruler. In doing so, Banzan follows the usage in section 7 of the *Great Learning*. Other Confucian texts such as the *Mencius* occasionally used the same terminology. The *Mencius* (7A/31) notes that when "worthies serve as the people's ministers," they will please the people by expelling rulers who abandon virtue, if they do so for the sake of rectifying misrule. If that is not their intent, Mencius declares, then such a move against a ruler amounts to usurpation. Mencius' reference to "the people's ministers" thus suggests the power of the people at large in relation to both their rulers and their ministers as long as that power is wielded for the sake of virtuous rule. In this, Mencius was not typical of Confucian theorists so much as one of the most if not the single most confrontational and threatening. In alluding to the *Mencius* and the *Great Learning*, Banzan positioned himself similarly.

Along related lines, Banzan affirms that there is a way to predict when a state will prosper and when one will collapse into ruin. Simply put, Banzan states that if the channels of communication are open between the people's ruler and the people's ministers, then all will be well within the state. If the ruler shuts those channels, silencing the people's ministers, then the beginning of the end will have been set in motion. Banzan explains that heaven will send down various calamities, warning the ruler that he is endangering the polity if he does not allow open communication with the people's ministers. Banzan does not dilute his prognosis. If rulers are obstinate and refuse to listen to the people's ministers, then a decline into ruin will ensue. Well-known examples from Chinese political history are cited in this context.

Equally controversial is the heavenly-decreed duty Banzan attributes to the people's ministers. In addition to assisting the ruler with compassionate government, the people's ministers are to remonstrate, as needed, with the ruler when his commitment to compassionate government wanes. Provided that the ruler heeds remonstration, his rule might last. But if the ruler silences his ministers and closes channels of communication, Banzan states that heaven will send down its judgment with effective finality, and then offer hope once again for compassionate government in the realm as guided by a new line of rulers.

Banzan's remarks draw on the *Great Learning*, section 14, which quotes the *Book of History* and its emphasis upon having a minister who is sincere, simple, and honest and, most importantly, recognizes the talents and capabilities of others. With such a minister, the *Great Learning* explains, a state will be well governed. On the other hand, when there are ministers who deceive and refuse, due to jealousy and worse, to recognize the talents of others, then the end of the state is soon announced by calamities sent by heaven. Although Banzan does not cite section 14, there the *Great Learning* links open, honest communication between the people's ministers and the people's rulers, as well as the people's ministers and the people below, as crucial to the prosperity of the state. The *Great Learning* also threatens that if such openness is not present, the state faces doom. To the extent that Banzan's remarks in Chapter 2 of *Responding to the Great Learning* are related to the *Great Learning*, they most conspicuously echo section 14 and its discussions of ministers and the state.

Chapter 3, "Revering Good Counsel," offers a brief discussion of the nature of good counsel, noting that it does not consist of philosophical discussions of the way so much as advice on the extent to which a ruler's policies and administrative initiatives are effective at the ground level. Once again, Banzan emphasizes the importance of maintaining openness in communication between the ruler and those offering good counsel to keep the realm from falling into a vortex of ruin. Here, as in the preceding chapter, Banzan draws on the ideas of the *Great Learning* as developed in section 14 where the ideal minister and his antithesis are described, and the consequences of each are laid bare.

Chapter 4, "A Grand Project for Growing Wealth," emphasizes the importance of wealth for compassionate government, suggesting that without it, government cannot help the helpless in society, including the increasing number of rōnin, as well as those in the countryside facing starvation due to flooding, drought, and bad harvests. To rightly achieve wealth for the realm, Banzan calls for a major overhaul of the socio-economic system realized via "the great way." The latter includes initiatives such as relieving daimyō of various financial burdens including regular ceremonial service in Edo to the shogunate. Such relief would allow daimyō to provide relief for the people below. Banzan also proposes recognition of rice as a currency, on par with gold and silver, at a fixed rate of exchange in relation to the latter. If implemented, daimyō would not have to sell their rice in Osaka or Edo to gain gold and silver currency necessary to finance their service to the shogunate. Also, the waste due to shipwrecked cargo and rot in port granaries would end, resulting in more rice for consumption, transactions, and storage to alleviate hunger during times of trial.

Banzan's emphasis on wealth for effective, compassionate government clearly echoes the *Great Learning* on this count, as well as the *Mencius* and its remarks linking compassionate government to the well-field system of land redistribution. However, Banzan's specific proposals – that daimyō be relieved of most of their Edo service requirements for the shogunate and that rice be made, officially, a form of currency alongside gold and silver – are his own contributions to the discourse, not ones found in either the *Great Learning* or the *Mencius*. These are two of the viable, practicable regulations that he proposes which, according to his foreword, were unprecedented in ancient and modern times, in either China or Japan. While Banzan does not make this point, these two proposals alone would have revolutionized the socio-economic and political order, reversing the flow of resources into the shogun's capital resulting from daimyō service to the shogunate, and laying the foundations for enhanced daimyō power and wealth in the hinterlands. Economically, a rice-based currency, alongside silver and gold, would have, if implemented, undercut the rice markets in burgeoning economic centers such as Osaka and led to a more locally centered economic order providing, presumably, for better material interests of the rice producers, that is, the peasants in the countryside. Banzan later proposes returning samurai to the countryside to live and labor alongside the peasantry, a move that would have furthered the empowerment of the hinterlands as opposed to the shogunal center in what would have amounted to a major reorganization of the socio–economic and politico–military order of the realm.

Chapter 4 emphasizes the onerous burden for daimyō of rendering service to the shogunate, suggesting that such service needs to be rethought along more economic lines. Banzan also criticizes peasants for devoting good farmland to cash crops such as tobacco instead of rice because, in Banzan's view, this results in a reduction of rice yield so essential to the overall well-being of the economy. Banzan's strategy of returning samurai to the countryside is adumbrated in this chapter as part of a shift Banzan envisioned for a reorganized early-modern Japan away from burgeoning urban centers and their commercially dominant interests, and toward the countryside and the rice fields wherein Banzan saw enormous wealth potential of a most fundamental sort. If these initiatives meant to maximize rice productivity were implemented, Banzan projected that greater levels of agrarian wealth would be produced for everyone and the problems of poverty and starvation solved throughout the realm.

Banzan's thinking on the grand project for growing wealth expands on the *Great Learning*, section 15, which states:

> There is a great way for the production of wealth. Let there be many producers and only few consumers. Let the producers be quick in production, and the consumers consume in moderation. Then wealth will be constantly produced.
>
> Compassionate rulers, by means of their wealth, make something of themselves. Yet rulers who are not compassionate compromise themselves to accumulate wealth. Never has there been a ruler above who was fond of compassion while those below were not fond of righteousness and justice. Never has there been a ruler fond of righteousness and justice whose projects were not brought to completion.

Banzan's thinking about the importance of maximizing wealth in the realm is much more detailed than the *Great Learning* passage above. In the latter passage, however, Banzan found ample Confucian justification for government concern with wealth, allocation of resources, and the economic welfare of the realm. Rather than advance a robust agenda meant to promote economic diversity, commercialization, and urbanization as keys to growing wealth, Banzan's thinking was, like the *Great Learning*, focused mostly on maximizing agrarian production while simultaneously reducing non-essential consumption by the people at large. By expanding the number of rice producers and their rice yield, and minimizing unnecessary expense, there would be, in Banzan's view, more than enough for all.

Banzan's discussion of the great way is also precedented, in Confucian literature, in the opening passage of the *Book of Rituals*' chapter, "Evolution of the Rites." It relates:

> Confucius said, "When the great way is practiced, everyone below heaven will share in common. Men of talents will be employed [in government] and men of ability will be promoted as well. Their words will be honest, and they will cultivate harmony and friendly relations with all. As a result, people will not simply love their parents, [they will love the parents of other people as well]. Nor will people simply treat their own children as their offspring, [instead they will treat other people's offspring as their own as well].
>
> "Suitable provisions will be secured for the aged, employment for the able-bodied, and support for the young. Those in government will show kindness and compassion to widows, orphans, childless men, and the disabled, so that everyone will be sufficiently cared for. Men will have their responsibilities, and women will handle domestic affairs.
>
> "People will accumulate wealth because they dislike seeing things going to waste, not because they seek wealth for their own selfish advantage. They will work because they dislike being indolent, not for selfish profit. As a result, conspiracies will no longer be hatched. Robbers, thieves, rebels, and traitors will be no more. And people will feel free to leave their doors open. Realization of the great way will lead to what can be called an age of great equality."

In *Responding to the Great Learning*, Banzan refers to "the great way" often, suggesting that his proposals overall were meant to realize, in contemporary times, the Confucian utopian vision of "the great way" and the age of "great equality." The *Book of Rituals* passage includes many themes at the heart of Banzan's *Responding to the Great Learning*, most importantly his emphasis on the need to employ men with "talents" in government, as well as men of ability. By doing so, Banzan hoped his series of reforms would contribute to the realization of his idyllic vision of an agrarian utopia wherein all shared according to their station enabling a common cultural harmony that provided for all.

Chapter 5, "Eliminating Anxieties over Flooding and Relieving Droughts," develops Banzan's conception of compassionate government along two very practical lines: (1) preventing floods and droughts by way of civil engineering projects such as the construction of reliable retention ponds, and (2) using unhulled rice as a form of currency. While the first draws on Banzan's experiences in Okayama domain and reveals the extent to which his understanding of problems and their solutions was experientially grounded rather than simply the product of ivory-tower book learning, the second line of reform, currency reform, would have been, socio-economically, more widely consequential on a daily basis in early-modern Japan.

In Banzan's view, the Tokugawa economy had become severely inefficient as daimyō sold much of their domain's rice yield for gold and silver coins to finance their service in Edo as part of the alternate attendance duties required of them by the shogunate. When rice was shipped to major urban centers – Osaka and Edo – to be sold, large quantities ended up being lost at sea, or, once in granaries, to insects and rot. The result was that much of the fundamental foodstuff of the country was being, in effect, wasted. Banzan proposed eliminating that by having the value of a *koku* of rice fixed in relation to silver so that the *koku* could be used for business transactions of all sorts, precluding the need for shipping rice to urban centers and running the risk of incurring losses along the way.

Banzan does not, however, adequately address the practical, logistical issues involved in taking to market, for example, 50 *koku* of rice to do one's shopping. Then again, he seems to have envisioned a simpler, less commercialized economy wherein consumption patterns would have been few and essentially basic, so that large quantities of rice would not need to be transported to markets to make purchases. That aside, Banzan's diagnosis of the problems facing the Tokugawa economy are striking for both their revolutionary and reactionary character. Banzan's call for rice as currency is a prelude to his proposal that samurai be returned to the countryside as part of a massive, de-urbanization program shrinking urban areas and reducing the economic waste that he saw in them. Similarly, Banzan proposed reducing (1) the saké industry because it required excessive rice, (2) the tobacco industry because it displaced rice farming, and (3) cotton manufacturing because it, like tobacco, displaced rice as a crop. For Banzan, a healed Tokugawa economy, free from massive debt and chronic waste, would have been one that returned to its origins in the soil and largely operated via barter exchanges wherein rice was swapped for the most basic necessities. While the arc of these proposals was reactionary, implementing them would have required revolutionary levels of social engineering, forcing samurai to return to the countryside, and those already in rural areas to forsake alternative economic activities that added spice and variety to their otherwise arduous existence.

Chapter 6, "Preparing for Northern Barbarians, Emergencies, and Bad Harvests," forecasts what Banzan apparently thought was an inevitable invasion of Japan by a shadowy group of people he consistently identifies as "northern barbarians." An early translation of Banzan's text cast this group as the Mongols because they had earlier invaded Japan and conceivably could have done so again. However, it is far more likely that Banzan's fears were directed at the Manchu peoples who in 1644 entered China to put down an anti-Ming uprising, but then proceeded, once the rebellion was quashed, to take control of the land and declare themselves the founders of a new imperial regime, the Qing (1644–1912). Tokugawa Japan learned of these events through Dutch reports coming in from Nagasaki as well as by way of Ming emigres fleeing their homeland, determined not to serve a dynasty that had conquered the one to which they felt an undying loyalty. Several of the emigres were outstanding Confucian scholars known to the Japanese scholarly elite of Banzan's day. Banzan possibly heard reports from them about an impending invasion of Japan, and rather than respond with caution, emerged as the most vocal prophet of Japan's coming doom. The only hope for the realm, in Banzan's view, was making immediate preparations for war.

Sounding very much like an alarmist, Banzan warned that if something were not done quickly, Japan would descend into defeat, ruin, and utter chaos. Yet more than a matter of military equipment and training, Banzan saw his country unprepared because it lacked the basic provisions, that is, rice, necessary to feed an army fighting in the field in defense of the realm. The result, he predicted, would be desertion and then defeat, largely due to Japanese domains having insufficient stores to field and feed an army for any length of time.

Yet an invasion never occurred and so Banzan ended up appearing somewhat deluded and out of touch with political and international realities. On the other hand, approximately a century and a half later, as barbarians began appearing in Japanese waters, this time coming from both the north (Czarist Russia) and the south (Europe and America) rather than simply the north, Banzan's calls seemed more prescient than paranoid, even if his policies for achieving military readiness, using rice as currency and returning samurai to the fields, were profoundly antiquated and askew. Then again, in the early twentieth century some two hundred years after his passing, Banzan's warnings about northern barbarians seemed even more clairvoyant as Czarist Russia returned, seeking to check Japan's ambitions in northeast Asia. With that late-Meiji period moment, Banzan's status as a farsighted political thinker rose to new heights. Not surprisingly, the late-Meiji period witnessed a relative explosion in Banzan-related scholarship just as the imperial nation then sought to deal with foreign threats more aggressively.

Chapter 7, "Filling Shogunal Coffers with Gold, Silver, Rice, and Grain," continues Banzan's emphasis on measures necessary to prepare the country militarily for an invasion by northern barbarians. Banzan's specific proposals have little basis in either the *Great Learning* or the *Mencius*, or any other Confucian text for that matter, except insofar as the theme of compassionate government crops up time and again. Banzan's most interesting proposal here is his reiteration that the shogunate modify its alternate attendance rule requiring daimyō to remain in Edo while serving the shogun six months out of a year, or every other year, depending on the distance of the daimyō's domain from Edo. Banzan recognized that requirement as a major drain on daimyō and domain resources and so advocated a return to something akin to the Kamakura shogunate's model of alternate attendance which only required of daimyō fifty days of service once every three years. By Banzan's estimations, this approach would both ensure the loyalty of the daimyō and cost all parties involved considerably less, allowing them to store more provisions in preparation for a foreign invasion.

Chapter 8, "Eliminating Debt from the Realm below Heaven," discusses how debts owed by daimyō, retainers, and peasants might be either paid off or refinanced along reasonable lines. Banzan's key point is that with a reduction in daimyō expenses due to severely reduced alternative attendance demands, daimyō would have extra resources available to devote to repaying debts. Also, as they would need less money, they could allow peasants to turn over a smaller fraction of the total yield of their produce. The peasants could then use the additional rice to pay off their debts. In some cases, adjudication of debt repayment might be necessary. This, as well as debt-management generally, would be supervised by the shogunate, with the intent that it all contribute to the realization of compassionate government, that is, socio-economic and political peace and prosperity for all in the realm. Lenders would also be regulated, but only to enable them to remain in business making a good, though not extravagant, living. Through this plan, Banzan thought that the realm would realize overall prosperity and economic well-being, as well as, at the personal level, contentment and peace of mind.

Chapter 9, "Helping Rōnin, Vagrants, the Unemployed, and the Impoverished," proposes means of alleviating poverty among rōnin by allowing them stipends sufficient to support their parents, wives, and children, allotted according to the number of individuals in each rōnin family. In modern parlance, Banzan proposes unemployment relief, as well as relief for those with fiefs but insufficient resources to provide for their families. Funds for such government assistance would be expected of daimyō who, no longer burdened annually by alternate attendance expenses, could devote a portion of their domain resources to rōnin assistance. If enacted, Banzan's plan for rōnin relief, along with helping homeless rōnin, would be, in his view, among the greatest achievements of compassionate government. With this chapter, the meaning of compassionate government becomes even clearer. Hardly a set of platitudes or mystic-metaphysical visions of oneness with all things, Banzan's understanding of compassionate government meant to provide material assistance to those in need. His sympathy for the downtrodden and outcast possibly issued from his feeling of oneness with all things, but his practical expression of it was grounded in the relief work he oversaw in Okayama domain following its earlier devastation due to flooding.

Chapter 9 is arguably an expansion of the *Great Learning*, section 12, which explains that "bringing peace to all below heaven is a matter of governing the realm." It adds that when the ruler has pity on the aged, the elderly, orphans, and those without others to assist them, then all below heaven will be decent and filial as well. While the *Great Learning* expresses concern for the less fortunate, it assumes that their care extends from the ruler's good example and humane sentiments. In Banzan's view, being a moral exemplar is not enough: material provisions in the form of stipends are necessary for the sake of truly assisting those in need. Also, Banzan's concern is most obviously for the rōnin population and their strained circumstances, though it surely extended well beyond the socio-economic confines of his own group.

Chapter 10, "Making Mountains Luxuriant and Rivers Run Deep," expands Banzan's understanding of compassionate government by relating it to maintenance of a healthy environmental balance for the sake of the welfare of the socio-economic and political realm. Banzan begins by addressing the proposition that mountains and rivers are the foundations of the state. While he concurs with this, Banzan notes that mountains have been ravaged for the sake of harvesting their timber, and rivers choked with sediment from mountains stripped bare of forests. Banzan blames these problems on the high demand for lumber, resulting from unbridled construction of temples, shrines, castles, and samurai mansions. Widespread consumption of forest timber as firewood for hearths is also to blame. As a solution, Banzan calls on commoners to use field straw for cooking rather than timber. He also suggests that the number of temples and shrines be reduced, and that repairs to remaining shrines and temples be made with timber recycled from dismantled shrines and temples closed down or consolidated. With decreased demand for timber, mountain tops will have a chance to recover and, once again, emerge as well-forested forces in the ecological and political order. With established forests, sediment will no longer clog riverbeds, enabling rivers to flow well into the sea. The result will be, in Banzan's mind, another achievement of compassionate government, this time in the form of a well-balanced environment that serves as the foundation of the realm.

Neither the *Great Learning* nor the *Mencius* affirms that mountains and rivers are the foundations of the political order. However, in the *Book of Rituals*, the chapter "Rules for Sacrifices" recognizes in passing that mountains, forests, valleys, and rivers provide people with sustenance, but it stops short of declaring them the foundations of the polity. The *Mencius* (2B/10) denies that mountains and rivers provide for the security of the state, but in the denial offers the hint that such a relationship might well have been broached. Rather than do so, however, the *Mencius* recognizes the importance of harmony and good relations among people as the decisive factor in securing the state. Nevertheless, the idea – even if denied – does appear in the *Mencius*. With *Responding to the Great Learning*, Banzan takes these notions to the next level, affirming that mountains and rivers are the foundations of the state and so, matters of absolute political importance.

Chapter 11, "The Ebb and Flow of the Ruler's Blessings," addresses a question asking whether there are government measures ensuring that the shogunate and all domains and provinces enjoy prosperity together. Banzan's questioner asks because he has heard a saying that the shogunate does best when the domains and provinces are in dire straits. Banzan responds that poverty in the provinces and domains leads to poverty throughout the realm and that in turn results in a withering away of the blessing of the decree of heaven, and so the ruler's tenure. When that happens, nothing can be done. Banzan insists that it is shallow, even despicable to view poverty in the domains and provinces as advantageous to the shogunate. Recalling shogunal rule in Japanese history, Banzan praises the Hōjō regents of the Kamakura period as the wisest because they required their vassals' attendance in Kamakura only once every three years, and then for only fifty days. When in Kamakura, daimyō were warned against excessive spending lest the resources of their domains be wasted there. The Kamakura model is one that Banzan later returns to and advocates as part of his proposals for restructuring the Tokugawa polity.

Banzan's view that the fate of the domains and provinces is inseparable from the fate of the shogunate has, incidentally, an overall founding in the *Great Learning* insofar as that text sees governing states – or domains and provinces in Japanese terminology – as intrinsically related to bringing peace and prosperity to the realm below heaven. While the political order historically relevant to the *Great Learning* was that of the Zhou dynasty kingdom and its vassal states, the political logic of part and whole integrally and inseparably related in prosperity and decline, makes that text relevant to this chapter of *Responding to the Great Learning*.

Chapter 12, "Returning to the Old Farmer–Samurai Society," details Banzan's plan – already adumbrated – for reuniting farmers and samurai. Realizing that this major undertaking in socio–economic engineering of an armed population would be problematic, Banzan proposed measures, all under the guise of compassionate government, whereby the reuniting might be facilitated, including resolution of farmers' debts, return of lost land to farmers, and reductions in grain demands on farmers. These would be made possible largely due to the decreased burden on farmers once daimyō no longer must serve the shogun in Edo half of every year or every other year. In Banzan's scheme of compassionate government which here follows the Kamakura model for vassal service, daimyō would only spend fifty days in Edo, once every three years. The result would be a drastic reduction in daimyō expenses, and for farmers, considerable relief. With the peasant farming population in better economic condition, Banzan presumably imagined that samurai accustomed to living in castle towns would be more amenable to relocation to rural areas to live among the agrarian stock.

Banzan warns that rulers who are too permissive or too accommodating in implementing this will not be able to realize his vision of compassionate government. Put differently, reuniting samurai with the farming population would require shrewd, iron rule in the service of compassionate government. Banzan does not go into the details, but instead shifts to how samurai ought to behave in relation to farmers once they have been returned to the countryside. Banzan encourages consideration for the peasantry, especially since they will be neighbors to the samurai for generations to come. Banzan suggests that samurai take up the ways of the farmers in social behavior and pastimes such as hunting and fishing. Banzan emphasizes that samurai still need to practice the martial arts and engage in study and learning, but as much as possible they should live simply as farmers do. In several generations, for all practical purposes their descendants would have fully merged with the peasant population as farmer–samurai.

Banzan's vision for Edo is extraordinary if not downright incredible. He proposes a 90 percent reduction in Edo residential space and suggests that the vacated space once populated with daimyō mansions be converted to rice fields. In effect, Banzan thus proposes a massive de-urbanization of the shogunal metropolis as a means of economically strengthening samurai and the realm. New wealth, supposedly, would thereby be realized which, Banzan emphasizes, should be used for the sake of the realm, not for the shogunate and certainly not for any privileged group. Banzan's program of compassionate government thus entailed a colossal re-engineering of the Tokugawa polity, especially at the elite level of samurai, with the latter being downsized radically as they reunited with the agrarian elements in creating Banzan's utopian polity united in agrarian and military strength.

Chapter 13, "Eliminating Landless Income and Increasing New Fiefs," criticizes several peculiar practices hampering the overall prosperity of the realm. One is the tribute expected of daimyō on holdings that have no basis in land. Banzan calls this an undue and unfair imposition on daimyō which should be corrected with updated surveys of arable land or increases in the land-based holdings of a daimyō to make the "no-land" holdings less problematic. At the same time, Banzan admits that resolving this sort of issue will be difficult because the holdings, whether land-based or not, are combined and thus difficult to separate. Still, Banzan affirms that generally the fiefs given to daimyō should be based on arable land and not on other, amorphous factors. Banzan also criticizes transport fees that result in circuitous shipping routes that are preferred due to their lower costs as opposed to the safer land routes that are heavily taxed.

Banzan calls on the shogunate to allow those who bring new land under cultivation to till it for three years without taxation. Such leniency would make industrious farmers wealthier and encourage them in diligence for generations. Banzan also praises daimyō who, when their fiefs are near mountains and streams, take personal responsibility for them, ensuring that they are not ravaged or choked, thus becoming a source of disaster and hardship. Overall, Banzan's compassionate government proposals here are meant to enhance production of wealth and prosperity in the land, and contribute to social and political strength as well.

Chapter 14, "Lowering the Cost of Foreign Silk and Textiles," advocates efforts toward domestic production of silk rather than continued reliance on expensive imports from China. To facilitate this, Banzan proposes that mulberry bushes be planted around samurai dwellings so that silkworms can be raised and silk harvested. Recognizing that farmers are already burdened with growing rice, Banzan suggests that samurai women, high and low, find more productive ways of using their time than in frivolous pursuits. Banzan thus foresaw the emergence of a domestic silk industry driven by female labor that would, in approximately ten to fifteen years, compete with foreign products imported into Japan.

Banzan's thinking here is mercantilist in nature, seeking to cultivate a domestic industry and then protect it for the sake of enabling Japan to avoid having to pay foreign merchants in gold and silver. Yet Banzan is also a realist, recognizing for the moment that Japan had no choice but to import silk and other fine textiles. Additionally, Banzan criticizes the shogunate's decision to close Hirado as a port for foreign trade, leaving only Nagasaki open. Consequently, silk imports became more expensive. Instead of continuing that policy, Banzan advocates reopening Hirado. While Banzan's short-term forecast is that considerable efforts will be necessary to keep Japan from dependency on foreign silk, he envisions, optimistically, that with increased wealth and prosperity resulting from compassionate government, silk would eventually be produced and consumed by aristocrats, samurai, merchants, and artisans.

Chapter 15, "Eliminating Christianity," sets forth Banzan's critique of Christianity and his proposals for dealing with followers of the banned religion. Banzan claims that Christian teachings spread in Japan because of the poverty and ignorance of the people. The solution, in his view, is compassionate government. With the latter, poverty will be eliminated and enlightened teachings will prevail. By enlightened teachings

Banzan means those of Confucianism and Shintō, as well as rites, music, and martial arts. Evidence of the efficacy of Confucianism, he claims, is found in China, the land of sages and worthies, where Christianity never flourished despite the absence of any rules or regulations against it. Until compassionate government is practiced, however, Banzan thinks that shogunal strategies for eliminating the foreign religion, such as temple registration, waste the resources of the domains and provinces.

Even though Banzan was opposed to Christianity, he noted that reports from officials sent to apprehend those accused of being Christians stated that the suspects were more reverent and devoted to their beliefs than most Buddhists. To the extent that allowances of this kind typified Banzan's longstanding views of Christians, they possibly contributed to spurious charges that Banzan had secret leanings toward Christianity. That aside, Banzan's opposition to Christianity was shared by virtually all Confucian scholars of the day, and not a few went well beyond Banzan in denouncing the foreign religion and calling for its expulsion from the realm. In many respects, opposition to Christianity united Confucian scholars across virtually all lines, whether of the Zhu Xi, Wang Yangming, or other supposed lineages.

Chapter 16, "Reviving Buddhism," proposes that Buddhism be reinvigorated and restored by strict insistence on rigorous rules limiting entry into the clergy, and encouragement of frugal forms of Buddhist practice such as "sitting under trees and atop rocks" while wearing hemp-woven robes. Banzan admits that Buddhism appears to be flourishing in Japan due to the large number of Buddhist temples, priests, monks, and ceremonies associated with it. However, he claims that the clear majority of the clergy are immoral opportunists out for an easy livelihood rather than sincerely devoted practitioners of the three teachings: the Buddhist precepts, Buddhist mind control, and Buddhist wisdom.

Banzan even declares that most clergy are "robbers and thieves." During the coming invasion of northern barbarians or perhaps with a natural disaster such as a major drought, most of the clergy, in Banzan's view, would become thieves, abandoning their temples as soon as they encounter difficulties. Banzan predicts that if temples burned down, they would remain in ashes while most of the clergy deserted the faith to pursue their opportunism elsewhere. Yet out of the ashes, Banzan envisioned a rebirth of mountain forests and rivers, recovering from the environmental ravages caused by earlier overconstruction of Buddhist temples. Along with a revival of nature, Banzan predicted a revival of Buddhism, stronger and more authentic for having shed insincere clergy who earlier only sought food and shelter.

Chapter 17, "Reviving Shintō," criticizes earlier accounts of Shintō such as those in *Chronicles of Japan* (*Nihon shoki*) as nothing more than the writings of ancient clergy addressing matters of behavior and comportment, metaphysical topics, and other matters related to shrines and ritual beliefs. Banzan claims that these accounts addressed the outer shell of Shintō, not its whole substance. Rather than revere Japan's ancient writings as the textual basis of Shintō, Banzan claims that Shintō has no sacred writings at all, only the three sacred treasures, the mirror, the sword, and the jewel, which serve as its holy texts. To the extent that there are commentaries on these three texts, they appear in the Confucian classics and their commentaries. Although Banzan does not emphasize the foreign identity of these texts, they were the Chinese Confucian classics. In effect, Banzan thus proposes a more universalistic, multicultural understanding of Shintō, one more broadly affirming the importance of Chinese Confucianism in relation to Shintō than had typically been the norm.

Banzan extolled the *Middle Way* as the most important Confucian text related to Shintō because of its discussions of the three virtues – wisdom, compassion, and courage – therein referred to as the "utmost way." Banzan in turn paired the three virtues of the *Middle Way* with the three sacred treasures of Shintō, with the mirror exemplifying wisdom; the jewel, compassion; and the sword, courage. Banzan also claimed that what Chinese Confucianism called the way of the sages and worthies was in Japan known as the way of the divine rulers.

In one of his more detailed statements, Banzan explained Shintō in political terms, relating it to the mission of governing central to the *Great Learning* as well as to the virtues described in the *Middle Way*.

> In whatever age, Shintō consists of the ruler's virtuous actions in governing and bringing order to the realm below heaven, responding to human feelings, and transforming things according to their time, place, and circumstances, thereby illuminating the virtues of wisdom, compassion, and courage. The writings that record the deeds of these spiritual rulers should be considered sacred literature.

Banzan repeatedly returned to these topics in *Accumulating Righteousness, Japanese Writings* and *Accumulating Righteousness, Further Writings*, and in his other works. While an important portion of *Responding to the Great Learning*, Banzan's thinking on Shintō therein is by no means his most complete or definitive statement. It is significant insofar as it reveals that Banzan, like many Japanese political thinkers, viewed matters related to spirituality as an integral topic in any discussion of government and socio-economic matters.

Chapter 18, "Worthy Rulers Reviving Japan," soon becomes a discussion of whether Confucianism should be relied upon exclusively in a government that seeks to reinvigorate the realm. Banzan reveals, in his answer, the extent to which he meant *Responding to the Great Learning* to be an open-minded, non-doctrinaire analysis of how best to govern the realm and bring peace and prosperity to all below heaven. Despite his evident leanings toward Confucianism, Banzan explains that Japan can best be revived when wise rulers lack selfishness and partiality in governing, and draw on Confucianism, Buddhism, and Shintō as they are appropriate to the problems facing the country.

In explaining this further, Banzan warns against the six infirmities of the mind, each an expression of selfishness and partiality, that contribute to misgovernment of the realm, hampering Japan's vitality. The six infirmities are (1) promoting one's own views without considering those of others, (2) being reluctant to seek the advice and insights of others, (3) being partial in relation to Confucianism, Buddhism, or Shintō, (4) being inclined to rewards and punishments, (5) being obsessed with material wants and sexual passion, and (6) being too narrow-minded in searching for men of talent and ability.

In one of his few metaphysical remarks in *Responding to the Great Learning*, Banzan suggests that a realm well governed without selfishness and partiality is one wherein the way of humanity assists the creative processes (*zōkū*) of the universe. In this instance, Banzan draws, it seems, not from the *Great Learning* but instead from the *Middle Way*, sections 30–33, the final ones in that text. There, Confucius is described as one who harmonized with heaven above and merged with water and land below, and so was himself comparable to heaven and earth. In *Responding to the Great Learning*, Banzan imagined that the ruler without selfishness and partiality was such a person, embodying the very highest levels of sagacity and sincerity and so, like Confucius, could lead the realm in assisting heaven and earth in guiding the creative processes therein. However, if channels of communication were closed and these creative processes obstructed, Banzan warned that heavenly disasters and earthly eruptions would follow, as well as illnesses and diseases. With the latter, Banzan warned, upheaval and chaos would not be distant.

Chapter 19, "Governing with Education," notes that schools have a political role insofar as they teach the way of humanity integral to governing the realm and bringing peace and prosperity to all below heaven. Within the school system that Banzan envisions, the shogun, daimyō, and other government leaders play important roles in cultivating learning about the way of humanity and compassionate government. The shogun is especially important given his prestige and authority. Banzan suggests that with just a few words of praise for learning, the power of the shogun is such that he can transform the entire realm.

In addition to the way of humanity, schools should teach culture and military arts. Banzan outlines a detailed curriculum primarily though not exclusively for the sons of samurai, assigning subject matter for various age groups as appropriate to the seasons of the year. The subjects range from reading and writing to literature, mathematics, ritual behavior, hunting, horsemanship, and archery. By systematic instruction of samurai youth and others, led ultimately by the shogun himself, Banzan hoped to provide the realm with an educated elite whose cultural and practical knowledge fully qualified them for the socio-political status that hereditary right otherwise conferred upon them.

While the *Great Learning* also outlines a program of education, it is more centered on the imperial person than the people at large. Its assumption is that through his self-cultivation and refinement, the entire realm might be transformed by extension. Banzan modifies this view, suggesting that the shogun and the samurai elite are the crucially effective figures in the educational transformation of the realm. Also, while the *Great Learning* succinctly explains the emperor's education in terms of rectifying the mind, making thoughts sincere, investigating things, and extending knowledge, it provides few specifics beyond that terse curriculum. However, it must be admitted that in the *Book of Rituals'* sixteenth chapter, "Records on Education," a locally based school system and curriculum of instruction corresponding with the age of the students and the seasons of the year is outlined. Though hardly the same as Banzan's, it was likely the model that Banzan followed in outlining his thinking about government through education. Banzan's discussion of schools and their curricula is, of course, detailed in a manner appropriate to the time, place, and circumstances of his day.

Chapter 20, "Those Who Should Teach in Our Schools," suggests that rather than allow Buddhists to teach in the schools, the best course would be to have children from the Kyoto aristocracy and cultured families therein educated so that they might in turn be sent out into the countryside to serve as the teachers at schools established in the domains and provinces throughout the realm. The result would be a countrywide broadcast of the educational sensibilities and refinement of the imperial capital, in the form of teachers. By suggesting that imperial progeny, aristocratic sons, and scions of cultured families serve as teachers in the domains and provinces, Banzan was proposing what might be called a return of the aristocracy to the countryside, in an erudite and civil capacity, as the counterpart to his proposal that samurai be returned to the countryside to work alongside the agrarian peasantry.

Chapter 21, "A Little Kindness Provides Benefits," discusses alternatives to Banzan's ideal, realization of compassionate government and the grand project for growing wealth, that might serve to alleviate matters in the here and now for people at large. Banzan, willing to offer an expedient for the present, returns to his proposal that rice, pegged at 50 units of silver per *koku*,[113] be recognized as a currency suitable for use in all commercial transactions. Rather than allow extreme fluctuations in the price of rice, Banzan advocated government involvement in the market, buying up rice in years of abundance to maintain the 50 units of silver valuation per *koku*, and selling the earlier purchased surplus in years of poor harvest to keep the population fed and prices from skyrocketing. By calling for active market intervention, Banzan hoped to prevent wild swings in the price of rice, even while ensuring that in years of plenty rice did not go to waste and that in years of poor harvests, there was plenty available to avert hunger and starvation. As a stopgap solution, Banzan's proposal fell short, as he recognized fully, of solving all the glaring problems of the day, and in no way approximated, to his admitted regret, the benefits of full realization of compassionate government.

Chapter 22, "Wasted Rice and Grain," returns to Banzan's earlier discussion of the unnecessary loss of large quantities of rice and the wild fluctuations in the price of rice given the market as it then existed. In discussing the enormous loss of rice, Banzan makes the frequently cited remark, that Japan had more debt than all the gold and silver in the entire

---

[113] Although the rates varied, one unit of silver, known as a *me* or *ginme*, was the equivalent of 3.75 grams. Generally, 1 *koku* of rice was worth approximately 50 *me* in silver. However, in years of abundance, the price would plummet, and in years of scarcity, it would escalate.

country could possibly pay. Banzan's solution to the problem of waste and market fluctuations amounts to a recapitulation of many of the key ideas in the previous chapters, including using rice as currency in transactions, setting the value of rice at a fixed rate, and conducting business transactions without preferring gold and silver over rice. Also, Banzan proposes extended time for repayment of debts, ending saké brewing, reducing the population of Edo, and reductions in the amount of rice shipped and possibly lost at sea in the process. These and other administrative measures, such as ensuring that talented and capable individuals are given positions in government and that their counsels are heeded, comprise Banzan's final recommendations.

Translation of *Responding to the Great Learning*

KUMAZAWA BANZAN

Responding to the Great Learning: Part I

There are viable measures for saving the country from its contemporary predicament. These measures never circulated in antiquity or contemporary times, in either Japan or China. Even now, their realization depends upon having the right person in government. Once that person appears, they must be implemented. Until then, they should remain secret, not transmitted.[1]

[1] This translation is based on the text in the *Banzan zenshū* (*Complete Works of Kumazawa Banzan*), vol. 3, pp. 233–282, entitled, *Daigaku wakumon chikoku heitenka no bekkan*, or, in translation, *Responding to the Great Learning: Another Volume on Governing the Realm and Bringing Peace to All below Heaven*. Other versions of the text, including digitized woodblock editions and manuscripts, have also been referenced.

1 The Heaven-Decreed Duty of the People's Ruler

Someone asked, "What is the heaven-decreed duty[1] of the people's ruler?[2]"

Banzan replied, "The heaven-decreed duty of the people's ruler is to administer compassionate government[3] with a compassionate mind[4] as the father and mother of the people.[5] For the ruler of a single provincial domain,[6]

1 For more on "the heavenly-decreed duty" (*tenshoku*), see *Mencius*, 5B/12, p. 40. *Xunzi*, "Essay on Heaven," section 2. Xunzi (third century BCE), was one of the major Confucian thinkers of ancient China. He is best known for his assertion, contrary to Mencius, that human nature is originally bad. Because of that assessment, Xunzi was often viewed as a heterodox thinker within the Confucian fold.

2 "The people's ruler" (*jinkun*) alludes to the *Great Learning*, section 7, which states "the people's ruler abides in compassion." Also, *Mencius*, 1A/6, p. 2.

3 *Mencius*, 1A/5, p. 2. 1B/11,12, p. 8. 2A/1, p. 10. 3A/3, p. 19. 4A/1, p. 26. 4A/15, p. 28. Compassionate government (C: *renzheng*; J: *jinsei*) is the signature political notion in the *Mencius*. Confucius did not address it, though he often spoke of "compassion" (*ren*) and "government" (*zheng*). Mencius combined the words as a compound. Thereafter, "compassionate government" became one of the most distinctively Confucian political terms in East Asian history.

4 Banzan's reference to "a compassionate mind" (*jinshin*) alludes to *Mencius*, 4A/1, p. 26.

5 *Book of History* (*Shujing*), "Books of Zhou," "The Great Declaration" (*Tai shi*). "Heaven and earth are the father and mother of the ten thousand things. People are the most spiritual beings of the ten thousand things. The most brightly intelligent of them is elevated as their ruler, and he undertakes his work as 'the father and mother of the people'." Also, "The Great Plan" (*Hong fa*): "The son of heaven is the father and mother of the people, and so becomes the king of the realm below heaven."

6 Banzan refers to political units via a Confucian term – C: *guo*; J: *koku* or *kuni* – not infrequently translated as "state." In Japanese history, however, *kuni* was typically understood as an imperial province. Banzan does not refer to daimyō domains, or *han*, as such, but nevertheless he is addressing domain government when referring to *kuni*. In the Tokugawa period, both references were used in discussing the operative units of political authority and practice. Banzan's usage might indicate his tendency to privilege

3

heaven decrees[7] that he serve as the father and mother of the people of that domain. For the ruler of the realm below heaven, heaven decrees that he serve as the father and mother of the realm below heaven. It is the same for those ordered to perform various tasks for the people's ruler.

"[Because the ruler's duties might be neglected] heaven's decrees are not, therefore, granted for eternity.[8] It is said that when a ruler gains the minds and hearts of the multitudes, he gains the realm. When he loses the minds and hearts of the multitudes, he loses the realm.[9] The minds and hearts of the multitudes of people cleave to compassion and recoil from what betrays compassion. When a ruler tends to his heaven-assigned tasks, he retains the decree of heaven. When a ruler abandons his heaven-assigned tasks, he loses the decree of heaven. The decree of heaven always favors compassion and goodness. This is the unchanging nature of the decree of heaven which is otherwise not constant, but instead, changeable.

"Even if the people's ruler has a compassionate mind and heart, if he cannot administer compassionate government then his rule is 'merely good.'[10] Making compassionate government a reality comes down to getting the right people in government. If a ruler appoints wise men to high-ranking positions, has those with inborn talents[11] for governing take responsibility

the imperial regime and its nomenclature for political geography, but it would be naïve to imagine that he did not have domains in mind first and foremost. To capture these nuances, *kuni* is here translated as provincial domains, and occasionally, more simply as domains.

[7] The notion "the decree of heaven" or "heaven decrees" (C: *tianming*; J: *tenmei*) first appears in the *Shujing* (*Book of History*), and there some twenty-six times, referring to the commands of a providential heaven, presiding over the cosmos and ensuring the ethical goodness of the political world. Most pointedly, the decree of heaven was the directing force, ordering and sanctioning the overthrow of one dynastic line by another. According to the *tianming* narrative, when one dynasty forsook its virtue and thus its legitimacy, heaven recognized a ruling family line of virtue and decreed that it overthrow the one that had abandoned virtue and lost its legitimacy to rule. Thereafter, the new line would rule, with heaven's decree, but only if it maintained virtue (*toku*) as evident in its concern for the welfare of the people.

[8] *Shujing*, "Announcement to the Prince of Kang," 15, "The king said, '... The decree [of heaven] is not constant [*bu yu chang*].'"

[9] *Great Learning*, section 13. Also, *Mencius* 4A/9.

[10] *Mencius*, 4A/1, p. 26. "Mencius said, 'The way of Yao and Shun, if not enacted with compassionate government, cannot peacefully govern the realm below heaven. ... Therefore, it is said, 'Merely being good is not sufficient to govern.'"

[11] In his *Brief Commentary on the Analects* (*Rongo shōkai*), Banzan explains that one who has inborn talents for governing the realm below heaven and the provinces within it must also be educated and ethical. The notion of "inborn talents" (*honsai*), could be literally translated as "basic talents" or "fundamental talents," but given Banzan's appreciation for

for administering domains, and decrees that capable people[12] administer other tasks, then his compassionate mind would become all-encompassing and compassionate government would be fully realized."

Someone asked, "What does 'placing wise men in high positions' involve?"

Banzan replied, "The ruler is the very strength of the realm below heaven. However, even in strength he can go to excess. Even the high-flying dragon encounters regrets[13] and misfortune. The ruler therefore should temper his strength with gentleness. He should do this by appointing for himself an official tutor and guardian.[14] He should also establish an office for remonstration. He should additionally favor virtue, advance literary culture and the martial arts, and elevate people of refined and cultured sensibilities to supervise samurai officials and administrators. That is what placing wise men in high positions involves."

Someone asked, "What does it mean to have 'inborn talents' for governing?"

Banzan replied, "While there are various talents such as wisdom and cleverness, the talent for administering provincial domains and the realm below heaven is what I call an 'inborn talent.' Confucius remarked that people who have [this kind of] talent are rare.[15] Because they are rare, from olden times rulers who embodied the way had such people brought into service regardless of whether they were secondary retainers, commoners, or even rustics. In antiquity, Yi Yin was elevated from the laborers in the farm fields of the prince of Xin.[16] Fu Yue was elevated from the ranks of bricklayers building walls.[17]

"From past times, when the office of prime minister was established, people with such a talent for governing were promptly elevated, without regard to whether they were high-born or of the lowest station. Their offices and stipends were not hereditary. Instead, stipends were restricted

---

Wang Yangming's thinking about "innate knowledge" (C: *liangzhi*; J: *ryōchi*), and abilities that people possess without having learned them via books and reading, rendering *honsai* as "inborn talents" seems equally appropriate.

[12] *Mencius*, 2A/4, p. 12.   [13] *Book of Changes*, "Qian," section 7.
[14] *Shujing*, Tai Jia, II:6.   [15] *Analects*, 8/20, p. 15.
[16] *Mencius*, 5A/7, p. 37. "Mencius said, 'Yi Yin was a farmer working in the fields of the prince of Xin, but even so found happiness in the way of Yao and Shun.'"
[17] *Mencius*, 6B/15, p. 50. "Mencius said, 'Shun was called up to serve in governing even though he had been earlier working in the farm fields. Fu Yue was elevated to assist in government even though he had been previously working in construction.'"

to the period of their time of service only. By providing stipends for ministerial service corresponding to tenure in office, the early rulers who followed the way ensured that for over one hundred generations the wise and talented would not be excluded from high office and their method of elevating those with talents would be appropriate to the circumstances of later ages as well."

Someone asked, "I have heard of official stipends that are hereditary. What are stipends that are exclusive to one generation?"

Banzan replied, "Officials who have to manage vassals and fiefs [which they receive as hereditary compensation] end up spending all their energy doing so. That impairs their ability to serve as officials. This is especially true when ordinary people are appointed to offices with hereditary fiefs and, suddenly, find themselves in charge of many retainers and servants. They then devote their minds exclusively to managing their affairs and are not able to tend to their official duties, governing.

"Therefore, the prime minister's salary of 100,000 *koku*[18] should be paid in rice, wheat, gold, and silver. He should be allowed only as many servants and horses as are necessary for his personal livelihood and assistance. For his official duties, he should have lesser officials serving him just like they were his house retainers. Of his stipend of 100,000 *koku*, 10,000 *koku* should suffice for his family. He can use the remaining 90,000 *koku* to help relatives, friends, those in need, and to ensure the well-being of his descendants for years to come. When he becomes sick or elderly, he should resign his stipend and return to his family's home. For those without a homeplace, lodging would be provided for their retirement.

"When senior officials receive hereditary fiefs of one hundred thousand *koku* which they then bequeath to their descendants, after ten relatives have inherited the original fief, the expense will have grown to 1 million *koku*. Because the shogunate does not have enough resources to continue to support this method of payment, it is impossible to select men from a large pool of talent. Instead, high officials have to be chosen from those already possessing high rank and office. Because such high-ranking people are few, it is difficult to find any with a basic talent for governing. Those whose aptitudes and virtues are not appropriate to

---

[18] One *koku* equals 180 liters or 380 US pints, or five US bushels. Measured in terms of weight, 1 koku equals 150 kilograms, or approximately 330 US pounds. The *koku* was a standard unit of measure for rice income during the Tokugawa period.

their official positions and yet continue to receive large stipends generation after generation will be abandoned by heaven. Consequently, few competent men will be found among their descendants.

"Therefore, in the past it was said that for the sake of elevating those who are worthy, a ruler should search among the commoners. Hence, the ruler must keep channels of communication open so that good advice from the realm below heaven might come forth. Even critical remarks must be taken into consideration. Without privileging his own brilliance and wisdom, the ruler should enjoy seeking the counsel of others. This should be a primary concern for the people's ruler who seeks to govern as the father and mother of his people."

2 The Heaven–Decreed Duty of the People's Ministers

Someone asked, "What is the heaven–decreed duty of the people's ministers[1]?"

Banzan replied, "The heaven–decreed duty of a minister is to assist the ruler in implementing compassionate government. Some ministers will help guide the mind and heart of the ruler. Others will help him communicate and enact compassionate government. In doing so, ministers credit the ruler with all that is good, and take personal responsibility for any mistakes. Ministers should not covet authority and power for themselves but instead recognize those as belonging wholly to the ruler.

"The way of the minister is modeled on the way of earth which is gentle and yielding. However, the minister should not be excessively yielding, nor should he bend simply for the sake of gain. When a ruler forsakes goodness, his ministers should remonstrate with him. Doing so supplements the minister's gentleness. From above, [the ruler in following] the way of heaven provides for everything below, while from below [the minister in following] the way of earth brings activity to things above. When above and below interact, their purpose penetrates everything. Such are the right principles informing proper relations between rulers and ministers.

---

[1] Banzan refers to ministers as *jinshin*, literally, "the people's ministers," much as he referred to the ruler as "the people's ruler" (*jinkun*). In doing so, he is referring to ministers who help govern the people of the realm on behalf of the ruler yet do so for the sake of the welfare of the people. In using this term, Banzan alludes to the *Great Learning*, section 7, which states "the people's minister abides in respect and reverence." Also see, *Mencius* (7A/31).

"It is said that when a ruler is obsessed with strength and a minister is given over to gentleness, the ruler will become haughty and arrogant and his ministers will fawn and flatter, thus bringing disorder to the principles informing right relations between rulers and ministers. A beclouded ruler might fail due to weakness, while a ruler who brilliantly scrutinizes and fastidiously pries into matters might harm the realm when quick decisions are necessary. Such ill-advised approaches to governing might affect the entire realm below heaven and ultimately lead it to ruin. Therefore, the ruler above reveres wisdom but not mere cleverness. A bright and wise ruler is lenient and broad-minded, while his subjects below enjoy the gentleness and harmony of his rule. It is thus said that the ruler in following the way of heaven, all-encompassing and all-embracing, finds his virtue expressed."

Someone asked, "Can we know beforehand whether the realm below heaven will be well governed or fall into anarchy, persist or collapse into ruin, enjoy good fortune or suffer bad?"

Banzan replied, "There are ways of knowing these matters. When we consider examples from ancient and modern times, in China and Japan, we see that good government prevails when channels of communication are open. When those channels are obstructed, there will be upheaval. Slow-witted rulers and kings are not the ones who block channels of communication. Rather, it is rulers who rely on cleverness who obstruct channels of communication.

"For this reason, it should be noted, the *Book of Changes* positions *Li* (離) ☲ as the upper trigram of the hexagram, *Kui* 睽 (䷥). Now as a trigram, *Li* typically signifies "fire" and "brightness." However, only with the hexagram *Kui* does its meaning change to signify things that are deviant and contrary. When *yang* goes to an extreme, it signifies haughtiness. When firmness and strength go to an extreme, they express cruelty. When *Li*, brightness, is above, it represents clever scrutiny. Haughtiness, clever scrutiny, and cruelty are the most extreme nuances of *Kui*.

"The top trigram in *Kui*, which is *Li*, signifies fire proceeding upward. The lower trigram in *Kui* is *Dui* (兌) ☱, which indicates a swamp flowing downward. *Kui* thus symbolizes contrary and opposing channels of communication, and so a lack of empathy and understanding between superiors and inferiors. When superiors and inferiors do not empathize with and appreciate one another, the minds and hearts of the people below heaven become alienated. When the minds and hearts of the people below heaven are so alienated, that is tantamount to having no ruler. That is the origin of great upheaval in the realm.

"When a ruler on high relies solely on his own clever mind and despises the criticisms of the realm below heaven, he will eventually reject those who remonstrate, which in turn leads him down the path of upheaval. When a ruler executes ministers who remonstrate, he will bring upheaval and ruin to his realm. It has thus been said that while it is not in the best personal interests of a minister to speak honestly and directly to a ruler, doing so brings good fortune to the realm.

"In ancient China, the Qin dynasty (221–206 BCE) lost the realm below heaven because it made it a crime to criticize, thereby suppressing the severe but good and loyal words of those who would have remonstrated with the Qin emperors over their abuses.[2] The founder of the Han dynasty (221 BCE–206 CE), Han Gaozu (256–195 BCE), appreciated goodness and heeded remonstration. He brought together the wisdom of all below heaven and so consolidated authority throughout his empire. With respectfulness and frugality, Han Gaozu's son, Emperor Xiao Wen (202–157 BCE), brought peace and prosperity to the realm below heaven. Emperor Xiao Wen's grandson, Emperor Xiao Wu (156–87 BCE), favored those who offered loyal remonstration and was pleased to hear their utmost and honest words. These emperors thus laid the foundations for the 400-year reign of the Han dynasty.

"A ruler who is too clever and brilliant in scrutinizing things will end up punishing many people. That is not the way of heaven. It is said that *yang* always prevails during summer, nurturing life, while *yin* always prevails during winter, expanding in emptiness and inactivity. From this we know that the way of heaven relies on compassion and virtue, but not on laws and punishments.

"How awesome is the interaction between heaven and humanity! When a realm has lost the way and defeat is imminent, heaven sends down calamities and disasters to provide warnings. Calamities and disasters take the form of misfortunes caused by wind, water, and other natural forces. If rulers remain oblivious to the way of heaven, heaven produces strange aberrations that shock and frighten. Such strange aberrations

---

[2] The Qin dynasty was one of the most despotic and authoritarian in all Chinese history. While the First Emperor of the Qin did enact many policies that contributed to the unification of China, the brevity of the dynasty he founded resulted from popular dissatisfaction with its harsh rule. The Han dynasty continued many of the policies of the Qin but did so with greater lenience and flexibility and as a result endured for centuries.

are the extraordinary transformations of spiritual beings. Then, if rulers still have not come to realize the way of heaven, heaven sends down disastrous, ruinous defeat.

"The way of heaven exemplifies for the people's ruler compassion and love and thus seeks to preempt the need for disaster and ruin. Strict application of rewards and punishments should not, therefore, be integral to practicing the way. It is said that when the way is practiced, those who have committed crimes will only be punished by having to wear clothes with markings differentiating them from the rest of society, and yet even with such mild punishment no one will dare to violate any prohibitions.[3] Rites and music are the best way to gain people's consent. When the correct model is displayed and the crooked cast aside,[4] people will have a sense of shame that helps them to correct what is crooked. Such is the generous compassion integral to the way of the true king."

Someone asked, "The people's ruler has no greater virtue than utmost brilliance. Why, then, should he be cautioned about his brilliance in scrutinizing things?"

Banzan replied, "It is said that when a ruler's ultimate brilliance uncovers a single crime, one hundred others come to light. Nevertheless, a ruler can still be deceived by his own personal wisdom. Therefore, a ruler should employ the wise men of the realm below heaven, heed remonstrations, and listen to critical assessments of his rule. Enjoying peace of mind and heart, he governs his domains, brings stability to the realm below heaven, and enjoys a good reputation throughout later ages. That is possible due to his ultimate brilliance.[5]

"The way of the ruler thus follows heaven and so does not rely on strength excessively. By the same token, the *Book of Changes* observes that "when a group of dragons has no need for a dominating leader, things are auspicious."[6] Similarly, the way of the ruler makes no showy displays

---

3 Emperor Xiao Wen of the Han dynasty reportedly stated that the ancient sage ruler Shun punished criminals by having them wear garments marked to indicate their crime. Despite such light punishment, no one broke the laws. Sima Qian, *Shiji* 10: "The Basic Annals of Emperor Wen the Filial," *Records of the Grand Historian: Han Dynasty I: Revised Edition*, translated by Burton Watson (Hong Kong: Columbia University Press, 1993), p. 300.

4 *Analects*, 2/19, p. 3.

5 *Family Sayings of Confucius* (*Kongzi jiayu*), "Wang yan jie." "The brilliance of the realm below heaven consists in being able to elevate the utmost worthies of the realm below heaven."

6 *Book of Changes*, "Explanation of the Hexagram Qian."

of coercive power, nor is it overly rigorous in punishments. Instead, the ruler should be of humble mind in heeding the remarks of others. In dealing with his subjects below, he should be warm and respectful. It can thus be said that the way of the ruler enhances the ruler's strength by calming his brilliance in scrutinizing things."

3 Revering Good Counsel

Someone asked, "The sage emperor Yu reportedly revered good counsel.[1] What is meant by good counsel?"

Banzan replied, "Good counsel does not refer to philosophical discussions of the way, virtue, or scholarly topics. Those well below the ruler should not presume to teach sages [like Yu] about morality. Instead, they should offer counsel about effective and ineffective aspects of the administration of the country and the realm below heaven. Even though the ruler's decrees might be good, there are times when they might not be entirely appropriate to human feelings and circumstances. When the ruler heeds remarks about the pros and cons of his administration and revises things according to present circumstances, those governing will enjoy abundance and the common people will get their lot, find profit in what is beneficial, and experience happiness in what they should.

"Words of advice pertain to matters great and small. Just as those living on riverbanks know floodwaters well, the feelings of the lower people are best understood by those living among the lower elements. Insofar as they benefit the administration of the realm, their words should be greeted with pleasure. The sage emperor Yu revered good counsel even when delivered by one of lower standing who served, at least in that instance, as his teacher, precisely because it provided him with information previously unknown. Thus did the sage emperor Yu reverently receive good counsel.

"Accordingly, the sage's mind and body must be without selfishness in impartially welcoming what benefits the realm below heaven. The sage

[1] *Shu jing,* "Counsels of Gao-yao."

13

ruler maintains open channels of communication and is fond of questions, heeding remonstration and accepting criticism when considering the pros and cons of political administration. Knowing whether the realm below heaven will enjoy good fortune or bad comes down to knowing whether the channels of communication are open or closed. For that reason, rulers who bring together the wisest men of the realm below heaven into their service will prosper abundantly."

4 A Grand Project for Growing Wealth

Someone asked, "Why should there be a grand project for growing wealth[1]?"

Banzan replied, "Without wealth, a ruler cannot enact compassionate government in the realm below heaven. Today, there are many helpless people.[2] These people have no one they can rely on, nor anyone from whom they can seek assistance. They have neither parents, spouses, nor children with whom they can live. A compassionate ruler's government should first seek to assist these helpless people.

"Currently, the worst cases of helplessness appear among the rōnin. During repeated famines, countless have starved to death. Although the price of rice goes down during years of abundant harvest, lower prices do not benefit those whose budgets are already stretched to their limits.

[1] Banzan repeatedly discusses the "grand project for growing wealth" (*fuyū taigyō*) in *Responding to the Great Learning*. In earlier Confucian literature, wealth was not a standard topic, but neither was it absent. *Mencius* (5A/1) states, "what all people desire is that there be wealth in the realm below heaven." In the *Middle Way*, the ancient sage king Shun is praised for his great filial piety, his sagacity, his royal respect, and for having brought wealth to all within the four seas. The *Xunzi* also spoke of bringing wealth to the realm below heaven as something that everyone desires, and added in its chapter, "Enriching the Country," that it was essential for rulers to ensure the wealth of their realms. The "Great Commentary" on the *Book of Changes* uses the terms *fuyū* and *taigyō* in proximity in remarking that [growing] "wealth" is what is referred to as "the grand project" of the way. However, the *Book of Changes* does not use the four-character expression as a compound as does Banzan. The *Great Learning* only mentions wealth once, noting that "wealth makes a house shine." Banzan's thinking resonates more with the *Middle Way* and the *Xunzi* insofar as those texts emphasize that an ideal ruler should provide for the wealth of his entire realm. That aside, in emphasizing this along with his later emphasis on military preparedness in the event of foreign invasion, Banzan can be seen as a forerunner of later advocates of "enriching the country and strengthening its arms" (*fukoku kyōhei*).

[2] *Mencius* 1B/5, pp. 6–7.

15

Every year, many rōnin die of starvation, unknown. This results from daimyō lords of the domains and the district supervisors being strained in their resources and so cutting off stipends for their retainers. Furthermore, those retainers whose income has been cut must in turn cut off their own retainers' stipends.

"People surely realize this because right in front of their eyes such rōnin have multiplied. Even though they know that it is cruel to do so, when daimyō and their retainers have debts that exceed their incomes, year in and year out, they take more and more from the common people. For this reason, excessive debt levels among the common people are increasingly a fact of life. In this generation, everyone – high and low – is falling into excessive debt. If samurai and peasants fall into poverty, artisans and merchants will end up doing so as well. At that point, poverty will prevail throughout the realm below heaven.

"Even if all the gold, silver, rice, and grain stored in the shogunate's vaults and warehouses were dispersed without remainder, that would not even cover 1 percent of the debt. Why? Because the contemporary debt is over one hundred times the amount of currency in circulation in the entire realm below heaven. However, this problem could be easily resolved if government measures sought to address it. The solution was never realized in antiquity, nor in later generations. It consists of 'the great way,'³ which can be implemented now with exceptional ease."⁴

Someone asked, "What are government measures?"

Banzan replied, "Government measures are concerned with managing wealth. When someone in our society gains wealth and uses it for their own profit and advantage, that harms other people. Wealth brings those who have it personal pleasure, but others resent it. When the ruler of a domain amasses personal worldly wealth, people within that domain jealously resent it. When the shogun amasses wealth for himself, people of

---

3 Banzan's understanding of "the great way" derives from his familiarity with a utopian passage from the *Book of Rituals'* chapter, "Evolution of the Rites." For a translation of this passage, see the synopsis of Chapter 4 presented in the Introduction.

4 Here Banzan clarifies his foreword to the text. The "viable measures" there referred to, which he stated had not been realized in either ancient times or modern, in either China or Japan, are here identified, it seems, as those associated with "the great way," or its corollary, "the grand project for growing wealth." In concrete terms, these involve, in Banzan's thinking, drastically reducing the alternate attendance requirement and using rice as a form of currency. A number of other measures are related to these, but these are the keys, according to Banzan, to solving the socio-economic and political problems of the day.

the realm below heaven also resent it. But that is because common people covet petty personal wealth.

"However, if a daimyō gained wealth for all by implementing the great way, then his whole domain would be pleased by it. If the shogun gained it in such a manner, all below heaven would be pleased with it. The reason is that wealth for all is truly great wealth. If a ruler gained such wealth, his descendants would receive generous stipends for as long as heaven and earth continued, and he, having secured a good reputation for generations to come, would enjoy peace and contentment in mind and body.

"During the more than five hundred years of military rule, I regret that even the great shoguns worthy of that office never learned about the wealth for all produced by the great way. Great carpenters might have strong eyes and excellent skills, but when they do not have a compass and a carpenter's square,[5] they cannot build a house. Although renowned rulers might appear, unless they learn the methods of the early sage kings, they cannot bring lasting peaceful rule to all below heaven."

Someone asked, "The methods of the early sage kings are recorded in the Chinese classics and commentaries.[6] With such tools at their disposal, why have rulers not put them to use?"

Banzan replied, "Integral to the methods of the early kings is the 'highest good'[7] realized by responding appropriately to the circumstances of time, place, and social standing. However, explaining in writing how to realize the highest good is difficult. Hereditary rulers, including daimyō and shoguns, who possess innate sagacity are virtually unknown. Thus, it is difficult for them to comprehend the highest good by themselves. Yet those born into the lower orders of society who have attained insights into circumstances and human feelings, strength in learning, a true sense of purpose, and a basic talent for governing might well comprehend how to realize the highest good. Those who understand how to realize the highest good should be made the teachers of rulers."

---

5 *Mencius* 4A/1, p. 26.
6 The classics are the five classics of ancient Chinese literature, including the *Book of Changes*, the *Book of Historical Writings*, the *Book of Poetry*, the *Book of Rituals*, and the *Spring and Autumn Annals*. The commentaries refer to the various writings by later thinkers explaining the meanings and significance of the classics.
7 The *Great Learning* as a chapter in the *Book of Rituals* opens with the statement, "The way of the great learning consists in illuminating luminous virtue, loving the people, and abiding in the highest good."

Someone asked, "In recent years, tax rates have reached unprecedented levels reducing people to extreme poverty. From what source, then, might wealth be developed?"

Banzan replied, "The government can waive high tax rates throughout the realm below heaven thereby providing sufficient wealth for samurai of the various provinces. The granaries of the shogunate and the various daimyō lords of the realm will then become so full that there will be nowhere to store additional rice.

"Today, unlimited amounts of rice are lost without benefiting anyone. Nevertheless, the status quo allows this waste to maintain things as they are. After peasants have paid their taxes and samurai have collected them, even though large amounts of rice are lost, still relatively good circumstances seemingly emerge for both high and low. If all else remained the same and yet no rice were lost to waste, our society would become more impoverished. Indeed, if the loss of rice were prevented with things as they are now, then the price of rice would plummet.

"In recent years, due to abundant harvests, samurai and the common people have become increasingly impoverished. When samurai and the common people are in dire straits, the economy suffers. Artisans and merchants also become impoverished. Rōnin might see lower rice prices favorably, but when the grand samurai and the lesser samurai are in extreme circumstances, they find it difficult to help anyone and so employment in their service becomes rare. As a consequence, the number of rōnin grows even greater. Even those who live day-to-day selling their labor will find that as samurai, farmers, artisans, and merchants experience distress, they have to cut back their expenses and retain fewer people. Such overall distress results from even a slight excess of rice."

Someone asked, "Do the common people not want a year of abundant harvest?"

Banzan replied, "Recently, during years of abundant harvests, the common people have fallen into even more debt and extreme distress. Some borrowed money when 1 *koku* of rice was selling for 70–80 silver units, but because the price of 1 *koku* later dropped to 30–40 silver units, their debt on the original loan doubled. And, with interest included, their debt more than doubled. Even in a year of abundant harvest, their land will not produce double the amount of rice.

"Just the other year, when a person traveled to Gōshū [now, Shiga Prefecture] and purchased sardines, they could bring home two bundles of sardines for every bundle of rice they took to market. Now they must take two bundles of rice to bring back just one of sardines. This is because the price of rice has plummeted. Myriad other exchanges are similar so you can conjecture just how egregious things are. In bad years when the price of rice is high, it is of no use to the farmers because they have no extra rice to sell. In years of abundant harvest, because the price of rice is not good, it seems farmers cannot even breathe. Therefore, with the current circumstances, it would not be any better for the common people even if waste were prevented and new rice fields were brought into cultivation."

Someone asked, "If government measures could change the status quo, might something be done to prevent the loss of rice?"

Banzan answered, "Enormous quantities of rice are now being thrown away. However, if this waste were eliminated, the shogun[8] and the various daimyō lords of the realm would become very wealthy. Their granaries would have no more room for storage. But daimyō cannot initiate this change. If the shogun sought to implement the great way, the present situation could be easily changed. However, if things are not altered at all, our hope that the great way might be realized will come to nought.

"I will list some examples of waste.

"First, there is waste right before our eyes. Rice is lost throughout Japan[9] because reservoirs are not constructed in a manner consistent with the geographical features around them. As a result, in years of flooding, approximately 1 million *koku* is lost. In years of drought, because reservoirs are not built in suitable locations or are built poorly, they are useless.

"Second, an incalculable amount of rice is lost when cargo vessels carrying it to Edo or Osaka from Kyushu and Shikoku in the southwest, Saigoku in the west, and Hokkoku in the north, end up shipwrecked.

---

8 Annotations to the *Nihon shisō taikei* edition of *Responding to the Great Learning* (hereafter referred to as "NST") note (p. 418) that the 1788 text upon which it is generally based include the words *kōgi*, indicating the shogunate, while manuscript versions at Tokyo University (henceforth referred to as "manuscripts") have the word *kubō*, indicating the shogun rather than the shogunate. The NST text follows the latter. Since it was presumably closer to Banzan's draft, this translation follows the manuscripts' usage as well. The 1788 edition is more circumspect here, and in numerous other such passages.

9 The NST text here follows manuscript copies of *Responding* which include the words "throughout Japan" (*Nihon kokuchū*). The 1788 edition referred to the "sixty odd provinces" of the realm.

"Third, while taxes were paid, in ancient times, with unhulled rice, now they are paid with hulled rice. As a result, an incalculable amount is lost to insects infesting granaries and eating the hulled rice.

"Fourth, a vast amount is wasted because saké brewers now brew one hundred times as much saké as in ancient times, using large quantities of rice to make the beverage.

"Fifth, there is a loss of rice caused by farm fields being used to grow tobacco.

"Sixth, there is rice lost due to farmers using their fields to raise cotton rather than rice.

"Seventh, people have become physically weaker, resulting in less rice being produced in their fields.

"Eighth, one hundredfold more 'barbarian cakes' (*nanban kashi*) are being made, resulting in more waste.

"There are many other examples of such waste. Yet if this waste were stopped then prices would plummet and daimyō would not be able to finance their alternate attendance service to the shogunate in Edo by selling their rice. We must come to terms with the fact that in recent years even though harvests have not been bad and considerable quantities of rice have been sold, still the realm below heaven is poverty ridden."

Someone asked, "What government measures might prevent such waste, keep the price of rice from plummeting, and at the same time please everyone, high and low?"

Banzan replied, "Daimyō cannot finance their service obligations to the shogunate unless they sell their rice for gold and silver coins because the latter are used as currency. Since daimyō send their rice to Osaka and Edo to sell it in exchange for gold and silver currency, those ports are overflowing with rice. However, because there are only a few buyers, the price falls and poverty among the common people ensues. Yet with so much rice being shipped to the port cities to be sold for gold and silver coins, there is less rice in the core provinces than most would think.

"If the value of rice were established at a set rate in relation to metal currency, then in Kyoto, Osaka, Edo, and the provinces of the realm various items could be bought and sold with rice. If rice were used in transactions beginning with those at dry goods stores, then people in the lower occupations would soon be using it as well in purchasing various goods. Those in the eastern provinces would purchase items from the imperial capital, paying those in the western provinces with rice promissory notes.

There might be some challenges along the way, but, with time, resolving them should be easy enough. Circumstances will need to be adjusted so that daimyō are not in a bind even if they do not sell their rice for coins. If the rice which would have been lost to waste had it been shipped off to be sold were salvaged and stored, unhusked, in the provinces, then even in times of famine no one would starve to death. Even if the northern barbarians[10] attacked, there would be no dearth of provisions for our troops defending the realm."

Someone asked, "Should gold and silver currency be abandoned?"

Banzan replied, "We should continue to use them just as they are now. When rice alongside gold and silver coins are used as currency without discrimination, each of them will be useful."

Someone asked, "What should the price of rice be?"

Banzan replied, "One *koku* of rice should equal 50 units of silver. That should be the current average price. Hereafter, depending on circumstances, the price can be gradually adjusted, according to the average at a particular time."

---

[10] Here Banzan broaches a topic returned to repeatedly in *Responding to the Great Learning*: the threat of invasion by "northern barbarians," presumably the Manchu peoples who, following the collapse of the Ming dynasty, entered China and took control as the Qing dynasty (1644–1912).

5 Eliminating Anxieties over Flooding and Relieving Droughts

Someone asked, "How can we make reservoirs conform to the lay of the land so that flood damage is prevented?"

Banzan replied, "Crudely put, reservoir construction in the provinces nowadays is as ineffective as shooing flies away from rice. This is because reservoirs are poorly adapted to present-day geographic circumstances. Although it is said that the eternal way[1] holds that mountain forests should be luxuriant and rivers should flow deeply, realization of the eternal way will be difficult unless the shogun is truly intent on implementing the great way and enacting compassionate government. Even if the shogun sought to enact a plan for realizing the eternal way through compassionate government, it would still take at least fifty to sixty years before the results were apparent. However, once plans for realizing the eternal way are made, within fifty to sixty years anxieties over flooding should have subsided.

"Those who seek to make reservoirs conform to the lay of the land must first examine and understand the geographic contours of the rivers in the various provinces. Mapping this out will be challenging. However, if a start is made at the Yodo River in Osaka, might it not serve as a model for dealing with rivers in the various domains? But to do this, first there must be a commitment to compassionate government. As things stand at present, the unruly flows of our rivers and misguided efforts to build up riverbanks are simply bringing grief to many people.

---

[1] Banzan's reference to "the eternal way" (*eikyū no michi*) might be an allusion to a classical text, but it remains unidentified.

"Taira Kiyomori (1118–1181) sacrificed over a dozen people as 'human piers' in trying to build an island,[2] but only ended up causing suffering for people hundreds of years thereafter. Later generations did not follow his example as such, but surely people are still being sacrificed as human piers when hundreds even thousands are reduced to vagrancy because the productive capacity of their farmlands has been lost due to flooding, ultimately leading to hunger and starvation. Things might seem to go well, but success [in providing for the well-being of the people] has not been achieved. And how on earth can any ordinary person with only limited knowledge of things grasp the geographic principles of a particular time, place, and circumstance?

"In the past someone asked me, 'Fields that for the last thirty years have produced over 30,000 *koku* of rice annually recently fell victim to floods, ending up as swampland. We calculated that by draining water into the sea, the old fields producing 30,000 *koku* could be recovered and, additionally, new land producing another 30,000 *koku* could be gained. New drainage banks needed for draining the water will require use of approximately 10,000 *koku* of land from the old fields. However, if 10,000 were sacrificed to gain 60,000 *koku*, this would support a large number of people. Wouldn't that be for the best?'

"I replied that it seems advantageous to sacrifice 10,000 *koku* to gain 60,000. After all, those who might otherwise have ended up living on swampland would have become vagrants and starved to death. On the other hand, some of them might have remained to eke out a living. And if they had been able to recover their former lands, they would have been very happy about that. Since this happened years ago, those who could not even recover their lands will not be so upset. However, the men, women, and children who once lived on good farmland producing that 10,000 *koku* which was sacrificed to gain 60,000 *koku* probably would have numbered over 1,000 today. It is tragic that along the way many of them were reduced to vagrancy and starvation, having suddenly lost their homes and lands for the sake of building river drainage banks to recover other lands for other people. Regardless of the gain of 60,000 *koku*

---

[2] According to the *Heike monogatari*, Kiyomori initiated construction of an artificial island, Tsukishima, off the coast of Fukuhara to facilitate commerce. Following setbacks due to harsh weather, human sacrifices to appease the gods were considered. Instead, however, boulders with Buddhist texts inscribed on them were used as foundation stones for the island. Roberta Strippoli, *Dancer, Nun, Ghost, Goddess* (Leiden: Brill, 2018), p. 107. Nevertheless, presumably as part of the apocryphal tradition vilifying Kiyomori, it was said that he sacrificed people as "human piers" for his artificial island.

resulting from the sacrifice of 10,000 *koku*, a compassionate person would not have done this.

"There is a far better solution than requiring such a sacrifice. Every time there is extensive rain and flooding, some provinces lose around 150,000 *koku*. In addition to that, old farmland capable of producing approximately 50,000 *koku* might end up as swampland. There are construction projects which, if undertaken, could drain the swampland so that the loss of 150,000 *koku* would be avoided, but in the process 10,000–20,000 *koku* of superior farmland would have to be sacrificed. Along the way, there would also be a tragic sacrifice of one or two thousand human piers. But no one wants to acknowledge the human loss.

"However, if this project were based on compassionate government, the human sacrifice would have to be addressed. If 50,000 *koku* of submerged superior land could be recovered, in the short-term that would mean recovering at least half of the annual land taxes on it. On the other hand, if the taxes on 10,000 *koku* of this recovered land were returned so that people who lost land were provided some of the newly recovered land along with temporary tax exemptions for constructing homes, reestablishing rice fields, and growing crops, then they would be glad that their former land had been used for the project. Even if discussed simply in terms of profit, the shogunate would gain 40 percent of the 50,000 *koku*. On top of that, if the loss to flooding of land that once produced 140,000–150,000 *koku* were prevented, the amount of rice gained by all, above and below, would be difficult to calculate.

"Those who simply follow practices from past generations do not realize that compassionate government could indeed be implemented in this way. Yet even when measures based on compassionate government are discussed, shogunal officials are not of the same mind about them. As a result, the case for compassionate government never reaches those at the top.

"Nevertheless, if inundated areas were drained and floodwaters kept back with dikes, and if all this were done well, not even 10,000 *koku* of old land would have to be lost. However, when new fields below the swamplands are developed, many of the older fields are lost in the process. Opening a lot of new fields by sacrificing the old is not good for the domains. In fact, it would be better if the new fields were not opened. If the projects that domains undertake to manage river waters are based on compassionate government, then rice lands will not need to be lost to flooding and people will not have to worry about losing their homes.

"In a western province [Okayama], a castle stood just downstream from a large river. Below the castle were the residences of samurai and townspeople. Every so often there was flooding that devastated these homes. Because the riverbed grew higher and higher, people feared that more flooding would result in more people drowning. Samurai and townspeople were all worried about the destruction that might result from the river's currents.

"So, I taught them how to ward off the river. My instructions were not entirely acted upon, but because they were followed for the most part even after several flooding rains the homes below the castle were not damaged. Seeing these results, would not a clever person take heed of my approach to managing river flooding? The conventional wisdom on riverbank construction is very much at odds with my approach. While things might go well occasionally, unless efforts at flood prevention are based on compassionate government, they will not be fully successful."

Someone asked, "What about drought preparations?"

Banzan replied, "Even when there are large retention ponds nearby, drought preparations will be difficult to implement in drought-prone areas unless they are grounded in compassionate government. In drought-stricken areas in western provinces [i.e., Okayama], many large retention ponds have been constructed. Because compassionate government informed their construction, they have been effective. Even after thirty years, there have still not been any losses resulting from frequent droughts. Nor have there been breaches in the riverbanks, despite flood-waters. Yet even when retention ponds are built in suitable areas, if constructed poorly then floodwaters will break down their banks and ancient fields below will be reduced to perpetual wastelands. This is indeed a grave matter.

"I will outline the gist of my approach to constructing retention ponds here. When the banks hold like mountains of firmly packed earth and the pond-bed follows the natural flow of water, regardless of rain and flood-waters, the banks will not burst. First, find a low spot in the ground to serve as the pond's bed. Around a deep cavity wherein water tends to collect, the foundations should be laid. If gravel is on the top layer of ground there, make sure that there is solid earth underneath. Excavate the gravel down to the solid earth. Then bring more solid earth from nearby and pack it where the gravel had been, at the bottom of what will be the pond. Above that, build the banks of the new pond. Although the spot had not previously held water, from hundreds of yards inland water will flow down and collect there. That is because the banks will stop any water that previously flowed past that area. Accordingly, you can add piping so that when needed the pond's water can be channeled to irrigate fields.

"When building a retention pond by a dry, rocky river, the bed will often consist of a sheet of stones. Excavate the stones completely until you hit solid earth and then do as before. In most cases, if you think you need a 60-foot-wide dike, you should make it 120 feet wide. Because most people construct retention ponds by running a measuring rope across the width of the proposed dike from so-many feet to so-many feet, at a height of so-many feet, and then calculating the amount of labor and earth required to build it, the resulting dikes are not strong.

"For strong dikes, it is best to measure the earth to be excavated, from so-many feet to so-many feet, and so-many feet deep, next calculate how many men and how much earth will be needed, and then pack the earth atop the dike solidly without letting it get too high. From the middle of the dike, measure its thickness, depositing earth on one side, and then the other side. Next have workers pound and compress the earth hard with hoes, as other workers remove stones, bamboo, wood, and reeds from the earth being packed. This is necessary because if anything is mixed in with the earth, the dike will be weak. Then, as the ground is leveled off, have some earth from the east side piled on the west side, and that from the west side piled on the east. If each worker adds more than his share of the earth needed, the embankment should naturally end up as strong as a mountain.

"Generally, if the construction requires 30,000 men, you should plan on 90,000 to 100,000. Otherwise, the result will not be strong. Also, the workers should be employed lightly. Each man should receive, for one day's labor, at least three portions of rice. They should begin work at 8 in the morning and continue until 4 in the afternoon, with a two-hour rest in between. This is one expression of compassionate government. Another group of workers should cut the stones at both ends of the embankment to help form a stream for excess water to flow down. If a mountain juts out nearby, it is best to cut a stream for water to flow around it. This is the gist of how to build a retention pond."

Question: "This is all fine and good, but such projects require an extraordinary number of workers. Will the labor required not be contrary to people's sentiments these days?"

Banzan replied, "Construction of retention ponds that I have previously supervised requiring 100,000 days' labor could have been built makeshift with 30,000 days' labor. However, within a decade, repeated breaks would have occurred, requiring many more workers for repairs. Moreover, below the retention ponds, rice fields would have been lost had breaks occurred. The retention ponds that I have supervised using sufficient numbers of workers have never failed even though they were constructed over thirty years ago. So, construction costs for retention ponds should be weighed in light of such benefits and losses.

"Although I have supervised construction of many large retention ponds and from years past worked with various magistrates in the building process, I have never worried that the dikes built would fail when heavy rains brought powerful flows down from remote mountain valleys, reducing the rice fields below, with a total yield of 3,000–5,000 *koku*, to an eternal wasteland. Unless we build retention ponds so that they will not break, regardless of, as noted, the sentiments of the people today, then decades later people will fall victims to droughts resulting in hardships for the samurai and people at large. After overseeing retention pond construction, I have allowed the magistrates to proceed as they see fit. Since that time, over thirty years have passed and there has been no drought damage. I give the magistrates praise for that achievement.

"It is possible to end the droughts and floods that have damaged Yamato Province and to redevelop abandoned lands in Kawachi Province. However, I would not propose that we attempt to do so until there are adequate resources providing for compassionate government in the process because otherwise the common people adversely affected would probably deem me a criminal.[3] Yet when compassionate government is administered without delay, prevention of floods and droughts will contribute first and foremost to wealth for all. But given the present circumstances wherein there are no resources for implementing these initiatives in accordance with compassionate government, if old wastelands in Kawachi were redeveloped, it would only lead to greater distress and poverty for samurai and the common people.

"An analogy might be helpful. If you want to offer a padded robe to someone who has fallen into a river and lost their clothes, it would be best to get them out first, dry them off with a light robe, and then give them

---

3 *Mencius* 6B/7, pp. 48–49.

the padded one. If the person in distress were to put on the padded robe while still in the river, it would become heavy with water and might cause them to drown. Similarly, compassionate government should first ensure that samurai and common people have enough to repay their debts and live within their means, without having to sell their rice to do so."

Someone asked, "If rice were used as a form of currency, why should samurai and the common people not sell it?"

Banzan replied, "There are some problems related to their doing so. However, they should be easy enough to resolve."

Someone asked, "Since the population has become sizable, should people grow cotton in their rice fields? Cotton is easier for farmers to grow than rice. If cotton is not grown, would its price not rise and the common people end up freezing? And if farmers stopped growing cotton and simply grew rice, would they not increasingly fall short in paying their annual tribute."

Banzan replied, "As sumptuary laws have changed, even those who are above the samurai have been wearing cotton. And because wealthy peasants, artisans, and merchants wear cotton as well, even more is grown. As more cotton is grown, tribute payments have become easier to pay. Yet tribute rates have also increased so that ultimately growing more cotton is not helping people. Even though samurai with fiefs receive more due to higher tribute rates, because the price of rice is lower, their lives are worse than in the past when the tribute rate was lower.

"Simply by putting a stop to cotton cultivation and slightly reducing the tribute rate, compassionate government could provide, without obstacles, many financial benefits for samurai. Within ten years, debts of the various daimyō lords and their retainers could be paid off entirely. Along the way, cotton garments worn by those above samurai would become a wasteful expense. Humble sorts who only wear a little cotton, decorated with colored paper and combined with straw matting, would still fare well enough, even if cotton production were curtailed.

"Until fifty years ago, samurai and those above wore figured satin, silk crepe, silk gauze, and smooth silk. Even young samurai wore silk and pongee. Each wore garments according to their ranks. And those of middle and lower standing who served samurai wore pongee silk. At that time, no one was squandering their resources and falling heavily into debt as have so many today.

"If government measures can revive things as they were in the past, then even without growing cotton in rice fields, cotton might be produced in sufficient quantities and the commoners below would lack nothing. Moreover, wealthy commoners would wear, as they did in the past, jackets appropriate to their station. Wealthy peasants and townspeople might even dress more handsomely than lower-level samurai, wearing garments such as silk robes.

"High and low should be distinguished by the color of their clothing, not by whether it is expensive. Because there are many important matters that must be discussed first, Chinese and Japanese textiles can be addressed later."

Someone asked, "If saké breweries were closed, society would surely feel the loss. If the saké industry were lost, what would be the consequences?"

Banzan replied, "There is an approach that neither adversely affects society nor causes trouble for the saké houses. When rice is used as currency, even saké will be sold for rice. Rice would be used to pay for household needs. Excess rice could be used to make saké. If rice were no longer shipped off to be sold far and wide, there would be no loss of it at sea nor theft of it when transported by land. When saké is not shipped from different places but instead is made in each locality, there would be less produced. When the waste in brewing saké is eliminated, even without prohibiting saké, there would be no hardship on anyone. If we are to prepare for defense against the northern barbarians and store rice to guard against famine, then it might be necessary to forbid production of saké for a year or two."

Someone asked, "Tobacco is very profitable. But if growing tobacco were forbidden for the sake of growing rice, the resulting crop yield might not be sufficient to pay the annual tribute tax on land and meet people's living expenses. What do you propose on this count?"

Banzan replied, "This is a difficult matter to address right now. Later, circumstances calling for abolition of tobacco growing will probably arise on their own. When the granaries of the shogunal authorities and the various daimyō lords are overflowing with rice and grain and tobacco itself is not widely used, growing tobacco can be prohibited. Allowing tax-exempt rice to be grown instead of tobacco, at least for a while, will ease the transition. Even if rice were taxed at only one-tenth, the end of tobacco growing could still be achieved.

"In addition to those who shred tobacco, there are many others who earn a living by making utensils used in smoking. Once the realm has grown wealthy, there will be a census of households and rice stipends will be allocated for those who formerly worked in the tobacco industry, at least until they have taken up other work. The same approach should be used in dealing with the foreign cakes industry.

"Using unhulled rice to pay tribute and as a form of currency will not only eliminate the waste of rice occurring now, it will make an extraordinary contribution to people's diets. Minor obstacles might appear along the way, but they should be easy to resolve. Eliminating the loss of rice in shipping can be easily achieved once the shogun truly aspires to end it. This must be addressed."

6 Preparing for Northern Barbarians, Emergencies, and Bad Harvests[1]

Someone asked, "What sort of government measures might reduce poverty and bring prosperity, even while preparing the country for a possible attack by northern barbarians?"

Banzan replied, "It has been said that countries that promote culture and learning are also militarily prepared.[2] Promoting culture and learning means formulating political measures for governing the realm and bringing peace and prosperity to all below heaven. Being militarily prepared refers to having military power so that a country is internally solid while standing formidably against enemies externally. To be solid internally, a country must unite in embodying the great way and have plenty of provisions for its armies. To be formidable before our enemies, the most important thing is having renown as a martial country wherein samurai and commoners are truly proficient in archery, horsemanship, and military maneuvers.

"For now, the most urgent matter is storing up military rations. In the past, northern barbarians took control of the Middle Kingdom[3] and then invaded this country, Japan,[4] repeatedly. Now, the northern barbarians

---

[1] The full title to this chapter is "Preparing for northern barbarians, building up reserves to deal with any eventuality including bad harvest, and achieving all things by the grand project for growing wealth."

[2] Sima Qian, *Shiji* 47: "The Age of the Confucian Scholars."

[3] The 1788 text, which is the basis for the NST modern edition of *Responding to the Great Learning*, refers to China as "the land of the Tang" (*Tōdo*), but manuscript versions refer to China as "the Middle Kingdom" (*Chūgoku*). Here the latter is followed.

[4] The 1788 edition refers to Japan here as "this land" (*honbō*). Manuscript versions, however, refer to *Nihon*, or Japan.

have already taken control of the Middle Kingdom.[5] Simply hoping that they will not invade this country again does not amount to being militarily prepared.

"If the northern barbarians were to attack now, we would be no match for them in battle. We would not be because our storehouses are empty, and our minds and hearts are scattered. There are probably only one or two rare daimyō out of the twenty major lords of the realm who could field a well-rationed army. In the event of invasion, daimyō would surely have to request that any remaining rice earlier sent to the Osaka rice market be returned to their provinces. Moreover, if domains had silver on hand, they would probably use it to buy up all available rice.

"But then, within ten to twenty days, the price of 1 *koku* of rice would escalate to 100 units of silver, possibly 200 units. In twenty to thirty days, the price of rice would escalate further to 400 or 500 units of silver for every *koku*. If that happened, rōnin, townspeople, day laborers, and the clergy would face imminent starvation.

"With the realm in upheaval and people panicking, groundless rumors would multiply. Something akin to famine in times of safety would result, with some people dying of starvation. Bands of thieves – ranging from fifty to a hundred to as many as five hundred to a thousand – would soon run rampant. Some rōnin with exceptional military experience would be selected as their generals and then lead bands of marauders in unspeakable exploits.

"The powerful lumberjacks of the Yoshino, Kumano, and other mountainous areas number in the thousands. They make a living by cutting timber and exchanging it for rice. But in times of upheaval, most likely no one would want to exchange rice for timber. Lumberjacks would therefore have no choice but to leave their home provinces and become thieves. In the past, Yoshino was said to be a refuge where one could escape from the sadness of the world. In those days, many provinces had mountain forests and so there were only a few lumberjacks in Yoshino. Now, however, Yoshino has apparently become an extremely dangerous

---

5 The northern barbarians Banzan refers to first were the Mongols who completed their conquest of Song-dynasty China in 1279, and established their new dynasty, the Yuan (1279–1368). On two occasions in the thirteenth century, they attacked, but did not conquer, Kamakura Japan. Then, however, Banzan refers to the northern barbarians again, but in the second instance means the Manchus who had, decades prior, taken control of China and established the Qing dynasty. Banzan's fear was that the Manchus would follow the Mongols in eventually invading Japan. He uses the term "northern barbarians" to refer to both groups without, apparently, distinguishing one from the other.

place because of the many lumberjacks. People wealthy enough to carry silver coins now apparently think differently about Yoshino.

"In the past,[6] the annual land tax exacted from the farmer-samurai was minor. Moreover, because rice was widely used as currency, there was plenty of it everywhere. If a person carried gold or silver coins with them, then wherever they might go it was possible to purchase rice. These days, however, there seems to be no rice anywhere. Even though rice has become scarce in many provinces, circumstances overall suggest that rice should be plentiful. For that reason, people might be surprised when they discover that, even in times of apparent plenty, there is no rice. Even if one finds a little, the price ends up being so high that a hundred-day stipend might not be sufficient to purchase a twenty-day ration of rice.

"Ahead of us are the northern barbarians, yet along the way we also face starvation. In such circumstances, some of the lower elements, when sent to fight, will wonder whether to advance or retreat, and then flee for their lives and return home in secret. Even if they remain due to thoughts of shame, because they will be lacking horse attendants, spear carriers, armor carriers, water carriers and cooks, with nothing but themselves and their horses, starving, it will be impossible to make a stand. In truth, they will have no choice but to retreat to their home domains for sustenance.

"If only fifty or a hundred men deserted, they could be punished per the regulations, but what, other than nothing, can be done when the forces of an entire domain flee from battle and run back home? If the law were brought to bear on these men who believed they had in truth no other choice, province-wide uprisings would break out, followed by the eruption of one rebellion after the next. The gravitas of shogunal decrees that once prompted men to march out would vanish. Many people would have simply had enough, disgusted with everything.

"When there are no rations, no funds to cover deployment expenses, and the shogunate itself has no resources in reserve to draw on, is it not unreasonable to order troops to march into battle? Worse still, the military power and authority of the realm will begin to weaken even further as those who actually have provisions but claim to have none try to order people into battle without providing them with anything.

"The invasion of Japan by northern barbarians will bring ruin and destruction in its wake. Even if the barbarians simply invaded, retreated,

---

[6] During the Kamakura (1185–1333) and Ashikaga (1336–1573) periods.

and then withdrew, in the aftermath would not civil war ensue? Even if no one attacked the shogun,[7] if he exhausted his provisions and his military strength so that his orders, whether right or wrong, were not obeyed, then his inability from on high to rule would foreshadow power grabbing by the various domains. Yet that might be the best-case scenario. It is impossible to know what unimaginable disasters might ultimately be wrought by invasion and civil war.

"At this very moment, even as we consider these threats to the realm, we should begin preparing for them while there is still peace. When the time finally comes, even with great military strategists such as Zhang Liang and Kongming[8] as our guides, all manner of disasters might wrack the realm. Bands of thieves bringing irreparable ruin in their wake will take advantage of the depleted military provisions and exhausted troops of daimyō lords to seize their territories. Because they are thieves, they will seize rice in transport and oppress the common people to enrich themselves. If they spread their power far and wide, all sorts of unfathomable disasters might ensue. If an invasion by the northern barbarians were to bring about such turmoil, things would be far worse than they are now. Regretting this later will be to no avail."

Someone asked, "In Japan, we know there are several schools of military strategy, but they have only been tested inside this country. Would they be effective if the northern barbarians were the enemy?"

Banzan replied, "If the northern barbarians followed a poor strategy in their attack, then we could go on the offensive in battle. In that case, if one of our military strategists has a commander's character and a grasp of battlefield advantages that brings victory rather than defeat, might their skills not be somewhat useful in resisting the invasion?

"If the northern barbarians followed superior plans in their attack, our military strategists would be no match for them. But there is a military strategy that does not allow for defeat by even the northern barbarians' best military strategy.[9] While thinking about what would be best for our

---

[7] Here following manuscript versions of the text, rather than the 1788 edition that refers to the shogunate rather than the shogun.

[8] Zhang Liang (d. 186 BCE) was one of the most important commanders in the army of the first emperor of the Han dynasty. Kongming was the style name of Zhuge Liang (181–234), an outstanding statesman and military strategist of the Three Kingdoms period in ancient Chinese history.

[9] Banzan discusses how to prepare Japan for the coming invasion in the next chapter. The key is storing up sufficient provisions for Japanese troops in a prolonged war.

country, I discussed this a few years ago with the Prince of Kishū and some of the shogunal elders, but they have since passed away.[10] Perhaps their successors know of it. But at that time there seemed to be no need to act. Today, however, unless this military strategy were backed by abundant military rations, even it would serve no purpose."

---

[10] Tokugawa Yorinobu (1602–1671) was the tenth son of the founding shogun of the Tokugawa bakufu, Tokugawa Ieyasu. Yorinobu in turn founded the family line that presided over Kii Province, or Wakayama. The others referred to here were the shogunal elders Matsudaira Nobutsuna (1596–1662) and Itakura Shigenori (1617–1673).

7 Filling Shogunal Coffers with Gold, Silver, Rice, and Grain [1]

Someone asked, "Will eliminating the eight sources of waste[2] discussed earlier be adequate for realizing abundant military rations?"

Banzan replied, "What was previously discussed conveys the larger part of it. But unless we devote several years to accumulating resources, we will not succeed on the field of battle. Even if we began immediately, we would be off to a late start. The northern barbarians might invade next year in the spring or summer. So, unless we undertake preparations in the eighth or ninth lunar month of this year, by the twelfth lunar month or the first month of the next year, it will already be too late and, as a result, difficult to do anything effective. However, if an order went out promptly instructing all daimyō, without exception, to return to their domains, skip alternate attendance duties, postpone repayment of debts, and store tribute rice harvested in their domains, then we could plan an effective military strategy without worries over military rations.

"Those who have loaned silver to daimyō would temporarily have to suspend interest charges. Moreover, the lenders would be asked to calculate the original debt in silver based on an exchange rate of 1 *koku* of rice for 50 units of silver, and then collect payment in rice from the

---

[1] The title of this chapter, unabridged, is "Filling shogunal coffers with gold, silver, rice, and grain, and overwhelming provincial governors and the lords of castles with an abundance of the five grains."

[2] Here the reference is to Banzan's analysis of wasted rice, as discussed in Chapters 4 and 5. The eight causes are (1) reservoirs not being constructed in a manner consistent with geographical features around them, (2) shipwrecked cargo vessels, (3) insects infesting granaries and eating hulled rice, (4) saké brewing, (5) tobacco cultivation, (6) cotton cultivation, (7) physical weakness among the population, (8) production of "barbarian cakes."

domains as they are able to make them. Instead of metal coins, rice would be used as a means of payment in commercial transactions. Along with the wealthy, merchants would need to accept rice as a means of exchange, and artisans employed by merchants and the well-to-do would also be expected to take rice as payment. Rice would soon permeate commerce, especially if aristocrats and samurai in Kyoto were willing to make small purchases using rice as payment and the clergy were also willing to spend as currency the rice they receive.

"However, because there will be travelers and those carrying coins who want to make a purchase but have no rice with them, rice exchange shops would need to be established. Kyoto rice shops could sell 1 *koku* for 50 units of silver. For these shops to succeed, the price of rice in Osaka would need to be lower so that the Kyoto rice shops could make a small profit. There should be no problem with rice shops having enough rice to sell provided that daimyō sent the required amount from their granaries to Osaka and that shogunal granaries also supplied rice shops with rice.

"However, unless saké breweries are closed for one or two years, the amount of rice stored in the provinces will not be sufficient to counter a possible invasion by northern barbarians next year. Indeed, if the northern barbarians invaded, supplies would not be sufficient to prevent an outbreak of famine and thieving in Kyoto and Osaka. Saké shops have considerable financial resources so they should not be extremely distressed if, for a while, they were shut down completely. Even if their closure caused some trouble, that would be a small concern compared to the greater good. Accordingly, there is no real choice to make here. Depending on the size of the domain or fief, one in ten or twenty saké shops might be allowed to remain.

"Legal decrees could greatly reduce the amount of saké brewed. For a period of three years, saké gift-giving could be prohibited. Thereupon, saké would not be offered to guests and visitors. On special occasions, rather than a cask of saké, a substitute celebratory gift could be given. For religious rites and weddings, unfiltered saké might be brewed as was done in the past. For domestic use, home-brewed saké should suffice. Saké shops would be allowed for those who cannot make their own saké, or who need it for medicinal purposes.

"In the past, samurai and those above them did not drink saké purchased from a saké shop. Instead, they made it themselves and then stored it away. During a year, they would only have friends over a few times, in the spring when cherry trees were in bloom and in winter when snow had fallen. If we can live in that way, then even without sumptuary regulations, wasting rice on saké could be stopped. If we can do that for three years, even if the northern barbarians invaded and there were bad harvests and deprivation, there would be no domestic uprisings. A three-year supply of rice for Japan[3] today is more than the total amount of rice ancient Japan had in thirty years. Unless we have three years of rice stored, then we might be forced to conclude that 'our country will not continue to exist as our country.'"[4]

Someone asked, "Why do you say that a three-year supply of rice in storage today is greater than what was produced in thirty years during the age of wise rulers?"

Banzan replied, "Since the birth of humanity, neither in China nor in Japan[5] has there ever been as much annual land tribute tax collected as in recent years. Formerly, during the time when samurai were farmers, the annual tribute tax in Japan and China[6] was 10 percent of the harvest. Nowadays, if the lord of a domain worth 300,000 *koku* allotted 200,000 *koku* for his retainers, and 100,000 for his granaries, he would not be able to meet his public and private expenses. Earlier, the annual tribute on a 100,000-*koku* domain amounted to 10,000 *koku*. Today, the annual tribute on a 100,000-*koku* domain is half, or 50,000 *koku*.

"In the past, 10,000 *koku* stored in a granary was divided four ways, with three quarters covering public and private expenses and one quarter reserved for emergencies. The latter amounted to 2,500 *koku* per year. In ten years, it amounted to 25,000 *koku*. However, a 300,000-*koku* domain cannot help defend against the northern barbarians and alleviate a year of bad harvests with only 25,000 *koku*. By the same token, rice would therefore need to be stockpiled for thirty years to amass a total of 75,000 *koku*. Yet that amount would barely suffice for preventing emergencies. If an active daimyō with holdings of 300,000 *koku* stored 50,000 *koku* for his vassals, used 10,000 *koku* to settle his current accounts, and allotted 40,000 for provisions for defense and emergencies, then in three years,

---

[3] Manuscript copies refer to "Japan" (*Nihon*), while the 1788 woodblock edition refers to "our country" (*waga kuni*). Throughout this translation, the manuscript copies are followed.

[4] *Book of Rituals*, "The Royal Regulations," section II.

[5] Manuscript copies state *Chūka* and *Nihon*, or "China" and "Japan," while the 1788 edition states *Tōdo*, also read as *Morokoshi*, or "the land of the Tang," and *honbō*, or "this country." Here, the manuscript copies are followed.

[6] Manuscript copies reverse the previous order, referring to *Nihon* and *Chūka*, while the 1788 edition refers to *honbō* and *ikoku*, or "this country" and "the foreign country."

he would have 120,000 in stored provisions. Is that not more than was accumulated in thirty years in the past? In five years, they would have amassed 200,000 *koku*, or 400,000 *koku* of unhulled rice.

"Now in the western provinces, daimyō with domains of 300,000 *koku*[7] should store 50,000 *koku* in their domain granaries and 50,000 *koku* in Osaka granaries. If on top of that domains worth 400,000 *koku* could do the same, would there then even be enough storage space to store so much rice? Similarly, we can infer how things would be for holdings in increments of approximately 50,000 *koku*. Depending on the domains, some would store 100,000 *koku* of rice, and others, 200,000 *koku*.

"After three years, if the rice stored in preparation for disaster were not needed, then what might it be used for first? For unemployed samurai in Edo? For paying off debts. Even if defense against the northern barbarians were unnecessary, a leader intent on restoring Japan[8] would practice compassionate government and use available resources for such purposes. Later generations would surely deem him a wise ruler."

Someone asked, "If after three years, the shogunate were to expect daimyō to resume alternate attendance duties in Edo as in the past, how would things have improved?

Banzan replied, "If something like the Kamakura model were followed requiring daimyō to serve the shogun in his capital once every three years for a fixed period of fifty to sixty days, then for a daimyō lord of a 300,000-*koku* domain the cost would be about 5,000 *koku*. During the Kamakura period, daimyō were formidable men and among them were many high-ranking, fearsome grandees, yet still the shogunate took no hostages and only required fifty days' attendance once every three years. Even so, there were no problems. Rule by the Hōjō regents[9] on behalf of the Kamakura shogunate continued for nine generations, and then, following the Kamakura shogunate, the Ashikaga shogunate remained in power for fourteen generations. After its tenth generation, although the

---

[7] The 1788 edition states "100,000 *koku*." Again, this translation follows the manuscript versions which here state "300,000."

[8] Manuscript versions of the text refer to *Nihon chūkō*, or "the restoration of Japan," while the 1788 edition refers to *honbō chūkō*, or "the restoration of this country."

[9] Following the demise of the founding shogun, Minamoto Yoritomo (1147–1199), the Minamoto line continued nominally while a succession of male relatives of Yoritomo's wife, Hōjō Masako (1156–1225), known collectively as the Hōjō regents, were the effective leaders of the Kamakura shogunate.

Ashikaga shoguns ruled in name only, much as the imperial court does today, no one dared to attack the Ashikaga shogunate.

"Is not the shogunate even more secure today when the realm below heaven is unified and the families of the daimyō vassals, including their mothers, wives, and children, all reside in Edo? Moreover, there appear to be no troublesome people in the shogun's capital who are serious cause for concern. Why should there be anxieties over losing the great good fortune of heaven's decree and fears of some great misfortune from one's vassals? If the shogun[10] were to reduce the time vassals were required to spend in Edo, the vassals, thankful, would think it a gracious blessing, one that would serve as a foundation for their submission, mind and heart, to shogunal rule. If, however, daimyō ended up financially unable to bear the costs of rendering service in Edo per the status quo, and so had to request, from below, permission to be excused from service, that would not be good. The best course for the polity then is to reduce the costly Edo service requirements and thereby provide a great foundation for compassionate government."

Someone asked, "What will be done with the surplus rice of the daimyō and their retainers?"

Banzan replied, "Even though the shogunate will not simply seize the surplus rice, it will have its officials conduct an audit of daimyō management of resources, recording everything. Since the daimyō will have to comply with the shogunate's commands regarding debt repayment, the retainers of the daimyō will have to comply with daimyō orders regarding their debt repayment as well."

---

[10] Manuscript versions of the text give *kubō*, or "shogun," while the 1788 edition has *kōgi*, or "shogunate." Here, the manuscript versions are followed.

8 Eliminating Debt from the Realm below Heaven

Someone asked, "If the daimyō lords of castles and domains were excused from service in Edo, they would have much surplus rice. Some of their lesser vassals, however, currently have incomes barely sufficient to pay their family's expenses. Should the surplus rice be used to help pay their debts?"

Banzan replied, "The surplus rice belonging to daimyō lords of castles and provinces should be used to pay off the debts of their lesser vassals. Moreover, if compassionate government moved forward, everyone down to lower-level retainers would be relieved to know that some expenditures previously required were no longer necessary and that some things previously never imagined might be possible.

"However, daimyō and their retainers must obey the shogunate's orders. Shogunal officials, including those in Kyoto and in Osaka, would convey these orders. These officials would be responsible for keeping track of those who had lent gold and silver to the domains. In some cases, where the debt is large, shogunal officials might allow that repayment time be extended; where the debt is small, the repayment period might be reduced. Shogunal officials should allow, in some cases, repayments of 100–200 *koku*, and for others, of 30–50 *koku* so that even those who borrowed a large amount would not have to pay too much at one time. Payments could be financed for decades to come. Those who borrowed extremely large amounts might be permitted to make payments for countless years, providing the lender with an annual income, like an eternal fief, helping him to meet his expenses.

"If a lender made loans to three or perhaps even five daimyō, the lender would be paid by them as a group so that those making payments would not have to pay too much at one time. Shogunal magistrates should devise means whereby lenders could make loans and neither incur losses nor live in luxury, but instead enjoy peace of mind in conducting their business. In this way, even daimyō who have 40,000 *koku* of stored rice, but also considerable debt, might be allowed to repay it in 2,000–3,000-*koku* increments until the debt is repaid.

"Now, to repay the debts of the peasants, a considerable quantity of rice will be needed. However, if the debts could be repaid over a period of three to five years, those with 40,000 *koku* of stored rice could use 20,000 *koku* each year to liquidate the debts of a single district. Even at the current high rates, peasants generally have enough to cover the annual land tax. However, because their resources are not enough to meet loan payments on the principal and interest, they must borrow more money, going further into debt and ending up, as they are now, in extreme distress and poverty. If the authorities succeeded in liquidating their debts, then in some places, this would be comparable to a 10 percent tax reduction in their annual tribute.

"There are many different approaches to adjudicating debts in the different areas. Not wanting to go into all the details, I have kept to the basics here. If matters were resolved as I have outlined, however, there would still be considerable surplus rice and the various rōnin might once more gain a livelihood."

9 Helping Rōnin, Vagrants, the Unemployed, and the Impoverished[1]

Someone commented, "There are many daimyō and retainers. On top of that, there are a great many rōnin who once had fiefs. If we tried to give rōnin who no longer have fiefs stipends sufficient to support their fathers and mothers, wives and children, there would not be enough resources for this."

Banzan replied, "That is not the case. Because of the shogunate's grace, regardless of whether a rōnin had a fief or not, a count would be made of the number of family members and then provisions made, for example, for a rōnin family of ten, for a stipend for twenty people. For one hundred such rōnin, a stipend for two thousand people would be provided. For such a stipend, would not approximately 4,000 *koku* suffice?

"For rōnin who once received annually over 1,000 *koku* – including rōnin of good character and reputation – regardless of the number, even if they had a family including fifteen or twenty, they should receive a stipend for fifty or seventy people.

"Rōnin of lower standing who have a family of five or six and who provide support and lodging for a single manservant and maid, should receive approximately 5,000 *koku*. If this amount is not sufficient, surely no more than 10,000 *koku* should be provided.

"The various lords with 40,000 *koku* of stored rice should set aside 6,000-7,000 *koku*, and perhaps 10,000 *koku*, for rice stipends to provide rōnin. From this, the way in which provisions should be made in other cases can be inferred. If a lord wants to employ a rōnin, then he should

---

[1] Unabridged, the title for this chapter is "Helping all rōnin find work; putting vagrants and the unemployed in order; and assisting the distressed and impoverished."

either give him his old fief or, if the rōnin has relatives who still have fiefs, let him gradually assume them. If a rōnin finds a means of making a living, he should decline his stipend. Rōnin with resources to draw on, or with close relatives or friends they can rely on, should do so.

"Rōnin should be allowed, for now, to remain where they are currently dwelling. Calling them back to their domains and having them move and build houses would cause turmoil. One or two of the most outstanding rōnin should serve as representatives for the entire lot in a ceremonial audience of thanks with the daimyō of their domain. The others might meet their daimyō somewhere along the route to and from Edo while he is serving the shogunate. At some point, depending on circumstances, some rōnin might be gradually returned to their domains. This is the gist of it. The details should follow the circumstances of time and place.

"Due to their considerable debts, people throughout the realm below heaven, high and low, are impoverished and distressed. If the authorities could eliminate debts and provide for a debt-free future, nothing would bring greater joy and comfort to the various people of the realm. And if the helpless rōnin could be relieved of worries over hunger and cold, these two – debt relief and rōnin assistance – would stand as great achievements of compassionate government."

10 Making Mountains Luxuriant and Rivers Run Deep[1]

Someone asked, "Mountains and rivers are the foundations of the realm. But in recent years, mountains have been ravaged and rivers left shallow, that is, the country has been devastated. Formerly when such things happened, an age of chaos ensued and for a century or even two, civil war followed, and many lost their lives. Because rations for armies were strained, samurai were left without strength or pride. Timber was cut less frequently, and construction of new temples and grand halls ceased. However, during the chaos, mountains returned to their earlier luxuriant state and rivers again ran deep. Without waiting for such chaotic times finally to bring recovery, might not government measures ensure that mountains are luxuriant, and rivers run deep?"

Banzan replied, "From the start of the Warring States period,[2] nearly two centuries passed before mountains and rivers returned to their earlier state. However, compassionate government can restore mountains and rivers within a century. If compassionate government were practiced for five or six years, the debts of all below heaven would be eliminated. As a result, there would be a surplus of rice. This surplus would in turn facilitate enacting government measures for improving mountains and rivers.

---

[1] Unabridged, the title of this chapter is "How to reforest mountains and expand riverbeds in each province. Also, why the misery of the people leads to the destruction of forests."
[2] The Warring States period was a time of chronic warfare between contending samurai forces, lasting from the mid-fifteenth century through most of the sixteenth century. The name, "Warring States," alludes to a similar period in ancient Chinese history, from the fifth century BCE until the third, during which regional states struggled militarily for supremacy as the Zhou dynasty disintegrated. Out of the Warring States period in China, the first imperial regime, the Qin, emerged briefly, followed by the Han.

"Surplus rice could be distributed as a ration for woodcutters who ended up unemployed once timber harvesting in the mountains of Yoshino, Kumano, Kiso, and elsewhere ceased. Households that once cut shrubs and gathered wood from nearby mountains would instead burn the stalks from their field crops and leave the mountains alone. As they struggle to eke out a living, some people might sell their straw and gather firewood for themselves from the mountains. Rice should be given to these hard-pressed people so that they do not sell their chaff and then rely on mountain forests for firewood. In villages where there are no mountains, people should not buy firewood but instead make do the best they can morning and evening by burning chaff from their fields to cook.

"Some villages near mountains with more people than rice fields do not have enough chaff or firewood. In such cases, for example, if there were a village with fifty households, twenty would be sent somewhere else so that the remaining fields could be divided among the other thirty families. Moreover, their annual tribute could be lowered by 5–10 percent so that without cutting wood from the mountains, people would have enough fuel.

"Relocating people to other areas is entirely feasible because Kyushu has considerable land, but sparse population. People there are accustomed to providing sanctuary to even as many as five or ten thousand fleeing from other areas. Groups of fifty to one hundred people could be relocated to places such as Kyushu because it has superior fields and low annual tribute. A considerable amount of the surplus rice from that area could be provided to cover the initial daily expenses for the relocated population as well as the expenses involved in building new homes for them. Once settled, those relocated would soon come to prefer their new arrangements. Moreover, they would find that their new fields have none of the problems of their old fields. They would even be able to rehabilitate lands previously left fallow. Construction of reservoirs and river works should make possible extra rice land. In any event, harvesting wood from mountains would be stopped and people's hardships eliminated so that happiness and joy might prevail.

"Even bald mountains stripped of grasses and trees could be reforested. The breadth of the mountains ought to be surveyed and, unless impossible, one peak and then one valley at a time should be brought back to life. Depending on the extent of the valleys and peaks, 30, 50, 100, or even 200 *koku* of millet should be sown, and then on top of that, dry grass and reeds should be spread. Various birds would come to feed on the millet. Bird droppings would soon mix in with the soil so that trees planted would grow well there. The dried grass covering the millet would make it difficult for birds to get, forcing them to stay longer. Moreover, the millet would not be washed away by rain, and should grow well in the mountain soil.

"If done in this way, in only thirty years mountains would be covered with various trees. With luxuriant growth of mountain forests, nearby villages would not lack firewood. When this approach becomes well established and widespread, mountains will be lush and firewood in lasting abundance. Until such luxuriant growth is realized, pinewood cut from mountains and chaff from rice fields should suffice for fuel. Pines are not beneficial for mountain soil or arable rice land. But even in rocky, poor ground where grasses and trees do not grow, pine trees will.

"If we simply focus on what benefits us now, we will be ignoring the harm that comes in later years. When government measures for reforesting mountains are enacted, it will be best to cull new small pines while their roots are not deep. The existing pine forests on mountains would then spontaneously give way to mixed forests. After all, rain and dew that contact pines carry toxins so trees and grasses will not grow below them. Fields in which such tainted rain and dew flow turn bad. And pine-covered mountains do not draw evening rains.

"Cedar and cypress trees should be seeded on peaks and in valleys of large mountains such as Yoshino, Kongō, and others laid to waste by excessive timber harvesting. In the eastern and northern provinces as well as in other areas, seeds for cypress and cedar trees are said to be plentiful. If a competent person were ordered to follow this approach, with adjustments as needed, then mountains would soon become luxuriant.

"When mountains have many cypresses, cedar, and other trees, their spiritual energy will flourish in summer. As frequent evening showers follow, even in areas without retention ponds there should be no droughts. If soil from verdant mountain valleys no longer washed down clogging rivers, river currents would flow well, washing silt out to sea and causing riverbeds to deepen so that there would be no worries about flooding. It would be impossible to calculate the amount of wealth and prosperity produced through this great achievement."

Someone asked, "Timber cut from Kiso, Kumano, Tosa, and other forested areas produces revenue for daimyō comparable to that from rice and field crops. Will it not be difficult to stop harvesting trees?"

Banzan replied, "If the great way were realized, 90 percent of current official and private expenses would end. Once the grand project for growing wealth has begun, things people worry over today will make no difference at all. Moreover, revenue-producing commodities on mountains such as timber would then likely be replaced by other revenue sources. Even if all the revenue-producing commodities from mountain areas were combined, the total sum would not be enough to pay the interest on what daimyō of those areas currently owe. However, once debts are liquidated, many current expenses will be no more. Then, even without revenue-producing commodities such as timber, there should be enough for everyone."

Someone asked, "Some provinces have regulations protecting mountains and rivers, but increasingly mountains are ravaged and rivers are allowed to become more and more shallow. Why is this?"

Banzan replied, "Even though there are regulations against ravaging mountains, there are many people who do not even have a three-day supply of food. Nor do they have the means to buy wood to cook their meals. Even if their heads might be cut off tomorrow, today they feel forced to steal and cut timber. Although the village headman and the elders might know about these violations, they cannot but look the other way."

Someone asked, "If lumberjacks were stopped and timber no longer harvested, how would Shintō shrines, Buddhist temples, castles, samurai residences, Edo mansions, and the towns and villages of the various provinces be built?"

Banzan replied, "When the great way is practiced, even without cutting mountain forests, there is every reason to expect that there would be no shortage of timber. I have previously analyzed all these matters. However, since my earlier remarks were lengthy, I will abbreviate them here. First, regarding the construction of shrines: it is disrespectful to build multiple shrines in various locations all dedicated to the same deity. For that very reason, the ancients did not do so. Doing so diminishes the majesty of the deity. The only shrine for Amaterasu is in the village of Yamada in Ise Province. The only shrine for Hachiman is in the village of Usa. The only Kasuga shrine is in Nara. The shrine for Susanoo is only in Izumo. Ōanamuchi is enshrined in Miwa only. With the other deities, much the same should be true. While the mountains are being restored as they were in ancient times, new construction and repair of various shrines should be halted. If repairs can be made with wood taken from subordinate shrines, new timber would not be used up."

Someone asked, "Japan is a sacred country. How will local people worship guardian deities of their areas?"

Banzan replied, "In the Yamato region, the Kasuga, Miwa, Tatsuta, and Ikoma shrines house local guardian deities. In areas where widely worshipped deities are enshrined in shrine buildings but there are no shrines for the local guardian deities, the guardian deities should be enshrined and the widely worshipped deities should be relocated so that the shrine buildings previously devoted to them could be used for the worship of local guardian deities. This should be done much as small shrines are sometimes merged into one. This process must, in its particulars, follow the circumstances of the times. Once heterodox shrines are eradicated, authentic shrines will be regarded with heightened dignity and awe."

Someone asked, "What about Mt. Otokoyama and the imperially established Iwashimizu Hachiman Shrine[3] located there?"

Banzan replied, "It alone may be renovated and remain as it is."

Someone asked, "What of Buddhist temples?"

Banzan replied, "Nothing should be rushed. If hasty changes were made, the clergy would cause trouble. The ancient laws regulating entry into the priesthood should, however, be revived so that people are prohibited from simply deciding for themselves that they want to become a Buddhist monk. Thus, when someone from such-and-such a village, county, and province seeks to become a Buddhist monk, relatives from his village and surrounding areas should assemble to decide whether he is qualified to do so based on his mastery of the threefold training in Buddhist precepts, mind control, and wisdom. If he is deemed worthy of the priesthood, he should be presented to the district magistrate. After the district magistrate has investigated the matter, he should speak to the daimyō. The daimyō will then make his recommendation to the office of the magistrate serving the shogunate. If the proposal receives the shogunate's vermillion seal, then the candidate may become a Buddhist monk.

"If a monk violates the precepts, the high priest should examine the matter and report his findings to the shogunal authorities. The authorities would then relay the report to the monk's home daimyō and have him

---

3 The Iwashimizu Hachiman Shrine was founded on Mt. Otokoyama, south of Kyoto, in the late ninth century, reportedly for the protection of Kyoto and the imperial line. Dedicated to Hachiman, the protector deity of warriors and those defending Japan, the shrine was important to the major shogunal regimes, including the Kamakura and Tokugawa.

consider his negligence in the initial investigation of the monk leading to his, the daimyō's, recommendation of him for the priesthood. The village headman and district magistrate would also review their investigations for negligence in recommending the monk. The monk would then be returned to secular life and supported for life by his neighbors and kin. If procedures were conducted in this way, fewer would seek to become Buddhist clergy. Those who do become monks must follow monastic rules and regulations.

"Temples should be removed from villages by a distance of 15 chō [approx. 1,600 meters]. Moreover, temples should be separated from any area, including those that cannot strictly speaking be called a neighborhood, wherein just a few people dwell, by 15 chō. Buddhist law does not allow Buddhist halls and temples to be built right next to the homes of townspeople and the laity. Therefore, such temples should be torn down and the wood recovered from them used to repair mountain temples. Only Kannon and the sacred temple grounds of Kiyomizu in Kyoto and the Hase temple in Nara may remain. Others should be dismantled, one by one, as soon as circumstances permit. Yakushi, Inaba Yakushi, and other such renowned temples may be relocated on the vacant land of mountain temples. How the rest should be dealt with can be inferred from this.

"If mountain temples violate the laws by petitioning the shogunate for permission to include superior rice fields within the temple's confines and then recruit local people into their service, compassionate government need not be carried out in haste if, after all, such practices are customary. Instead, compassionate rule should seek a natural return to the way things were. In arranging for this, it would be best to discuss matters with priests who obey the precepts. I will leave complex issues abbreviated for now."

Someone asked, "What about construction and repair of samurai mansions?"

Banzan replied, "If the great way were practiced, farmers and warriors would soon return to the ways of antiquity. Then, even castles would not need to be as they are now. Not even a tenth of today's samurai mansions would be necessary. Surplus mansions could be dismantled so that there would be no shortage of materials for repairs. In recent years, we know that the shogunate demolished old shrines and temples that might have been repaired, and built new ones. However, because the new structures were built with poor quality timber and the carpentry work done carelessly, they too soon deteriorated. And, due to the shogunate's construction projects and the need for timber to complete them, mountains and wetlands have been increasingly ravaged, and riverbeds left shallower and shallower.

"In many cases, repairing buildings and restoring them to their original condition rather than building them anew resulted in structures that lasted three to five times longer. Nevertheless, the shogunate has often wasted its resources on unnecessary projects such as constructing buildings anew, and in the process left the realm's mountains and rivers increasingly ravaged.

"Bodhidharma, the first patriarch of Zen Buddhism, declared that there is no spiritual merit in building temples. Yet ordinary monks and lay people hold, on the contrary, that there is spiritual merit for such deeds. Following Bodhidharma's pronouncement, it is therefore best for both Shintō shrines and Buddhist temples to choose the way of major repairs and renovation rather than building anew.

"And, in the future, conflagrations will occur every so often. If these are quelled with compassionate government, it would be best for our mountains and our people."

Someone asked, "If those entering the priesthood per the regulations for becoming a monk must correctly follow the Buddhist precepts, then there will be fewer monks and neighborhood temples will be left empty. If there were fewer Shintō shrines as well, what would become of the senior priests' wives and children?"

Banzan replied, "There are few senior priests in rural shrines. Among the agrarian folk at large, there are only hereditary lines of associate shrine priests. They should be provided with some land from the shrine grounds. If there are hereditary shrine priests, senior priests, and others, then the shogunate should provide them with stipends and have them pursue scholarship. Later, they can serve as officials and teachers in the schools.

"Commoner homes do not require much timber. For the most part, timber near the village should suffice for their purposes. Since there are many mountains covered with pine forests, there should be enough wood for repair work needed in towns and villages. Pines growing on mountains with good soil would naturally be harvested first, and thereafter it would be best for mixed forests to replace them. There are some mountains with red sandy soil on which nothing will grow except pine trees. These mountains should henceforth be pine mountains.

"Recently, many men and women have suffered from cramps and convulsions. As a cure, they drink a medicinal decoction of tea. As a consequence, tea fields in the provinces have increased one hundredfold compared to ancient times. And, limitless quantities of firewood have been consumed to fuel this tea habit. Yet with compassionate government, depressed spirits will brighten, and, with education, people will not feel ill. Thereupon, as in ancient times, people will be happy to drink warm water in winter, and water in summer. Not only will many fields once devoted to tea start to grow the five grains and so increase the food supply, there will also be less demand for firewood. Everyone, high and low together, will enjoy a more comfortable life as needless haste ceases. Men and women might then pursue well their family responsibilities."

Responding to the
Great Learning:
Part II

11 The Ebb and Flow of the Ruler's Blessings

Someone asked, "Some say that when daimyō are impoverished and powerless, the shogunate does well. Are there government measures that would enable the shogunate and all domains of the realm to achieve wealth and plenty?"

Banzan replied, "When daimyō are of limited means and samurai are impoverished, even more is squeezed from the peasantry so that they will also fall into poverty. If the samurai and peasants are in poverty, the artisans and merchants end up impoverished too. And even more rōnin will be reduced to cold and hunger. All below heaven will soon be mired in poverty. When all below heaven are destitute, the ruler's divine blessing, the mandate of heaven, withers. When the decree of heaven withers, there is nothing that can be done.

"The ancient sage ruler Emperor Yao once observed, 'When all within the four seas are in distress and poverty, the rewards of heaven cease forever.' The worst thing that can happen to a ruler is thus the impoverishment of his vassal lords. Even from the perspective of a military hegemon,[1] it is shallow to think that poverty among the vassal lords would be a good thing for a ruler. The first shogun Minamoto Yoritomo, the Hōjō regents, and the Ashikaga shoguns were all hegemons. Of them, the Hōjō regents governed most excellently. During a three-year

---

[1] "Hegemon" refers to a military ruler who, although effective, is not a moral exemplar in governing. The *Mencius* (2A/3) contrasts the hegemon, known for a utilitarian approach to things, with the "true king," or the exemplar of ethical rule. That Banzan even briefly considers matters from the perspective of the hegemon rather than exclusively from that of the true king is evidence of his pragmatic relativism, i.e., his willingness to consider options other than the highest ideals that he no doubt considered preferable, if possible. When not, Banzan was ready to accommodate expedients that matched the times.

period, the Hōjō regents required daimyō to serve the shogunate in Kamakura only once, and then for just fifty days. And even then, daimyō were admonished not to spend excessively while in Kamakura. The shogunate's fear was that the abundant wealth of the provinces would be wasted in Kamakura."

12 Returning to the Old Farmer-Samurai Society

Someone asked, "Farmers and samurai have been separated for a very long time. Will it not be difficult to return to the way things were in the past?"

Banzan replied, "Unless the [great] way is realized, such a return would be extremely difficult. But if the [great] way were realized, it would be easy. Yet even for a ruler with a compassionate mind and compassionate sensibilities, if he is excessively permissive and accommodating, then trying to reunite farmers and samurai will indeed be difficult. Such a ruler would not be able to realize what I call compassionate government."

Someone asked, "What does it mean to be excessively permissive and accommodating?"

Banzan replied, "If daimyō were made to return to the ancient practice of serving the shogun in Edo once every three years for only fifty days but then were permitted to go back to their domains to live in luxury, that is, scrimping in the east while living it up in the west, then nothing would have been gained. On the other hand, just as parents provide for their children by teaching them how to behave, if the shogunate decreed that compassionate government be implemented, everyone would find that there is more grain than can be stored. Such abundance would make it easier to reunite farmers and samurai. However, if neither the samurai nor the farmers were happy with their prospects, it would be difficult to bring them back together.

"So, first, farmers' debts should be paid off, pawned rice fields should be returned, and fields earlier sold should be purchased by the shogunate,

57

at the sale price, and then returned to the farmers. If those who purchased rice fields already have many, but those who sold them only a few, then the fields should be returned to the sellers. If those who sold rice fields have many but those who bought them have only a few, then the buyers should keep them. Moreover, once samurai are reunited with the peasant farmers in the countryside, the tribute that they will pay would be reduced to one-tenth. As things are now, that is, with farmers separated from the samurai, high land tributes have, of course, left the farmers impoverished.

"Samurai should live here and there among the farmers. Moreover, samurai must understand that they should be careful never to mistreat farmers because their own children and grandchildren will live and die with them, dwelling alongside them generation after generation. In military service, when samurai lead farmers, they should never ask them to bear too much of the burden. Military support of about 20 or 30 percent of the rice produce should suffice. After all, in the countryside, samurai will not have castle guard duty or police duties.

"When visiting neighbors in the same village or one nearby, samurai should enter informally through the kitchen and begin conversing in a familiar manner so that their hosts will not feel that they must treat them lavishly as guests. If they don't mind a little manual labor, samurai might find pleasure and good health in assisting those below them with chores such as weeding vegetable gardens. Samurai should hunt in the mountains and fields, and fish in rivers and swamps, regardless of wind, rain, frost, or snow. In exerting themselves in the martial arts, they should also strive to be warriors who can better defend their lord. Administrative measures should address these matters in detail to match the times."

"Samurai with large fiefs and many sons, however, should be able, for the most part, to divide things equally among their children. By the time a fief has been divided among children and grandchildren, the samurai will become farmers and will have to pay an annual tribute of one-tenth of their income.

"When samurai dwell among the farmers, the duties assigned to the shogunal district magistrates and administrative assistants will indeed become important. These days, however, administrative assistants do not govern effectively. A samurai general and lieutenant might have to be assigned responsibility for the towns and villages, serving as true administrative assistants of the shogunate."

Someone asked, "Presently, the lord of a castle with a fief of 100,000 *koku* receives 50 percent tribute, or 50,000 *koku* annually, half of the produce of his fief. If the tax rate were reduced to 10 percent, the tribute would only amount to 10,000 *koku*. Would a tax rate that is one fifth of the current rate suffice?"

Banzan replied, "Of the 50,000-*koku* income currently remaining for the daimyō, retainer fiefs take 40 percent. Apart from that, if stipends and other expenses are figured in, then there would not even be 10,000 *koku* left to store in granaries. That is not enough for a daimyō to cover his expenses while rendering service in Edo. Now, daimyō must therefore borrow funds resulting in interest that must be paid, making their income even less adequate. Later, they might be forced to resort to various measures that are not compassionate, such as borrowing funds from their retainers or simply dismissing them.

"But, when compassionate government is implemented and there is a return to the Kamakura practice of having daimyō serve the shogun in Edo only once every three years, and then for only fifty days, daimyō would only need to put aside 1,000 *koku* per year so that in three years, they would have 3,000 *koku* to cover expenses for their service in Edo. Then there would be no need for storing 9,000 *koku* more a year in granaries to cover costs of service in Edo. Capable and talented individuals from nearby farming villages could be brought into service at the daimyō's castle and simply paid a service wage. Moreover, daimyō would not need to spend as much on their castles as they presently do. A main citadel and secondary citadel should suffice. Only one tenth as many samurai residences would be necessary.

"Most of the land previously occupied by samurai residences could become an enormous swath of rice fields. These fields would be tax exempt and should benefit those above and below. Those serving in the castles would be given dwellings and expected to plant bamboo across the front as a living fence, and mulberry bushes on the outer areas so their wives and children could raise silkworms."

Someone asked, "What would become of the shogun's direct retainers?"

Banzan replied, "Should not those residing in and around Edo live just as do farmers and samurai elsewhere? With compassionate government, the mothers, wives, and children of the daimyō vassals would be allowed to return to their home domains, provided that daimyō themselves remain obedient. Then, a single mansion for the daimyō while in

Edo would suffice. The number of neighborhoods within Edo would be one tenth of what they are today, and yet adequate for those remaining there. Direct vassals of the shogun and high-ranking persons would return to their respective domains. Samurai commanders from the shogunate's service in Edo would also be dispatched to oversee things in the various regions of the country.

"Vacant lots where daimyō mansions once stood in Edo would be numerous. Because Edo has a natural water supply, might not most of the land there be converted into rice fields? Because the land in Edo is level, could it not be divided up according to the well-field system?[1] Once farmer-samurai achieve peace, happiness, and prosperity in the countryside, lower-level shogunal retainers could return to the countryside as well to farm their fiefs. When schools are administered so that high and low come to understand the moral way, people's thoughts and minds will be changed for the better so that matters can be resolved by intelligent discussion.

"Only officials serving the shogun would be provided large mansions surrounding the shogun's castle. They would have hedges in front and mulberry bushes along the back to provide perpetual landscaping. Commanders of shogunal retainers should base their units 5–10 *ri* (1 *ri* = 3.9 km) away from Edo Castle. During their fifty to one hundred days of service, they would guard all four sides of the shogun's castle securely. The commanders of the archery and firearm units would do likewise.

"If troops were taught martial arts and the moral way while serving the shogun, they would gladly serve. Three hundred samurai devoting themselves exclusively to serving the shogunate, away from their wives and children, would be better than a thousand living below the shogun's castle with their wives and children. When compassionate government is realized and peace prevails, there would be no cause for worry. Literary studies and martial arts must not be forgotten, and morality and scholarly arts should also be pursued."

---

[1] *Mencius* 3A/3. Here, Mencius links the practice of compassionate government to the equal distribution of land to the agrarian population according to the so-called well-field system. The system is named for the Chinese character for a water well, which appears, in written form, like a nine-square grid wherein each square is of equal size. The middle square, or plot of land, was supposed to be the "public" plot, commonly farmed by those tending the other eight "private" plots. The produce from the public plot went to the authorities.

Someone asked, "If, after everything else is done, would not the 10 percent land tax leave the shogunate's coffers unable to meet the needs of the realm below heaven?"

Banzan replied, "Currently, daimyō lords do not benefit much from largesse the shogunate provides them. Nor does the shogunate benefit from largesse offered by the daimyō. In these exchanges, the daimyō are simply wasting resources. The shogunate and the daimyō should thus cease these exchanges. If this were done, the shogunate would have more than enough resources to cover its expenses. If there were deficits, the shogunate could follow the ancient practice of having daimyō pay one-fiftieth harvest tribute for the two years when they were not serving in Edo. That should resolve any shortfalls. From an income of 10,000 *koku*, that tribute would come to 200 *koku*. From an income of 100,000 *koku*, it would come to 2,000 *koku*. Additionally, the shogunate could resort to floating taxes on forests and swampland if need be.

"Guards stationed in Kyoto, Osaka, Suruga, and other places should be discontinued. As the number of Shintō shrines and Buddhist temples are reduced and maintenance to remaining structures done by simple repairs, the shogunate's expenses would not be excessive. Moreover, when the moral way thus prevails in the world, if there were valid expenses that the shogunate could not cover, it should confer with the daimyō regarding how best to meet them. The shogunate should not have any deficits even though it might have to request a little more tribute from the daimyō. That should not be a problem for the daimyō, since they will be relieved of most of their official duties in service to the shogunate. When a ruler treats his retainers as his own children, his retainers will regard him as their father."[2]

Someone asked, "Since the grand project for growing wealth will produce more grain and currency than can be stored, will the shogunate never again run a deficit?"

Banzan replied, "The wealth produced will be wealth for the sake of the realm below heaven. Since the abundant surplus grain will be spent on cultural learning and military provisions, the shogunate should never have insufficient funds. After poverty within the four seas has been relieved and all other matters attended to, the shogunate will no longer need additional wealth. Accordingly, there will be a return to the ancient way of the farmer-samurai, a revival of the one-tenth tax, a distribution

[2] *Mencius* 4B/3, makes a similar remark.

of wealth among the population, and a union of the minds and hearts of all the people[3] so that everyone will enjoy a degree of wealth, prosperity, and plenty and no one will ever again know want.

"If farmer and samurai are reunited, Japan's[4] martial courage will become exceptionally strong, validating the country's reputation as a land of true warriors. From the time that samurai and farmers were separated, however, samurai have ended up sick in body and physically weak. Although courageous in mind and heart, they never face enemies in battle and so become weak with age and then succumb to illness. Foot-soldiers and lesser sorts serving such weakened samurai have not thought highly of their masters. Such has been the decline of our military strength. Even in ordinary life, because there are no farmer-samurai, customs have become debauched and short-lived. Now is the time for returning to the old way of the farmer-samurai."

---

[3] *Great Learning*, ch. 10.
[4] Following manuscript versions of the text that state "Japan" (*Nihon*). The 1788 edition states, "this country" (*honbō*), NST p. 442.

13 Eliminating Landless Income and Increasing New Fiefs[1]

Someone asked, "In some provinces, there is 'landless income.'[2] This leads to distress and poverty for the peasantry, and causes losses for fief-holders. Is this not unreasonable?"

Banzan replied, "Absolutely. Land surveys should eliminate such irrational practices. However, even for fief-holders, because landless income is tied to the overall land tribute, it cannot easily be eliminated. When those who have landless income receive land-based fiefs that produce income, the landless income might be effectively eliminated by increasing the tribute on these lands. Landless income holdings in the shogunate's domains can be eliminated similarly. The others can be done away with easily through the bounty of compassionate government.

"There are also unfortunate consequences issuing from tributes on transportation services for various commodities. Taxes are levied on the land transport, by horseback, of rice from Obama Castle in Wakasa Province [now Fukui Prefecture] to Lake Biwa in Ōmi Province [now Shiga Prefecture]. However, because these taxes are included in the tax basis of the fiefs of these areas, they cannot be eliminated by the local daimyō. To bypass these taxes, carriers have rerouted large quantities of rice around western Japan to Osaka by boat, and consequently, the city of Otsu on Lake Biwa in Ōmi has declined. The daimyō of Obama Castle has also lost out. There are probably many such examples in the provinces. Taxes

---

[1] Unabridged, the title of this chapter is "Eliminating landless income and increasing new fiefs with compassionate government."

[2] "Landless income" refers to income not tied to the rice harvest of a particular piece of land.

on commodities transported by land should be administered by the shogunate. Daimyō and district lords, regardless of their standing, should only manage rice land. For the sake of the realm, various floating taxes such as the land transport tax should be lowered or eliminated. If this were done, it would be best for all of Japan.

"In ancient times, famous mountains and large swamps were not part of any daimyō's fief. Daimyō assigned responsibility for mountains and swamps did not let them suffer damage. Thus, evening showers and rain alleviated droughts. Even with great downpours making mountains verdant and rivers full, riverbeds remained deep so that there were no worries over flooding. Also, in ancient times, increases in land and reclaimed land were tax exempt for three years. Farmers became prosperous, which encouraged them to strive on relentlessly. It was much the same with those who were permitted their family's inheritance."

14 Lowering the Cost of Foreign Silk and Textiles[1]

Someone asked, "What government measures would enable Japan[2] to produce silks and textiles so that it does not have to import them from foreign lands?"

Banzan replied, "In Japan,[3] because farmers have had to find time for raising silkworms and harvesting silk while otherwise busy cultivating rice, they have had trouble producing good cotton and silk. In the end, too little is produced to meet the demand for finished textiles. All the while, the wives and children of high-ranking samurai spend their days pursuing frivolous amusements, while the wives of low-ranking samurai labor away over nothing of benefit and end up with no free time.

"When the [great] way is practiced and auxiliary regulations are in place, wives of low-ranking samurai will have free time and not have to engage in hard labor, while wives of high-ranking samurai can enjoy the arts of the way and set their minds on women's tasks. Then, mulberry bushes will be planted as fences and in vacant lots so that silkworms can be raised. Producing silk would occupy the hands not only of these well-born women, but of all who have free time. In a few years, as women master the details of their work, all kinds of silk and textiles might be produced. Cotton spun by the better sorts comes out a beautiful white

---

1 Unabridged, the title of this chapter is "The need to lower the price of foreign silk and fabrics. Also, how Japan, in ten to fifteen years, can produce cotton in abundance and silk in good quality."

2 Here, this translation follows manuscript versions of the text, cited in NST, which state "Japan" (*Nihon*). The 1788 edition states, "this country" (*honbō*), NST p. 444.

3 Ibid.

color, while that spun by those of lower standing is recognizably inferior, even though the cotton being spun is the same.

"Yet still, mulberry bushes planted today will take ten to fifteen years to reach maturity. During that time, if we do not import silk textiles, we will not have them. If, as in the past, good fabric could be imported inexpensively at two ports, Nagasaki and Hirado,[4] textiles would be limited to only one-fiftieth of the imports otherwise including medical supplies. When there is enough silk and cotton in Japan, wealthy aristocrats, samurai, farmers, artisans, and merchants could wear silk. Even though rice fields would no longer be used to grow cotton, it could be grown in gardens by poorer folk so that the lower elements would have plenty to wear."

Someone asked, "How might we import foreign products of high quality inexpensively?"

Banzan replied, "If the [great] way were practiced, such matters would become clear, the minds and hearts of shogunal administrators and merchants would be transformed anew, and the circumstances which they oversee could be changed for the better. However, things have only worsened since the port of Hirado was closed and Nagasaki alone remained open. Should we not, therefore, begin by trying to change that situation?

"It is not wise for Japan to pay foreigners for imports and yet expect to retain gold and silver at home. If we use our wealth to import items from abroad we will find that the quality of the goods purchased worsens. If the imported goods are then sold domestically at a higher price to recover the funds spent on them, the costs would be recovered but only at the expense of our own country, Japan.[5]

"We should not spend our wealth extravagantly purchasing items from foreigners shipped into Japan's[6] ports and then try to resell them for a profit. Instead, imports should be sent directly to textile shops in Kyoto. If the latter are regulated so that those working in them are allowed a modest, subsistence profit, then the price for silk and textiles could be kept low.

---

[4] In the early 1640s, the shogunate closed the port at Hirado, not far from Nagasaki, in an effort to limit Dutch presence in Japan to the confines of Dejima, located off the coast of Nagasaki. Banzan suggests that Hirado be reopened as a port of trade.

[5] Following manuscript versions of the text which state "Japan" (*Nihon*). The 1788 edition states, "our country" (*wagakuni*), NST p. 444.

[6] Manuscripts state "Japan" (*Nihon*). The 1788 edition states, "this side's," NST p. 444.

"If we reduce purchases of damask fabrics, figured satin, and silk crepe while buying good quality imports, then relatively little gold would be spent paying foreign countries for those products. That would be a good thing for Japan.[7] Even if the price paid to foreigners for good quality imports was somewhat high, as long as buyers did not then engage in underhanded practices such as reselling the commodities in Japan[8] for a profit, and instead sent them to Kyoto, domestic prices might be relatively low. But if we insist that foreigners sell their goods at a sacrifice, they will only export inferior quality goods. For now, prices are not low, and it must be acknowledged that there are many unfortunate practices on both sides."

[7] Manuscripts state "Japan" (*Nihon*). The 1788 edition states, "this country" (*honbō*), NST p. 444.

[8] Ibid., p. 445.

15 Eliminating Christianity

Someone asked, "How might Christian teachings be eliminated?"

Banzan answered, "Christians spread their teachings by taking advantage of people's ignorance and poverty. If enlightened Confucian principles were taught throughout the realm resolving people's spiritual confusion while compassionate government ended people's poverty, then it would be impossible to spread Christian teachings even if those promoting those teachings redoubled their efforts. Proof is found in China,[1] the country of Confucian sages and worthies. Because China is enlightened, it has been impossible to spread Christian teachings there even though there are no regulations forbidding them.

"As with the proverb, 'only snakes know the way of snakes,' so it is said that 'unless you are a Christian, you will not recognize a Christian.' The present system requiring that people register themselves at Buddhist temples to prove they are not Christians is of no use whatsoever. For the domains, it amounts to another considerable expense.

"A report by a shogunal official sent to Kyushu to arrest suspected Christians relates the following:

> Those accused of being Christians are, when at Buddhist temples, more devout and faithful worshipers than ordinary people, and they have a greater desire for the afterlife. Even their neighbors do not think they are Christians. When questioned, they deny that it could possibly be true and so ask to be excused so they can return home. Yet when brought to the magistrate's office, they are confronted by more evidence than they can explain away.

[1] Manuscript copies refer to China as *Chūka*, while the 1788 edition states, *Tōdo*, also read as *Morokoshi*, or "the land of the Tang," NST p. 445.

"It should be added that unrighteous, immoral Buddhist monks supervise and administer the Christian registration process, and their work
with it is destroying the true essence of Buddhism. Because the measures
for eliminating Christianity are very detailed and lengthy to recount, this
summary statement should suffice: Christianity will be eliminated with
the practice of compassionate government."

16 Reviving Buddhism

Someone asked, "Buddhist teachings have never flourished in Central Asia and China as they are doing in Japan[1] today. What, then, do you mean by reviving Buddhism?"

Banzan replied, "When we look at how many temples and monks there are, it does seem that Buddhism has never flourished as it currently is doing in Japan. Yet when you consider the Buddhist teachings, they are on the brink of ruin. Some of the more thoughtful Buddhists have even said that contemporary monks are robbers and thieves.

"Monks who truly live by the Buddhist teachings probably number no more than one hundred out of every ten thousand. Perhaps as many as a thousand monks out of every ten thousand became monks due to a physical handicap that rendered them unable to work as samurai, farmers, artisans, or merchants. The rest are all clever, cunning sorts who plotted to gain a livelihood as clergy even though they harbor more lewd desires and eat more meat than do lay people. Many monks living together in major temples, supposedly still in training, studying, and practicing, are actually rascals, robbers, and thieves. Lay people realize this and have said as much. When the northern barbarians invade and there is a great famine, one hundred thousand monks will likely join the ranks of robbers and thieves.

"Those impoverished by the Christian temple-registration requirement are confused by this, and those who have not been reduced to poverty and are, moreover, somewhat perceptive, think it is regrettable. The poor are dumbfounded because if they do not give the monks gold and

---

[1] Manuscript versions state "Japan" (*Nihon*), while the 1788 edition states, "our country" (*wagakuni*), NST p. 445.

silver, they will not receive a certificate of temple registration. Those who are more perceptive are invariably disgusted with their home temples because of the corrupt, sham monks who reside there.

"If there were an invasion by northern barbarians or the onset of an age of chaos, few people would pay monks gold and silver for a temple-registration certificate establishing that they are not Christians because at that point no one will care about tracking down Christians. Ignorant Buddhists will be lured away by the many non-believers. With the perilous, chaotic times, temple duties will be neglected. During the anarchy, the one hundred true monks out of ten thousand fake ones would have to draw on the power of their faith in Buddhism to save themselves and others from daily starvation. Of those thousand monks who entered the clergy because of physical handicaps, some might rely on the sympathy of the people, scraping by living as beggars. Some might die of starvation. The rest would meet death and destruction as robbers and thieves. If burned down, temples would not be rebuilt. Those temples that remained would become dwellings for foxes and badgers. Is it not the decree of heaven that those egregious, profligate monks who once flourished would then meet their end? Not realizing this inevitable principle of fate, some imagine that the corrupt Buddhist clergy might enjoy prosperity forever, but that is just an empty dream.

"If our mountains and forests end up ravaged, people will lose their faith in Buddhism. Burdened with military expenses incurred during chaotic times, the shogunate and daimyō will not be able to muster the strength needed to rebuild Buddhist temples. No one is likely to seek temple registration during the confusion of military upheaval, given that high and low will have become disgusted with those worthless certificates. Although today the rich, in pursuit of reputation, give generous amounts of gold and silver to monks to build temples and halls, that would end when their gold and silver is stolen by robbers and thieves and their lives are taken as well. Similarly, the world cannot continue to exist while mountains and forests are being ravaged and rivers and streams are left shallow. Nor can monks continue to enjoy such immoral luxuries as they currently do. Once mountains and rivers have been devastated and yet a corrupt clergy remains, a major upheaval will surely ensue.

"If an age of chaos and disorder were to last for one or two hundred years, mountains and forests would come to flourish again as they did in the past, and rivers and streams would grow deep once more as in ancient times. During the age of chaos, immoral expressions of Buddhism that previously flourished would end, and only sincere priests would remain. Would not Buddhist teachings thereby be restored? If heaven rectifies the immorality of Buddhism, it might do so by means of war and chaos. During that time, for one or two hundred years, there would be much pain and suffering. However, if people followed the way of humanity and right order were realized through compassionate government, both high and low would enjoy a happiness and joy akin to that felt by people suddenly freed from the topsy-turvy of bondage and upheaval."

Someone asked, "If the temple-registration requirement were stopped and everyone below heaven allowed to believe or not believe, then most people would probably have no ties to a temple. If so, then would that not result in priests facing starvation?"

Banzan replied, "Due to that eventuality, compassionate government would provide surplus rice to feed priests who have no food. Moreover, people should be forbidden from simply deciding for themselves to become monks. As discussed earlier, if established rules governed admission to the priesthood, there would probably be one thousand times fewer monks. Within thirty years, with the passing of a number of monks, there would be even fewer. Many who entered the priesthood did so simply to gain a living and so should be forced to return to secular life. Lots of monks probably would return to secular life if only they could make a living by doing so. Those with literacy and learning might teach here and there at village schools.

"In the past, the Buddhist day of remembrance for the deceased occurred only once a year, and then only on the month and day of the deceased's passing. There was no reason for having a day of remembrance every month. When standards for entry into the priesthood were correct and monks few, annual remembrance services for the deceased brought enough rice to feed the clergy. However, when standards deteriorated and the number of monks increased, rice provided from the annual memorial services was not enough to feed them. As a result, temples began monthly memorial services.

"If the old Buddhist standards were deemed correct, then monthly memorial services would be halted and there would be a return to the practices of antiquity that prevailed when the Buddha lived in the world. With fewer priests and the right standards for entry into the priesthood, monks would not be greedy. Instead, they would live by the strength of the Buddhist teachings. If there were a return to simple Buddhist practices of sitting under trees or atop boulders, wearing hemp clothing and sitting on grass-woven mats, and if the clergy fully observed the threefold training in the Buddhist precepts, mind control, and wisdom, would that not amount to a revival of Buddhism?"

Someone asked, "For many imperial princes and princesses, it appears that they would have no means of livelihood if they were not given positions as priests and nuns. The same is true for the illegitimate children of the five regent houses and the aristocracy. It does not seem right to prevent them from becoming clerics. What is your view?"

Banzan replied, "When the [great] way is practiced, even though there are many imperial princes, princesses, and illegitimate children, there will be means of providing a living for them without having them become monks and nuns. With this approach, which involves having imperial princes and princesses serve as teachers in the countryside, the customs and culture of the provinces will be uplifted. The details on this will be discussed separately, in a later chapter on who should serve as teachers for the realm."

17 Reviving Shintō

Someone asked, "How would Shintō be revived?"

Banzan replied, "What people today call Shintō, or 'the way of the deities,' amounts to nothing more than the ancient laws and teachings of shrine clergy. That, however, is not Shintō. Instead, those teachings only convey the practical rules of mental and spiritual comportment for professional clergy. That material was simply cast in rhetoric, bound as sacred scriptures, and referred to as Shintō.

"The *Chronicles of Japan*[1] has been considered the foremost scripture of Shintō, but it only skims the surface, addressing *yin* and *yang* and the great ultimate.[2] Other matters such as purification[3] do not even appear in the opening chapters of the *Chronicles of Japan* discussing the age of the gods.

---

[1] *Chronicles of Japan* (*Nihon shoki*), dating from the early eighth century, is one of the first compilations of historical and quasi-historical records narrating the supposedly legitimate and divine succession of the imperial line as well as its activities as the country's ruling regime. The opening chapters of the work trace the beginnings of the imperial line to successive generations of deities and their divine procreative activity leading to the birthing of the first emperor, Jinmu. The work presents a spiritual narrative purportedly establishing the sacred standing of the imperial line.

[2] *Yin, yang*, and the great ultimate are metaphysical notions discussed widely in East Asian thought during the Han period and thereafter. They appear in the ancient *Book of Changes*, but only became prominent in philosophical writings in Han times.

[3] The dichotomy of pollution and purification is central to Shintō thought and practice. Purification refers primarily to spiritual purification but is often symbolized in mundane ways by practices such as washing hands before going into a shrine area. Contrary to Banzan, the story of Izanagi's efforts to cleanse himself after encountering his deceased wife's corpse is an early statement of Shintō thinking about purification, and indeed appears in the opening chapters of the *Nihon shoki*.

"Writings that could truly be deemed Japan's[4] sacred literature are nowhere to be found. Instead, the three sacred treasures – the jewel, the mirror, and the sword – alone are this country's sacred texts. In remote antiquity, there were neither written words nor recorded literature. Instead, the three sacred treasures communicated symbolically the virtues of wisdom (*chi*), compassion (*jin*), and courage (*yū*). The jewel in its warmth and brilliance symbolizes compassion. The mirror's luminosity symbolizes wisdom's spiritual luminosity in distinguishing right from wrong. The sword's strength symbolizes the divine martial spirit of courage in deciding matters. The three sacred treasures are comparable, as symbols, to the line-figures used in the *Book of Changes*, that is, the eight trigrams and sixty-four hexagrams.

"Wisdom, compassion, and courage are the three utmost virtues of all below heaven.[5] The Chinese classics and their commentaries[6] explain the symbolism of the three treasures. Surely there are no sacred writings in Shintō that surpass the Chinese classics and their commentaries on this count. In explaining and analyzing the symbolism of the three treasures, no single work surpasses the *Middle Way*. The sages of China[7] and the divine rulers of Japan taught the same virtues; their ways were not different. The three treasures of Japan and the Chinese classics and commentaries are like bamboo tallies that match one another.

"The person who knows and governs the realm below heaven is a spiritual lord (*kami no aruji*). In whatever age, Shintō consists of the virtuous actions of the ruler of all below heaven in governing and bringing order to the realm, responding to human feelings, transforming things in accordance with various times, places, and circumstances, and illuminating the virtues of wisdom, compassion, and courage. Writings that record the deeds of these spiritual rulers should be considered sacred literature.

"The age of Amaterasu was one of virtuous rule. If by expanding virtuous rule we could make this an enlightened country, a revival of Shintō

---

4 Manuscript copies refer to "Japan" (*Nihon*), while the 1788 edition refers to "this country" (*honbō*), NST p. 448.

5 *Middle Way*, section 20.

6 The classics and commentaries refer to the ancient classics of Chinese Confucianism, including the *Book of History*, the *Book of Changes*, the *Book of Rituals*, the *Book of Poetry*, and the *Spring and Autumn Annals*, as well as commentaries on them. In referring to the *Middle Way*, Banzan presumably means that text as it appeared in the *Book of Rituals* as a chapter, as well as to Zhu Xi's commentary on it as one of the so-called Four Books.

7 Manuscript copies cited in the NST text refer to China as *Chūka*, while the 1788 edition, as well as other manuscript copies, state *Tōdo*, also read as *Morokoshi*, or "the land of the Tang," NST p. 448.

would be realized. We must realize that what the world now refers to as Shintō is only one aspect of Shintō, not its entirety. The way is the spiritual way of heaven and earth (*tenchi no Shintō*). The way of the sages in China[8] is the way of the divine rulers of Japan.[9] Both are expressions of the spiritual way of heaven and earth.

"In Japan,[10] the word *kami* (spiritual being or deity) is an abbreviation of the word *kagami* (mirror), minus the syllable *ga*. *Kami* thus refers to a person who exhibits luminous wisdom, just like that of a mirror. Similarly, in China the word "sage" refers to a person possessing spiritual sagacity. This spiritual nuance came to be associated with sages because they manifested spiritual luminosity. Spirits (*kami*) typically have no form but are active. People have form and behavior. Spirits do not usually manifest behavior issuing from form. Most people do not display the mysterious functioning issuing from formlessness. However, sages can combine both the spiritual and human."

Someone asked, "If you cite the *Middle Way* in explaining the three treasures of Shintō, does that not amount to suggesting that Shintō borrowed from Confucianism?"

Banzan replied, "China[11] is the country that has taught everyone within the four seas. Every country therein has taken China as a model. In ancient times, virtually everything in Japan including official ranks, titles, clothing styles, and rites and music came from China.

"Chinese written words did not spread among the southern barbarians, the western barbarians, and the northern barbarians. However, they were introduced to Japan,[12] Korea (*Chōsen*), and the Ryūkyū Islands. That is why, from antiquity, we have studied Chinese writings and made them the basis of Japanese learning.[13]

"Since ancient times, Kyoto's aristocracy has had an institution of higher education, powerful families had schools, and the provinces had academies. However, during the Warring States period, such learning

---

[8] Ibid.

[9] Manuscript copies cited in the NST text refer to "Japan" (*Nihon*), while the 1788 edition refers to "this country" (*honbō*), NST pp. 448–449.

[10] Ibid.

[11] Manuscript copies refer to China as *Chūka*, while the 1788 edition states *Tōdo* also read as *Morokoshi*, or "the land of the Tang," NST pp. 448–449.

[12] Manuscript copies refer to "Japan" (*Nihon*), while the 1788 edition refers to "this country" (*honbō*), NST pp. 448–449.

[13] Manuscript versions state "Japanese learning" (*Nihon no gaku*), while the 1788 edition states, "our country's learning" (*wagakuni no gaku*), NST pp. 448–449.

was cut off for a very long time. When samurai were worshiping Emperor Ōjin[14] as the deity of the bow and arrow at Hachiman Shrine, Confucian scholars were invited from the [Korean] Kingdom of Baekje to teach the Chinese classics and their commentaries, as well as the ethical teachings therein. Had Japan not relied on Chinese[15] characters, it never would have become enlightened in the moral way.

"Buddhists borrowed extensively from Confucianism in spreading the Buddhist way. Even though Chinese characters were never in India, Buddhists in China borrowed Chinese[16] writing and the discourse of the Song Confucian School of Principle in promoting Buddhist teachings. Today, Buddhists do not speak of these borrowings and instead see the words of Confucius and Mencius as expressions of Buddhism. Even more so, this is evident insofar as the symbolism of the three treasures of Japan is explained via the teachings about wisdom, compassion, and courage emphasized in the Confucian school's transmission of methods of mind cultivation.

"If Confucianism is taken as the foundation, we can revive Shintō without omitting anything. However, supporters of Shintō are reluctant to borrow from Confucianism. For that reason, Shintō's theoretical discussions remain narrow and its practices seem like minor arts, isolated and insignificant, lacking anything comparable to Confucianism and Buddhism. Unless a worthy ruler emerges, reviving Shintō will surely be difficult."

---

[14] A legendary emperor dating, supposedly, to the third and early fourth centuries.
[15] Manuscripts refer to China as *Chūka*, while the 1788 edition states *Tōdo*, also read as *Morokoshi*, or "the land of the Tang," NST pp. 448–449.
[16] Ibid.

18 Worthy Rulers Reviving Japan[1]

Someone asked, "If a worthy ruler sought to revive Japan today, should he take advantage of the way of Confucianism in doing so?"

Banzan replied, "Why must a ruler intent on reviving Japan choose between Buddhism and Confucianism? Compassionate government administered by a worthy ruler should cultivate the essence of both Confucianism and Buddhism. The sage emperor Yao said, 'Truly hold fast to the middle way.' Utmost goodness is realized by doing what is appropriate to the times. What Yao called 'the middle way' allows for neither selfishness nor partialities. Holding fast to the middle way consists of following the principles of heaven in doing what should be done in accordance with time, place, and social circumstances."

Someone asked, "What do you mean by 'selfishness' and 'partialities'?"

Banzan replied, "Selfishness and partialities refer to infirmities of the mind and heart that make it difficult for the shogun and the various daimyō lords to hold fast to the middle way. One such infirmity consists in promoting one's own views without taking into consideration the good points of others. A second is being ashamed of seeking advice from one's inferiors, and generally despising having to ask anyone questions. Suffering from these infirmities, a ruler will have a narrow understanding of things and remain ignorant of human feelings and social circumstances. Government measures will go awry, and people will end up grieving, suffering, and resentful. This upsets the divine luminosity of heaven

---

[1] The title for this section in the 1788 edition is "Worthy Rulers Reviving Compassionate Government." Manuscript copies in the Tokyo University Library give another title, "Worthy Rulers Reviving Japan." Here, the latter is followed. Also see the NST text, p. 449.

and earth and obstructs the creative processes of the cosmos. The way of humanity should assist the creative processes of the world. However, when these processes are obstructed, heavenly disasters and earthly calamities erupt, as do illnesses and diseases. Most egregiously, selfishness and partialities lead rulers to close channels of communication and shut out criticism. When such occurs, upheaval and chaos are not distant.

"The third infirmity consists in preferring Confucianism, or Buddhism, or Shintō to the point of being partial and one-sided. While each teaching conveys goodness, when one alone is favored with partiality, good government is harmed. Although it is said that Confucianism conveys the basics of the way of the true kings, these days Confucians simply claim that they are right, and others are wrong. Ignorant of the fullness of virtue, they only amount to a small, solitary stream conveying a petty grasp of the way. They are not capable of bringing about the profound transformations that issue from grasping great virtue.[2]

"The fourth infirmity involves relying too much on rewards and punishments. Being too rigorous and excessive in punishing people harms the generative intent of heaven and earth. It gives people no peace of mind. Nor is it good simply to reward what one likes. Worse still, some people are rewarded out of proportion to their achievements. Rulers must not be fond of rewards and punishments, nor should they think that governing the realm and bringing peace to all below heaven can be achieved simply by correctly administering rewards and punishments. Rewards and punishments should be used when there is no other choice. They are not, however, an absolute necessity in governing.

"In antiquity, the three sovereigns and five emperors[3] relied on neither rewards nor punishments. Their people took pleasure in goodness and did not know any evil. Thus the age of the three sages and five emperors was one of superlative virtue and superlative rule.

---

[2] *Middle Way*, ch. 30.
[3] Here Banzan refers to a group of figures in ancient Chinese political thought who supposedly established the beginnings of civilized society. Today, these figures are considered legendary. Nevertheless, as exemplars of humanistic, civilized leadership, the three sovereigns and five emperors played powerful roles as ideal rulers in East Asian political thought. One of the earliest listings of the three sovereigns includes (1) the sovereign of heaven, (2) the sovereign of earth, and (3) the sovereign of humanity. In another listing, the three sovereigns are (1) Fuxi, the inventor of writing, (2) Shennong, the inventor of agriculture, and (3) Nüwa, wife of Fuxi and the mother of humanity. The five emperors, by one account, include (1) the Yellow Emperor, who promoted domestic, agrarian life, (2) Zhuanxu, the inventor of the calendar, (3) Ku, inventor of music, (4) Yao, the first ruler of ancient China, and (5) Shun, the second ruler of ancient China.

"Emperor Yu of the Xia dynasty[4] punished people but did not reward them. He thus continued the superlative rule of the sage emperors, Yao and Shun, but not their superlative virtue. In Yu's day, everyone below heaven was good, so there was no need to reward anyone. Had those who excelled been rewarded, then even unselfish people might have become obsessed over profit. Soon, their profit-driven minds would have led them to wickedness. On the other hand, if even one person out of ten thousand brought upheaval to the constant, well-ordered realm, Yu would have punished them. Such was Yu's great wisdom and his practice of ruling without going to excess.

"King Tang of the Shang dynasty[5] rewarded people but did not punish them. At the end of the Xia dynasty, wicked kings brought disorder to the customs of the world and people thereby learned of malicious ways. Wicked men soon became so numerous that they could not all be punished. For that reason, when there were good men, rulers like King Tang rewarded them.

"While wicked men were set aside, the focus was not on them. Instead, King Tang made evident the practice of compassionate government by 'elevating the upright and setting aside the crooked to make the crooked straight.'[6] In later ages, that model of compassionate government was often followed. But the great way was subsequently abandoned, and rulers increasingly relied on rewards and punishments, resulting in the decline of virtue. Ever since, rulers have not assisted the spiritual work of the creative processes of things."

Someone asked, "Was not an early form of rewards and punishments evident during the time of Yao and Shun?"

Banzan replied, "There were indeed things like rewards and punishments. In ancient Japan, the practice of giving land to people of rank

[4] According to the ancient Chinese *Book of History*, Yu was the founder of the Xia dynasty. While many historians today recognize the Xia (2070–1600 BCE) as a historical line preceding the next dynasty, the Shang (1600–1046 BCE), Yu is generally viewed as a legendary figure. The *Book of History* credits him with having controlled the floodwaters of ancient China. For that reason, Shun, recognizing Yu's contributions to the betterment of the emerging polity, abdicated the throne in his favor.

[5] According to the *Book of History*, Tang founded the Shang dynasty by following heaven's decree that he overthrow Jie, the last king of the Xia dynasty, described as a debauched, inhumane ruler. While the Shang is recognized as a historically credible dynasty in ancient Chinese history, Tang is considered a legendary ruler. It is curious that Banzan states that Tang did not punish people given that it was Tang who carried out heaven's decree in overthrowing Jie.

[6] *Analects* 12/20.

and to government officials was akin to giving rewards. When people of talent were assigned rank or government positions, they received a stipend commensurate with their rank and office. While these resembled rewards, they were not actually rewards. When heaven confers rank on someone, heaven also provides them with a stipend. Those who received rank and stipend did not think of them as favors, nor were they overjoyed about them. Instead, the recipients felt even more obliged to do their work. On the other hand, the sons of dukes, lords, nobles, and grandees who, foolish and unworthy, could not correct their mistakes, recognize their errors, and govern their people, were reduced to commoner status and made to work as farmers, artisans, and merchants. Although such practices resembled punishments, they were not punishments.

"The fifth infirmity is the love of material things and the love of passion. The passion of a common rustic for material things only benefits one person. When the shogun and daimyō of the realm are as fond of material things as are common rustics, then they acquire and waste things unreasonably, which is the root of disorder in the realm. People covet material things for themselves because they have small-minded desires. Compassionate rulers are fond of material things magnificently, for the greater good. Once the realm below heaven has initiated the grand project for growing wealth, it will be pleased with a compassionate ruler's fondness for material things. A compassionate ruler can thus enhance his standing in the realm by means of material goods.

"There is also a way for loving women. There have been rulers whose love for only one woman brought down their realm. There have also been rulers who loved ten women and yet did no harm to their polity. The Tang dynasty emperor, Xuanzong (685–762), was a ruler who loved only one woman, but nevertheless brought his country to ruin. He loved Yang Guifei (719–756), and soon his favors were also extended to her cousin, Yang Guozhong (d. 756). Xuanzong's misguided trust in Yang Guozhong brought ruin to the realm below heaven.[7]

[7] The first half of the reign of the Tang dynasty emperor, Xuanzong (685–762), was reportedly one of diligent rule. It was followed, however, by a disastrous second half, during which Xuanzong came to be obsessed with a female beauty, Yang Guifei. As a result of his neglect of imperial rule in favor of his passion for Yang Guifei, Xuanzong's reign ended with the rebellion of a Tang general, An Lushan, and the destruction of Changan, the capital of the Tang dynasty. Yang Guifei's cousin, Yang Guozhong, the chancellor during Xuanzong's later years, was blamed by many for the An Lushan Rebellion. Guozhong's elevation was a function of Xuanzong's infatuation with Yang Guifei, not Guozhong's talents for governing. Both Yang Guifei and Yang Guozhong were executed as Xuanzong and his entourage fled Changan escaping the armies of An Lushan.

"According to the correct way, a ruler should love one woman, but should not extend his passion to her relatives. A ruler's favors should stop with the one woman he loves. When there are poor relations, some kindness might be provided by a ruler acting as a private individual. Immoral relatives should not be allowed stipends so that they can live in luxury.

"A ruler does not have to be a sage or worthy to bring peace and order to the realm below heaven. Even if a ruler thinks like a commoner in his fondness for material things and sexual pleasure, if he also has a compassionate mind as the father and mother of his people and can thereby implement compassionate government, employ exceptional people, and assist in the creative processes of the ten thousand things, then he can indeed be a compassionate ruler. By fulfilling the responsibilities of his heaven-decreed work, the ruler will receive heaven's rewards for a very long time.

"The sixth infirmity relates to how men are chosen for official posts. One way involves selecting from a designated pool composed of a specific number of men. Yet when the pool is narrow, it might be difficult to find a suitable person. Unless one makes exceptions, including allowing for a broader, unlimited number of applicants, then worthies, men of ability, and men of talent will be hard to find. That is the meaning of the saying that one should look for worthies among the people at large.

"Governing the realm and bringing peace to all below heaven involves finding the right people. Everyone knows this, but still it is difficult to put into practice. Is this because there are few men who have a compassionate heart and think in terms of serving as the father and mother of their people or is it that they fall into the common ways of ordinary sorts and then lack the courage to respond with passion and do the right thing?

"These are the basic points regarding how Japan should be revived. Now is the time for initiating the grand project for growing wealth in the realm. Now is indeed the time for a worthy ruler to revive Japan. In this, if only a tenth of what the ancients did were accomplished, the consequences would be ten times as great. Everything discussed above concerns reviving Japan. I will now address governing with education."

19 Governing with Education

Someone asked, "Schools are places for learning and culture. What do you mean by 'governing with education'?"

Banzan replied, "Schools are places where people are taught the way of humanity. Governing the realm and bringing peace to all below heaven are based on correcting the mind and heart [in accordance with the way of humanity]. Teaching the way of humanity and correcting the mind and heart should thus be the priority for those in government. If the shogun, in following the way of humanity as taught in the schools, appreciated the daimyō lords of the realm, then their minds and hearts would submit to him just as sons do to fathers. This is the work of schools.

"A schoolmaster should be a man of virtue who clearly understands the principles of things. Under his guidance, those of broad learning and accomplished virtue would lecture on the Chinese classics and their commentaries. The shogun would lead his elder ministers, daimyō, and upper and middle samurai in lectures, discussions, and debates. One incisive remark on virtue by the shogun would surpass a thousand, even ten thousand words by all others, and would move the minds and will-power of daimyō and samurai into action. When communicated to the provinces, the shogun's words would elicit the intrinsically good mind of the masses. His flowing virtue would quicken goodness faster than express couriers transmitting orders.

"Even sages and worthies, when relegated to lowly station, can only bring about few benefits. And it is difficult for daimyō to achieve but so much. For this reason, sages view men of high rank as a great treasure.[1]

---

[1] *Book of Changes*, "The Great Treatise," part II (*Xici*), section 1.

'Men of high rank' are leaders such as the shogun. A sage cannot transform all below heaven unless he has gained access to a person of that rank. Even if a shogun is neither virtuous nor worthy and still has not escaped the vulgar lot, his compassionate mind as the father and mother of the people and his reverence for the way and virtue provide him, as shogun, with an ethical charisma and power that enables him to transform the realm. When the shogun gains a teacher who has mastered the methods of the mind,[2] then he, as the great ruler, will reflect inward [to realize his virtuous power]. Although there have been rulers in Japan and China fond of reading and writing, because none have practiced, internally, the methods of the mind, they have been unable to benefit the realm greatly."

Someone asked, "Are schools only concerned with matters such as teaching the way of humanity and correcting the mind?"

Banzan replied, "Those are the most important concerns of schools. But schools should also have students study cultural and military subjects. Yet in keeping with human sentiments and the circumstances of our day, samurai who are already thirty or forty years old will no longer be expected to attend school.

"At ages eight to nine, the sons of samurai should begin school and first be taught matters easy to master. They should learn to write, for example, one word per day. Learning to write is easy if the teacher is skillful with the brush. Lessons in propriety should include comportment in relations with one's father and elder brothers, one's elders, and hosts and guests. Students should learn how to serve others, enter and exit, welcome people and bid them farewell, receive and respond to messages, as well as other such forms of etiquette.

"From ages eleven to twelve, students will be introduced to reading the Chinese classics and their commentaries. They should be taught one phrase per day. For example, the sentence, 'The way of great learning consists in illuminating luminous virtue, loving the people, and dwelling in ultimate goodness,'[3] should be taught in four days. Afterwards, learning should proceed at this pace. Reading should not be made difficult. At

---

[2] "Methods of the mind" (*shinbō*) could be interpreted in relation to Buddhism as well as Confucianism. Here, most certainly Banzan refers to the notion as he understood it in relation to Wang Yangming's teachings. The same notion, however, was an integral part of Zhu Xi's teachings about correcting the mind. With Confucians – including followers of Zhu Xi and Wang Yangming – methods of the mind were preparatory to governing.

[3] This quotation of the opening line of the *Great Learning* is one of the few direct, overt allusions to that text in Banzan's *Responding to the Great Learning*.

this stage, students should be taught so that they will want to read more. Students who are eight to nine years old who have not yet learned to read might naturally benefit from listening to others read.

"Reading and writing should be taught on alternating days. Because exercises in propriety help relieve tensions that develop when learning to read and write, students who are thirteen to fourteen years old should be taught the most important aspects of propriety on the same day as reading and writing so that they gradually come to learn, one after the next, how to receive and deliver a sword, how to convey official messages, how to serve as an envoy, how to serve as an emissary, how to present a report, and how to deliver an oral report. They should also be taught how to handle a bow and arrow, a saddle, stirrups, and how to ford a river. Additionally, they should be taught how to behave as host and guest during a 7-5-3 course banquet and a 5-5-3 course meal. One can infer the rest of the curriculum from this.

"Music should be taught on other days. Students from ages eight to nine through those ages eleven to twelve should be taught to chant following sheet music for the flute, the double-reed flute, and the free-reed flute. They should learn from a musically talented instructor who can teach ten to twenty students at a time. From ages twelve to thirteen forward, they should be taught the three kinds of flutes individually. Of the string instruments, the harp (*koto*) should be taught first. Students ages eight to nine who listen to music will, in years to come, naturally reap the benefits.

"From ages fourteen to fifteen, students should be taught archery and horsemanship. Archery should be taught early on with a soft bamboo bow, and horsemanship should begin with a wooden horse, with instruction focusing on how to mount and dismount, how to saddle, and how to use the bridle and reins. After such techniques have been taught, students should ride a calm horse, at a moderate pace, so that they do not fall off. When archery and horsemanship are taught according to their respective ways, students should attain proficiency quickly.

"After mastering archery and horsemanship, students should, first, be taken on long rides in the spring. Students should not shoot arrows while mounting, dismounting, or riding a horse. Unless they are well accustomed to shooting them, bows are difficult for students to manage. Summer is the best time for riding a horse through water. Both horse and rider must learn how to swim before they go into water or cross a stream. Good samurai are often lost in battle while crossing a river on horseback.

"Autumn is the best time for training a horse. Riders should not over-burden their horse's legs, nor force them on challenging trails. Instead, while training a horse, riders should pay attention to the horse's breathing. Winter is a good time for keeping a horse well fed. During the eleventh and twelfth lunar months while hunting wild game, students should become proficient in horseback archery. However, simply rounding up animals for a hunt – a practice that developed in recent generations – is not very beneficial. This involves driving animals down from the mountains into an expansive area so that the horseback-samurai can make his kill. Also, students should learn to hunt deer and fowl with bow and arrows. Hunting these animals is best done on foot. This summarizes the basic curriculum for horsemanship and archery.

"By putting their minds to it, students can gradually learn arithmetic at home in their leisure time when they have long stretches of time, either during the day or at night, when they can focus on it. They should also study it in school.

"From ages fifteen to sixteen, students should attend school lectures about the ethical principles and literary import of the books they read. Around age twenty, students should be reading books on their own and asking their teachers about unclear passages they have noted. Those students who have already learned to read should teach those who have not. Gradually, this would be beneficial for both the student-teacher and the beginning student. And moreover, the master teacher would not be overworked.

"For instruction in the martial arts, there should be a teacher with advanced proficiency in that field. Unless the teacher is proficient, the students will not make progress. The techniques for using the long sword, the pike, and firearms would be taught among other subjects. With firearms, students should be introduced to target practice. However, they should not fire at birds or deer. If birds and deer are killed off with firearms, then hunting expeditions, by which samurai maintain solid physical training in archery, would be compromised.

"Samurai educated in this way from age eight to age thirty will become proficient in cultural and martial arts and equipped with learning useful for governing provincial domains and commanding armies. Some will grasp moral issues and others will develop other excellent talents and capabilities. There will be no lack of people capable of governing the realm and all below heaven. Even parents who never themselves had a chance to learn will find their hearts at peace upon seeing that their children have learning in moral and technical ways. Moreover, [exposed to their children's learning] they will not be confused by crude discussions of moral principles. Those who never had the chance to learn despite being clever at birth will, even as elder students, quickly grasp the classics. Youths who have studied will eventually become parents who, with age, can teach others. As youths, they should learn to be obedient and respectful; as mature adults, they should be active; as seniors, they should teach. Within fifty years, we would be a country of refined princes (*kunshi*). Would this not amount to a revival of Japan?"

Someone asked, "What standards of ritual behavior should be established?"

Banzan replied, "Those from the samurai estate who understand the way and appreciate human sentiments and contemporary circumstances should see to it that rituals and matters of etiquette are set forth. They should work with others who are broadly learned in matters related to Japan and China. Together, they should draft dozens of articles on ritual behavior. The shogun along with his elder ministers, upper-level samurai, middle samurai, and lower-level samurai should discuss and analyze the proposed rituals in terms of their advantages and disadvantages. The shogun and his ministers in charge of rituals should then produce a white paper outlining principles to be set forth. Still, heed should be given to various rules and human feelings prevalent within the provinces, their differences and similarities. Also, the valuable opinions of worthies and talented persons should be heard regarding the advantages and disadvantages of the proposed rituals and forms of etiquette. Within fifty years, this would bring about a minor transformation in the behavior of the world. Within five hundred years, a major transformation would have come about.

"Some of the ancient rituals could still be practiced, but others should not be. Rituals and etiquette are not laws. With laws, it is best to keep their number low. The founder of the Han dynasty, Han Gaozu, only recognized three laws,[4] but thereby brought order to the world below heaven. If rituals are carefully established, the world will achieve undisturbed centrality and those of high and low birth will live in peace. People who disobey laws should be punished, but those who turn their backs

---

[4] Han Gaozu reportedly abolished the many punitive laws of the Qin dynasty. His opposition to the inhumane legalism of the Qin was supposedly one of the reasons the Han dynasty won the support of the Chinese population.

on rituals should not be. Instead, they should be put to shame. If they are brought to shame time and again, they will find it difficult to face other people. Thus, even without punishments, peace and order could be realized."

Someone asked, "Are there rituals from antiquity that might still be used today?"

Banzan replied, "When a ruler sends a gift to a minister, the minister should bow before the bearer of the gift upon receiving it. When the bearer of the gift leaves, the minister should accompany him to the inner side of the front gate. After the bearer of the gift has returned, the minister should go to the ruler's residence and bow in gratitude personally for the gift.

"When a great minister sends a gift to a samurai, the samurai should bow upon receiving it. The samurai should accompany the bearer of the gift to the door as the latter departs. The samurai need not go to the great minister's residence to bow in appreciation. If the bearer of the gift arrives when the samurai is not at home and leaves a gift for him, then the samurai should go to the great minister's residence to bow as an expression of his gratitude for it.

"When someone calls on a sick person or offers condolences upon another's passing, these should be reciprocated when appropriate. A ritual expression of gratitude for the visit is not needed. When one is visited for propriety's sake, then one should return the visit for propriety's sake as well. When gifts are given for propriety's sake, the same should be done in return. Gifts given as an expression of a person's sense of purpose need not be matched by another.

"When a family receives gifts for a family member's coming of age ceremony or wedding, they should respond in kind for the family of the giver when the occasion arises. Virtuous people should respond to gifts given them by others with gracious words. Wealthy people should help others by giving of their resources. The aged should not strain themselves to repay gifts. The poor do not need to repay material gifts given.

"When one receives a visit from a person who has been out of touch for a long time, one should call on them, after an interval. If someone calls at one's house but no one is there, one should go to visit the caller and bow in appreciation. If those who made the first call are not at home when the visit of appreciation is made, there is no need to go again. Nor need one send a messenger. When one goes to visit someone, but they are not home, one need not make a return visit. If one is asked to agree to visit on another day, then one may do so.

"According to ritual propriety, offers, invitations, and proposals should only be extended three times.[5] The first time, if the other person declines, they are being polite. If they decline a second time, they are being definite. If they decline a third time, that should be considered final. When a host treats a guest politely and offers the guest an appropriate seat, the guest should initially decline. That is a polite decline. When the host politely offers again, the guest should take the seat without declining. However, if the guest declines again, they are being definite. When the host strongly insists on propriety, the guest should not decline. If the guest has reasons and declines a third time, that should be considered the final declination. Without insisting further, the host should take a seat inferior to that offered the guest. When a seat that should be taken is declined with finality, that does not follow propriety. Declining with finality when one should accept is embarrassing for the host.

"The same applies when one declines gifts or an official stipend. When there are reasons not to accept something, then one should decline with finality. When something is presented that one should accept, then one should not decline a third time. The rest can be inferred from this.

"If rituals and propriety are established, protocol for behavior can be set forth in minute detail. Some daimyō families have kept records of rituals and forms of propriety used in Kamakura times. Among them are some that might be used even today. Kamakura period daimyō were, for example, divided into three groups with each group attending the shogun in his capital once every three years. Other than the agricultural seasons, proximity to the shogun's capital determined their rotation. They were scheduled so that everyone would not be on the road at the same time. Nor were they supposed to be in a rush to arrive. While in their domains, daimyō were supposed to send a messenger once a year to deliver a present to the shogun, such as a long sword rather than horses as were given during the Muromachi shogunate.

"These messengers generally arrived in the shogun's capital during the first lunar month. Messengers from the colder provinces left their home provinces during the second month or perhaps at the beginning of the third month. Travel typically took a specified number of days.

---

5 *Book of Rituals*, "The Significance of Ceremonial Drinking in the Districts" (*Xiang yin jiu yi*).

Messengers from the daimyō of the five provinces around Kyoto arrived in Kamakura in eleven or twelve days. For those who encountered flooding along the way or sickness, a late arrival was no cause for worry. However, arrival days in advance of their expected time was not permitted. If difficulties were encountered along the way, they extended their travel time. The extension was based on how near or far they were.

"When Kamakura ritual protocol was established, every single matter was recorded in minute detail. Generally, messengers traveled around 9, 10, or 11 *ri* (1 *ri* = 3.9 km/2.4 miles) in one day, or, in some cases, 7 or 8 *ri*. Express couriers covered 12 to 15 *ri* per day. This was based on figuring 1 *ri* as 36 *chō* (1 *chō* = 109 m/357.6 ft).

"Envoys sent by daimyō were not allowed to make more than one trip per year. If there were a reason for doing so, guidance would come from the shogunate. If an envoy were sent when there was no reason for doing so, it was viewed as groveling, and a clear violation of propriety.

"Major lords were allowed to send express couriers to Kamakura once a month to inquire about the well-being of the shogun and to report on circumstances in the provinces. Middle-level lords were permitted to do this once every two months, and lesser lords, once every three to five months. Couriers did not go directly to the shogunate, but instead to vassals of the shogun who understood the circumstances.

"Subsequently, because envoys and express couriers were permitted to arrive late but were not warned against arriving too quickly, they began speeding to and from the shogun's capital as though they were carrying news of major misfortune and disorder in the realm. As there were no prohibitions against doing so, messengers were sent to the shogun's capital more and more frequently. As messengers became faster and more frequent, sending them caused distress and poverty for some domains. Many messengers also ended up falling ill, while others died prematurely.

"In ancient times, those of high and low birth were distinguished by the colors of their garments. They were not distinguished on the basis of the cost of their clothing. Among the people of high birth, some were poor. Among those of low birth, some were wealthy. The homes, furnishings, and wardrobes of the wealthy were beautiful. Court attire for samurai and those above was black with red trim. Townspeople, foot-soldiers, and footmen did not, therefore, wear black. Nowadays, however, black is even worn by mid-level pages. White attire was only worn by people with official court positions and rank.

"If ritual attire including caps, ceremonial robes, and formal divided skirts were revived, no one would note whether the undergarments were beautiful or unsightly. Simplicity should inform matters of ritual attire. For samurai, one small sword would suffice, whether at home or in public. When circumstances required it, a large sword might be worn in addition to a small sword. A short sword with a round scabbard tip could be worn by townspeople, footmen, and people of lower status. If there were cause for such, townspeople, foot-soldiers, and foot men could carry a large sword. However, those of lowly status should only be allowed the short sword.

"When ritual propriety prevails, status accoutrements need not be numerous. Things should be simple, not to mention frugal. The fundamental purpose of ritual propriety is that the world be at peace and those of high and low birth live long lives with ease, generation after generation."

20 Those Who Should Teach in Our Schools

Someone asked, "If only those who are committed, mind and heart, to Buddhism and practicing the threefold training in the precepts, mind control, and wisdom, may enter the priesthood, what will become of imperial princes and sons of the aristocracy? Few are likely, from the very depths of their hearts, to choose the path of Buddhism. What, then, might they do?"

Banzan replied, "If the [great] way were practiced throughout the realm, there would be options for imperial princes and the sons and daughters of the aristocracy even if they did not want to become Buddhists. Indeed, there would be plenty of opportunities for them.

"At one point during the upheaval of the Warring States period, the imperial court and aristocracy were not receiving land tribute and so many aristocrats ended up in the countryside seeking support. I have heard that among them was one[1] who envisioned the following:

> Hopefully, the person who unifies the realm below heaven and becomes shogun will appreciate the study of the Confucian way. Otherwise, if the schools that once existed in Kyoto and the provinces were revived, there would surely not be enough teachers for them. Even the Ashikaga school,[2] which has barely survived over the centuries, had to rely on Buddhist monks for teachers because there were no others. However, Buddhists should not oversee schools that teach ethics.

[1] Here, Banzan is apparently referring to Ichijō Kaneyoshi (1402–1481). During the Ōnin War, he fled Kyoto to live in Nara with his son, the abbot at the Kōfukuji.

[2] The Ashikaga School, one of the oldest in Japan, was known for its focus on Confucianism and Chinese learning. Its name comes from the village, Ashikaga, where it began, now in Tochigi Prefecture.

In order to provide teachers for the provinces, schools in Kyoto should first educate imperial princes and the sons of the aristocracy before assigning them hereditary rank and office. The same goes for the sons of commoners: everyone should be enrolled in a school. Students should first study literature and music. The sons of musicians and the sons of clergy should be allowed in schools to serve the imperial princes and sons of the aristocracy meals and work as their pageboys. The shogunate would cover the cost of their schooling. While studying, everyone would sit together in the same classroom. Music would be a good subject for them to learn together.

From the ranks of the student body, the most compassionate and virtuous of the imperial princes would be elevated in imperial rank as heir to the throne. Of the sons of the aristocracy, those with the most talent and wisdom would eventually be appointed heads of their families. Those talented in literature and music would be sent out to the provinces.

The imperial princes sent into the provinces would be given a rank corresponding to that of the children of regents and ministers of state. The children of regents would be assigned rank corresponding to the aristocracy. With their office and rank thus lowered, these former princes and high-born progeny would become guest-instructors of the domains to which they were assigned.

Large domains should be able to provide 2,000 *koku* for living expenses; a mid-sized domain would allot 1,500 *koku*; and the next could budget 1,000 *koku*. A small domain might offer 500 *koku* in living expenses. Would it not be possible even for domains with incomes of approximately 10,000 *koku* to combine resources to attract a teacher?

Domains with incomes totaling 100,000 *koku* or more should be able to support a school with a guest-teacher, as well as sons of musicians and clergy to help teach music and literature. A large domain could also support five or six assistants, while mid-sized domains might support four or five, and small domains, two or three assistants. And, fiefs would be granted to the teachers to provide for their income.

Imperial princesses and the daughters of the aristocracy should marry imperial princes who become guest-teachers in the provinces. Their standing as imperial princes serving as guest-teachers would be limited to one generation. Their sons would become commoners who might later serve as elementary school teachers in the domains or, if talented, as domain officials.

Teachers for the domain schools should be brought in regularly from the imperial capital. If this were done, the customs of the domains would become more genteel, rid of vulgarities. Rulers of the domains would benefit once proper rites and music were practiced since the latter would tend to preempt bad behavior.

Instructors who attained the very highest degree of excellence would serve as guest-teachers for the shogun, receiving his patronage. They would be known as teachers of the realm. It would be wrong to have Buddhist priests serve in this capacity as was the practice of the Ashikaga shogunate.

Because samurai are retainers serving for the sake of the shogun, they are bound by strict rules of propriety, making it difficult for them to speak their minds. However, since members of the aristocracy would be treated as guests of the shogun, much good would issue if learned and talented aristocrats served as the shogun's teachers, and those with talents in music served as his music tutors. Because daimyō lords are the rulers of their domains, everyone in their domains serves them. However, if the rulers of the domains invited sons of the aristocracy to serve as guest-teachers in the domain schools, they would get along amiably.

This man's reasoning is on target.

"Virgin princesses should serve at the Ise and Kamo Shrines. However, this practice ended during the Warring States period and was not resumed thereafter. After samurai reunified the realm, there was an inquiry into the cost necessary for reviving this practice. The response of the nobility was that anything less than 30,000 *koku* would be insufficient. But at that time, the imperial house only had 30,000 *koku* in fiefs. Deemed too expensive, the practice of having virgin princesses serve at the Ise and Kamo Shrines was not resumed. However, the response of the nobility was comparable to a musician trying to fix a harp and ending up 'gluing the strings to the bridge.'[3] The ignorance of some court nobles regarding human feelings and circumstances seems akin to this nearly every time. Yet when practices that were once commonplace, such as that of the service of the virgin princesses, no longer are, it is not easy to bring them back.

"Today, 30,000 *koku* would be as much as the income of one of the five home provinces such as Izumi or Kawachi during the age of impe-

---

[3] *Shiji* 81: "Biography of Lian Po and Lin Xiangru." Movement of the bridge enables a stringed instrument such as a *koto* to produce a range of harmonies. In gluing the strings of the *koto* to the bridge, the musician, in attempting to fix the instrument, leaves it in worse shape than before. Banzan suggest that the nobility, in asking for such extravagant support for vestal virgins, is making their service even more unlikely than ever.

rial rule. During the imperial age, the five provinces provided enough income for the imperial line to govern all below heaven. If the cost of imperial princesses serving at the Ise Shrine had exhausted the tribute of one entire province, how could the imperial line have brought order to the ten thousand things of the realm below heaven? What required 30,000 *koku* in tribute in ancient times can be done for 3,000 *koku* today. Despite the cost, in the imperial age the expense was indeed covered so that princesses could serve at these shrines.

"Today, 3,000 *koku* should suffice to maintain the virgin princesses. Since half would be paid in taxes, 1,500 *koku* would remain for their support. For samurai, such an amount would suffice to support twenty young samurai, twenty laborers, five horses, ten pages – in all, approximately fifty men. In the inner chambers, these funds could also support ten or fifteen women. Also, a samurai could support his father and mother, wife and children, and have enough for service rendered in the shogun's capital.

"Virgin princesses do not need so many men and horses. It would suffice for each princess to have three ladies-in-waiting, one of upper standing, one middle, and one lower. Each would also need two or three senior-age servants, and four of five subordinate servants. In addition, each would need seven or eight lady-musicians and three percussionists whose purpose would be to perform music and thereby appease the deities. Three lady officials who were daughters of the aristocracy would play the flute, the *biwa*, and the zither. In addition, each would need an older woman knowledgeable in literature and poetry to teach matters related to Japanese and Chinese topics, as well as ethical principles.

"If 3,000 *koku* in land produce, or a net tribute of 1,500 *koku* were deemed a sufficient allotment, the service of imperial princesses at the Ise Shrine could be revived. Because the Ise Shrine enshrines Japan's great progenitor and the Kamo Shrine enshrines the first progenitors, it stands to reason that the practice of having imperial princesses serve at those shrines should not be abandoned."

21 A Little Kindness Provides Benefits

Someone asked, "The grand project for growing wealth that you explained earlier is an enormous undertaking. Such an initiative might be difficult to realize any time soon even if compassionate government, itself a rarity in history, were achieved. Yet for the sake of the present, is there not something that might be done to make life better even if it does not fully prepare the realm for a coming invasion by the northern barbarians?"

Banzan replied, "Even with the recent abundant harvests, those of high rank and low as well as the samurai and common people have suffered extreme poverty. When the harvest is good, farmers cannot make ends meet because the price of rice ends up plummeting. In bad years, when the price of rice rises, it brings no benefit to farmers because they have so little to sell. For daimyō and their retainers, things are much the same.

"A middle-sized domain will send, in fair to poor years, 30,000 *koku* of rice to Osaka to be sold. If, however, in years of abundant harvests, the same domain had a yield of 50,000 *koku* and, in anticipation of bad years, sent 30,000 *koku* to Osaka to be sold, it could store up 20,000 *koku* for defense against the northern barbarians as well as famine in years of crop failure. Domains should manage their resources in this way. To facilitate this, the price of 1 *koku* of rice could possibly be set at 50 units of silver. Prices might, on occasion, rise slightly higher.

"Currently, 50 units of silver for 1 *koku* of rice is a fair, average price. If that were set, then samurai and those below them would never face hardships. However, as has been the case in recent years, plans for storage of surplus rice have been of no benefit because rice must be sold quickly to keep hardships from ensuing. If, however, rice had a fixed value just like the unit of silver, with the price for 1 *koku* set at 50 units of silver, it could be used, without issue, in all transactions, as a form of currency, for small purchases as well as for paying interest on loans or paying for dry goods.

"If high and low were living well and loan repayments extended, daimyō would then provide lenders with only as much rice payment as the lenders needed. In order to pay interest on a loan of 10,000 *koku* with silver, selling 1,000 *koku* of rice should suffice. If the remaining 9,000 *koku* were valued at a rate of 50 units of silver per *koku*, that amount of rice would be sufficient even to cover the costs of alternate attendance in Edo today.

"In Edo and Osaka, the price of rice could be set at between 50 and 60 units of silver. If it went up to 61 units, it should be sold down to 59. If it fell to 49, it should be bought up to 51. Rice shops would make their profits in the 10-unit margin as the price of 1 *koku* fluctuated between 50 and 60 units of silver. If shogunal granaries and daimyō granaries took turns buying and selling rice to adjust the price, there would be no problems in maintaining it. If this approach resulted in problems, they could be resolved easily enough.

"If the price of 1 *koku* of rice went much beyond 50 units of silver, it might become too high for rōnin and those living day-to-day. Yet if all samurai tried their best and helped their relatives and close friends, this should be easy to fix. When those living day-to-day, as well as the samurai and the common people are all doing well, the artisans and merchants will also do well. When employment is high, prices will rise a little which is, to an extent, acceptable. Things will, of course, differ according to the household. However, if the price of rice rises above 60 units of silver, that would be excessively high for many and so some people would end up starving.

"By controlling the price of rice as described above through storage of the surplus and buying and selling as prices escalate or decline, the price of rice should not exceed 60 units even during years of bad harvests. Is not this approach better than leaving things as they are and then suffering distress and poverty while ultimately facing the prospect of upheaval?

"Admittedly, the proposed ad hoc measures do not address the circumstances of rōnin, vagrants, and the helpless. Nor do they settle the debts of samurai, farmers, artisans, and merchants. Nor do they provide sufficiently for defense against the northern barbarians. Indeed, the proposed measures hardly approximate the far grander benefits of compassionate government."

22 Wasted Rice and Grain

Someone asked, "Earlier you discussed the grand project for growing wealth and other measures to be undertaken in good years to provide against bad years. While this and that might be done, if this year the seasons were irregular and the grain harvest meager, then the supply of rice in the provinces would be reduced as well. In some places, depending on the circumstances, there might seem to be plenty. But if the price of rice suddenly rose, would not many face hunger and starvation? The rōnin population has apparently doubled over the last decade. On top of the extreme distress and poverty endured by the various estates of the realm, might some upheaval be in the offing as well? This is indeed troubling. Are there not measures that might be taken to alleviate the problems facing the present generation?"

Banzan replied, "If we encountered a succession of bad years, it would indeed be difficult to realize compassionate government and the grand project for growing wealth. And it would be even more difficult to help anyone during a time of upheaval.

"Yet what if abundant harvests and plummeting prices continued for another five or six years? If we calculated, in currency, the amount of rice that would be wasted during that period, then for a daimyō with a fief valued at 100,000 *koku* – and a net income of 50,000 *koku* based on 50 percent tribute – the loss would be:

1,000 units of silver lost by the daimyō and his retainers,

2,000 units of silver lost in farm villages,

500 units of silver lost in the castle town.

Total loss: 3,500 units of silver.

Over a five-year period, the total loss would be 17,500 units of silver. For daimyō with incomes over 100,000 *koku*, more and more of their annual tribute tax would end up lost to waste. The waste at shogunal granaries would be even worse.

"Lower-ranking retainers would end up wasting rice in proportion to their stipends. Those with a 100-*koku* fief paying 40 percent tribute annually would lose 10 *ryō* (approx. 41–42 g) in gold annually. For the holder of a 1,000-*koku* fief, the loss would be 100 *ryō*. Over five years, this would come to a loss of 500 *ryō*. The various daimyō, their retainers, and the shogun's lower retainers would end up hard pressed as well. Losses in urban areas would be similar.

"The misery and suffering of rōnin and vagrants would be unspeakable. Yet if governmental administrative measures assisted the creative processes of the cosmos in working with the seasons by buying and selling rice to maintain supplies and prices, there would be no such waste and people would be well provided for. But no one is discussing administrative measures necessary for our times, and so waste brings distress and poverty to everyone in the realm below heaven."

Someone asked, "If that is so, then the losses suffered by the various provincial domains are surely enormous. There must be an incalculable amount of gold and silver lost. Surely the domains do not have such quantities of gold and silver to lose."

Banzan replied, "Japan's total debt is more than one hundred times the amount of its gold. For that reason the extent of the loss is so egregious."

Someone asked, "In bad years, people say that it is difficult to do anything. Yet rather than simply continue along and wait for turmoil and disorder, are there measures the government might take to preempt upheaval?"

Banzan replied, "The measures that might preempt disorder include having daimyō use rice as currency in transactions in their domains, setting the value of rice at a fixed rate just as a unit of silver has a fixed value, and conducting business transactions without preferring gold and silver over rice. As noted previously, if the period for debt repayment were extended, saké brewing stopped, Edo's population reduced, frantic travel ceased, rice shipping cut, and waste in general minimized, would not things improve somewhat?

"Because upheavals are often hard to forecast, it is difficult to discuss them much in advance. Even in setting the price of rice, although we may say that it should be 50 units of silver on average, with a bad year circumstances will differ so that unless 1 *koku* could rise to 55 units of silver on average, then things might not go well. Measures initiated after the eighth or ninth lunar months just before the rice harvest might help prevent upheaval, but if things were delayed until mid-winter, that is, well after the harvest, then regardless of the ruler's concerns, the same measures would not be easy to put into practice.

"How much worse would things be if bad years continued and the price of rice rose to 70 or 80 units of silver per *koku*? Unlike a few years ago when the price rose to 80 and 90 units per *koku*, there would be, given today's strained circumstances, even more cause for concern about the welfare of the people and the possibility of upheaval. Many would soon regret having sold rice cheaply during years of abundance.

"Instead of allowing rice to be sold for 30–40 units of silver per *koku* as occurred during the five to six years of prior abundant harvests, the price should be fixed at 50–60 units of silver per *koku* and the surplus accumulated. If that were done, then even if bad years came and continued for three to five years, the price of rice would never again rise to 70 or 80 units. The way of assisting the creative processes of the world is realized when people of talent store abundance to supplement shortages. Time and again, measures that should have been followed were not. As a result, shogunal vassals, daimyō, retainers, farmers, and townspeople have fallen into strained circumstances while rōnin, Buddhists, and vagrants multiplied.

"Although they did not have sage rulers and worthies as did the three dynasties of antiquity, the Han, the Tang, the Song, and the Ming dynasties continued for three or four hundred years each because they entrusted the prime minister's position to worthy and capable men, enacted policies addressing the urgent needs of their times and followed ethical approaches in doing so. The prime minister was a man who embodied a basic talent for governing. While a basic talent for governing is the premier talent of all below heaven, without virtue, it is useless. Although it need not be the spiritual virtue of sages and worthies, the virtue of the prime minister must consist of being pleased to heed criticism, admonishments, and good counsel."

Bibliography

Primary Sources, Including Modern Editions

Akiyama Kōdō. *Bokenroku.* Edited by Narita Genbi. Okayama: Okayama ken, 1901. A digital version is available in the Kokuritsu kokkai toshokan dejitaru korekushon at http://dl.ndl.go.jp/info:ndljp/pid/781327.

Chan, Wing–tsit, translator. *A Source Book in Chinese Philosophy.* Princeton, NJ: Princeton University Press, 1963.

Hara Nensai. "Kumazawa Banzan." In Minamoto Ryōen and Maeda Tsutomu, eds., *Sentetsu sōdan*, Tōyō bunko, vol. 574. Tokyo: Heibonsha, 1994.

Hayashi Razan. *Razan sensei bunshū*, vol. 2. Kyoto: Heian kōkogakkai, 1918.

Itō Jinsai. *Daigaku teihon.* 1685 woodblock edition. https://kotenseki.nijl.ac.jp/biblio/100160961/viewer/30?ln=en.

Kumazawa Banzan. *Banzan zenshū*, edited by Masamune Atsuo. 5 vols. Tokyo: Banzan zenshū kankōkai, 1940–1943.

Chūyō shōkai. Woodblock edition. Publisher unknown. No date of publication. https://www.wul.waseda.ac.jp/kotenseki/html/ro12/ro12_01576/index.html.

Daigaku shōkai. Bukō (Edo), Nihonbashi minami: Sugiura Saburobei, publisher. Undated. https://www.wul.waseda.ac.jp/kotenseki/html/ro12/ro12_00009/index.html.

Daigaku wakumon. In Gotō Yōichi and Tomoeda Ryūtarō, eds. *Kumazawa Banzan.* Nihon shisō taikei (NST), vol. 30. Tokyo: Iwanami shoten, 1971.

Daigaku wakumon. Nakamura Naomichi manuscript, dated 1815. https://archive.wul.waseda.ac.jp/kosho/io4/io4_00775/io4_00775_0188/io4_00775_0188.pdf.

Daigaku wakumon. In Nishida Taichirō, ed. *Fujiwara Seika, Nakae Tōju, Kumazawa Banzan, Yamazaki Ansai, Yamaga Sokō, Yamagata Daini shū.* Tokyo: Chikuma shobō, 1970.

Daigaku wakumon. Osaka: Sūkōdō, 1788. https://kotenseki.nijl.ac.jp/biblio/100209409/viewer/7?ln=en.

Daigaku wakumon. Undated manuscript, including notes throughout in red ink. https://kotenseki.nijl.ac.jp/biblio/200018535/viewer/85?ln=en. DOI 10.20730/200018535.

Daigaku wakumon. Undated manuscript of the 1788 edition. https://kotenseki.nijl.ac.jp/biblio/100199929/viewer/85?ln=en.

Daigaku wakumon. Undated woodblock. https://kotenseki.nijl.ac.jp/biblio/100132667/viewer/1?ln=en.

Daigaku wakumon: ichimei keizaiben. Tokyo: Keizai zasshi sha, 1894.

Kōkyō shōkai. Honchō (Edo): Nishimura Genroku, publisher. 1788. https://www.wul.waseda.ac.jp/kotenseki/html/ro12/ro12_01584/index.html.

Kumazawa Banzan shū. Vol. 1 of Kinsei shakai keizai gakusetsu taikei, edited by Nomura Kanetarō. Tokyo: Seibundō shinkōsha, 1935.

Shūgi gaisho. In Itō Tasaburō, ed., *Nakae Tōju Kumazawa Banzan*, Nihon no meicho, vol. 11. Tokyo: Chūō kōronsha, 1976.

Shūgi gaisho. Manuscript copy by Nakamura Naomichi, 1825–1826. https://www.wul.waseda.ac.jp/kotenseki/html/io4/io4_00775_0151/index.html.

Shūgi washo. In Gotō Yōichi and Tomoeda Ryūtarō, eds., *Kumazawa Banzan*, Nihon shisō taikei, vol. 30. Tokyo: Iwanami shoten, 1971.

Nakae Tōju, *Okina mondō.* In Itō Tasaburō, ed., *Nakae Tōju Kumazawa Banzan*, Nihon no meicho, vol. 11. Tokyo: Chūō kōronsha, 1976.

Nakae Tōju shū Kumazawa Banzan shū. Tokyo: Dai Nihon shisō zenshū kankōkai, 1934.

Sima Qian. *Shiji.* Chinese Text Project. https://ctext.org/shiji/zh

Secondary Sources

Armstrong, Robert C. *Light from the East, or Studies in Japanese Confucianism.* Toronto: University of Toronto Press, 1914.

Bowring, Richard. "Fujiwara Seika and the *Great Learning*," *Monumenta Nipponica*, vol. 61, no. 4. Winter 2006.

In Search of the Way: Thought and Religion in Early-Modern Japan, 1582–1860. Oxford: Oxford University Press, 2017.

Chan, Wing-tsit, trans. *Instructions for Practical Living and Other Neo-Confucian Writings by Wang Yangming.* New York: Columbia University Press, 1963.

De Bary, Wm. Theodore and Irene Bloom, eds. *Principle and Practicality: Essays in Neo-Confucianism and Practical Learning.* New York: Columbia University Press, 1979.

De Bary, Wm. Theodore, Carol Gluck, and Arthur E. Tiedemann, eds. *Sources of Japanese Tradition*, vol. 2: *1600–2000*, 2nd ed. New York: Columbia University Press, 2005.

Fisher, Galen M., trans. *"Dai Gaku Wakumon* by Kumazawa Banzan." *Transactions of the Asiatic Society of Japan*, 2nd Series, vol. 16. 1938.

"Kumazawa Banzan, His Life and Ideas." *Transactions of the Asiatic Society of Japan*, 2nd Series, vol. 16. 1938.

Bibliography

Gardner, Daniel K. *Chu Hsi and the Ta-hsueh: Neo-Confucian Reflection on the Confucian Canon.* Harvard East Asian Monographs. Cambridge, MA: Harvard University Asia Center, 1986.

Gotō Yōichi. "Kumazawa Banzan no shōgai to shisō no keisei." In Gotō Yōichi and Tomoeda Ryūtarō, eds. *Kumazawa Banzan.* Nihon shisō taikei, vol. 30. Tokyo: Iwanami shoten, 1971.

Gotō Yōichi and Tomoeda Ryūtarō, eds. *Kumazawa Banzan.* Nihon shisō taikei, vol. 30. Tokyo: Iwanami shoten, 1971.

Haboush, JaHyun Kim and Kenneth Robinson, trans. *A Korean War Captive in Japan, 1597–1600: The Writings of Kang Hang.* New York: Columbia University Press, 2013.

Honjō Eijirō. "Development of the Study on the History of Japanese Economic Thought." *Kyoto University Economic Review,* vol. 29, no. 2, 1959.

Inoue Michiyasu. *Banzan kō.* Okayama: Okayama-ken, 1902.

Banzan sensei ryakuden. Kogamachi, Ibaraki-ken: Kogakyō yūkai, 1910.

Banzan sensei shokanshū. Tokyo: Shūseidō, 1913.

Inoue Tetsujirō. *Nihon Yōmei gakuha no tetsugaku.* Tokyo: Fuzanbō shoten, 1900.

Ishida Ichirō and Kanaya Osamu, eds. *Fujiwara Seika/Hayashi Razan,* Nihon shisō taikei, vol. 28. Tokyo: Iwanami shoten, 1975.

Itō Tasaburō, ed. *Nakae Tōju Kumazawa Banzan.* Nihon no meicho, vol. 11. Tokyo: Chūō kōronsha, 1976.

Kimura Mitsunori. "Nenpu." In Kimura and Ushio Haruo. *Nakae Tōju/Kumazawa Banzan.* Nihon no shisōka, vol. 4. Tokyo: Meitoku shuppansha, 1978.

Lidin, Olof. *Ogyū Sorai's Discourse on Government (Seidan): An Annotated Translation.* Wiesbaden: Otto Harrassowitz, 1999.

McMullen, Ian James. "Courtier and Confucian in Seventeenth-Century Japan," *Japan Review,* no. 21. 2009.

Genji gaiden: The Origins of Kumazawa Banzan's Commentary on the Tale of Genji. Oriental Institute Monographs, 13. Oxford: Ithaca Press, 1991.

Idealism, Protest, and The Tale of Genji: The Confucianism of Kumazawa Banzan (1619–91). Oxford Oriental Monographs. Oxford: Clarendon Press, 1999.

"Kumazawa Banzan and 'Jitsugaku': Toward Pragmatic Action." In Wm. Theodore de Bary and Irene Bloom, eds. *Principle and Practicality: Essays in Neo-Confucianism and Practical Learning.* New York: Columbia University Press, 1979.

"The Life and Thought of a Seventeenth-Century Japanese Confucian." Ph.D. thesis, University of Cambridge, 1969.

Minamoto Ryōen. *Edo no Jugaku Daigaku juyō no rekishi.* Tokyo: Shibunkaku, 1988.

Miyazaki Michio. "Kumazawa Banzan no kirishitan ron." *Kokugakuin zasshi,* vol. 85, no. 9, 1984.

"Kumazawa Banzan to Ogyū Sorai." Parts 1–2. *Kokugakuin zasshi,* vol. 84, nos. 1–2, 1983.

"Kumazawa Banzan to Yamaga Sokō." *Kokugakuin zasshi,* vol. 82, no. 8, 1981.

Bibliography

Najita, Tetsuo. "Political Economism in the Thought of Dazai Shundai (1680–1747)." *Journal of Asian Studies*, vol. 31, no. 4, 1972.

Soeda Juichi. "Conditions of Study of Political Economy in Japan." *Kokka gakkai zasshi*, Vol. 6, no. 79, 1893.

Soum, Jean-François. *Nakae Tōju (1608–1648) et Kumazawa Banzan (1619–1691). Deux penseurs de l'époque d'Edo.* Paris: Collège de France, Institut des Hautes Études Japonaises, 2000.

Questions sur La Grande Étude: Daigaku wakumon. Tokyo: Maison Franco-Japonaise, 1995.

Strippoli, Roberta. *Dancer, Nun, Ghost, Goddess.* Leiden: Brill, 2018.

Tucker, John A. *Itō Jinsai's Gomō jigi and the Philosophical Definition of Early Modern Japan.* Leiden: Brill, 1998.

"Skepticism and the Neo-Confucian Canon: Itō Jinsai's Philosophical Critique of the *Great Learning*," *Dao A Journal of Comparative Philosophy*, vol. 12, no. 1, 2013.

Wajima Yoshio. "Kanbun igaku no kin, sono Hayashi mon kōryū to no kankei," in *Nihon Sōgakushi no kenkyū.* Tokyo: Yoshikawa kōbunkan, 1988.

Yamashita, Ryūji. "Nakae Tōju's Religious Thought and Its Relation to 'Jitsugaku.'" In Wm. Theodore de Bary and Irene Bloom, eds., *Principle and Practicality: Essays in Neo-Confucianism and Practical Learning.* New York: Columbia University Press, 1979.

Index

CAMBRIDGE TEXTS IN THE
HISTORY OF POLITICAL THOUGHT

Titles published in the series thus far

Aquinas *Political Writings* (edited and translated by R. W. Dyson)

Aristotle *The Politics and The Constitution of Athens* (edited and translated by Stephen Everson)

Arnold *Culture and Anarchy and Other Writings* (edited by Stefan Collini)

Astell *Political Writings* (edited by Patricia Springborg)

Augustine *The City of God against the Pagans* (edited and translated by R. W. Dyson)

Augustine *Political Writings* (edited by E. M. Atkins and R. J. Dodaro)

Austin *The Province of Jurisprudence Determined* (edited by Wilfrid E. Rumble)

Bacon *The History of the Reign of King Henry VII* (edited by Brian Vickers)

Bagehot *The English Constitution* (edited by Paul Smith)

Bakunin *Statism and Anarchy* (edited and translated by Marshall Shatz)

Baxter *Holy Commonwealth* (edited by William Lamont)

Bayle *Political Writings* (edited by Sally L. Jenkinson)

Beccaria *On Crimes and Punishments and Other Writings* (edited by Richard Bellamy; translated by Richard Davies)

Bentham *A Fragment on Government* (edited by Ross Harrison)

Bernstein *The Preconditions of Socialism* (edited and translated by Henry Tudor)

Bodin *On Sovereignty* (edited and translated by Julian H. Franklin)

Bolingbroke *Political Writings* (edited by David Armitage)

Bossuet *Politics Drawn from the Very Words of Holy Scripture* (edited and translated by Patrick Riley)

Botero *The Reason of State* (edited and translated by Robert Bireley)

The British Idealists (edited by David Boucher)

Burke *Pre-Revolutionary Writings* (edited by Ian Harris)

Burke *Revolutionary Writings* (edited by Iain Hampsher-Monk)

Cavendish *Political Writings* (edited by Susan James)

Christine de Pizan *The Book of the Body Politic* (edited by Kate Langdon Forhan)

Cicero *On Duties* (edited by E. M. Atkins; edited and translated by M. T. Griffin)

Cicero *On the Commonwealth and On the Laws* (edited and translated by James E. G. Zetzel)

Comte *Early Political Writings* (edited and translated by H. S. Jones)

Comte *Conciliarism and Papalism* (edited by J. H. Burns and Thomas M. Izbicki)

Condorcet *Political Writings* (edited by Steven Lukes and Nadia Urbinati)

Constant *Political Writings* (edited and translated by Biancamaria Fontana)

Dante *Monarchy* (edited and translated by Prue Shaw)

Diderot *Political Writings* (edited and translated by John Hope Mason and Robert Wokler)

Diderot *The Dutch Revolt* (edited and translated by Martin van Gelderen)

Diderot *Early Greek Political Thought from Homer to the Sophists* (edited and translated by Michael Gagarin and Paul Woodruff)

Diderot *The Early Political Writings of the German Romantics* (edited and translated by Frederick C. Beiser)

Emerson *Political Writings* (edited by Kenneth S. Sacks)

Emerson *The English Levellers* (edited by Andrew Sharp)

Erasmus *The Education of a Christian Prince with the Panegyric for Archduke Philip of Austria* (edited and translated by Lisa Jardine; translated by Neil M. Cheshire and Michael J. Heath)

Fénelon *Telemachus* (edited and translated by Patrick Riley)

Ferguson *An Essay on the History of Civil Society* (edited by Fania Oz-Salzberger)

Fichte *Addresses to the German Nation* (edited by Gregory Moore)

Filmer *Patriarcha and Other Writings* (edited by Johann P. Sommerville)

Fletcher *Political Works* (edited by John Robertson)

Sir John Fortescue *On the Laws and Governance of England* (edited by Shelley Lockwood)

Fourier *The Theory of the Four Movements* (edited by Gareth Stedman Jones; edited and translated by Ian Patterson)

Franklin *The Autobiography and Other Writings on Politics, Economics, and Virtue* (edited by Alan Houston)

Gramsci *Pre-Prison Writings* (edited by Richard Bellamy; translated by Virginia Cox)

Guicciardini *Dialogue on the Government of Florence* (edited and translated by Alison Brown)

Hamilton, Madison, and Jay (writing as 'Publius') *The Federalist with Letters of 'Brutus'* (edited by Terence Ball)

Harrington *The Commonwealth of Oceana and A System of Politics* (edited by J. G. A. Pocock)

Hegel *Elements of the Philosophy of Right* (edited by Allen W. Wood; translated by H. B. Nisbet)

Hegel *Political Writings* (edited by Laurence Dickey and H. B. Nisbet)

Hess *The Holy History of Mankind and Other Writings* (edited and translated by Shlomo Avineri)

Hobbes *On the Citizen* (edited and translated by Michael Silverthorne and Richard Tuck)

Hobbes *Leviathan* (edited by Richard Tuck)

Hobhouse *Liberalism and Other Writings* (edited by James Meadowcroft)

Hooker *Of the Laws of Ecclesiastical Polity* (edited by A. S. McGrade)

Hume *Political Essays* (edited by Knud Haakonssen)

King James VI and I *Political Writings* (edited by Johann P. Sommerville)

Jefferson *Political Writings* (edited by Joyce Appleby and Terence Ball)

John of Salisbury *Policraticus* (edited by Cary J. Nederman)

Kant *Political Writings* (edited by H. S. Reiss; translated by H. B. Nisbet)

Knox *On Rebellion* (edited by Roger A. Mason)

Price *Political Writings* (edited by D. O. Thomas)

Priestley *Political Writings* (edited by Peter Miller)

Proudhon *What is Property?* (edited and translated by Donald R. Kelley and Bonnie G. Smith)

Pufendorf *On the Duty of Man and Citizen according to Natural Law* (edited by James Tully; translated by Michael Silverthorne)

Pufendorf *The Radical Reformation* (edited and translated by Michael G. Baylor)

Rousseau *The Discourses and Other Early Political Writings* (edited and translated by Victor Gourevitch)

Rousseau *The Social Contract and Other Later Political Writings* (edited and translated by Victor Gourevitch)

Seneca *Moral and Political Essays* (edited and translated by John M. Cooper; edited by J. F. Procopé)

Sidney *Court Maxims* (edited by Hans W. Blom, Eco Haitsma Mulier and Ronald Janse)

Sorel *Reflections on Violence* (edited by Jeremy Jennings)

Spencer *Political Writings* (edited by John Offer)

Stirner *The Ego and Its Own* (edited by David Leopold)

Emperor Taizong and ministers *The Essentials of Governance* (compiled by Wu Jing; edited and translated by Hilde De Weerdt, Glen Dudbridge and Gabe van Beijeren)

Thoreau *Political Writings* (edited by Nancy L. Rosenblum)

Tönnies *Community and Civil Society* (edited and translated by Jose Harris; translated by Margaret Hollis)

Tönnies *Utopias of the British Enlightenment* (edited by Gregory Claeys)

Vico *The First New Science* (edited and translated by Leon Pompa)

Vitoria *Political Writings* (edited by Anthony Pagden and Jeremy Lawrance)

Voltaire *Political Writings* (edited and translated by David Williams)

Weber *Political Writings* (edited by Peter Lassman; edited and translated by Ronald Speirs)

William of Ockham *A Short Discourse on Tyrannical Government* (edited by Arthur Stephen McGrade; translated by John Kilcullen)

William of Ockham *A Letter to the Friars Minor and Other Writings* (edited by Arthur Stephen McGrade; edited and translated by John Kilcullen)

Wollstonecraft *A Vindication of the Rights of Men and A Vindication of the Rights of Woman* (edited by Sylvana Tomaselli)